240 BEST-EVER
Chilli Recipes

240 BEST-EVER
Chilli Recipes

A tongue-tingling collection of fantastic chilli recipes from around the world shown in more than 245 fiery photographs

Consultant Editor: **JENNI FLEETWOOD**

southwater

This edition is published by Southwater,
an imprint of Anness Publishing Ltd, Blaby Road,
Wigston, Leicestershire LE18 4SE

Email: info@anness.com

Web: www.southwaterbooks.com; www.annesspublishing.com

If you like the images in this book and would like to investigate
using them for publishing, promotions or advertising, please visit
our website www.practicalpictures.com for more information.

Publisher: Joanna Lorenz
Project Editor: Anne Hildyard
Design: SMI
Production Controller: Christine Ni

Previously published as part of a larger volume, *500 Chilli Recipes*

ETHICAL TRADING POLICY

At Anness Publishing we believe that business should be
conducted in an ethical and ecologically sustainable way, with
respect for the environment and a proper regard to the
replacement of the natural resources we employ.
As a publisher, we use a lot of wood pulp to make high-quality
paper for printing, and that wood commonly comes from spruce
trees. We are therefore currently growing more than 750,000 trees
in three Scottish forest plantations: Berrymoss (130 hectares/320
acres), West Touxhill (125 hectares/305 acres) and Deveron Forest
(75 hectares/185 acres). The forests we manage contain more than
3.5 times the number of trees employed each year in making
paper for the books we manufacture. Because of this ongoing
ecological investment programme, you, as our customer, can have
the pleasure and reassurance of knowing that a tree is being
cultivated on your behalf to naturally replace the materials used to
make the book you are holding. Our forestry programme is run in
accordance with the UK Woodland Assurance Scheme (UKWAS)
and will be certified by the internationally recognized Forest
Stewardship Council (FSC). The FSC is a non-government
organization dedicated to promoting responsible management
of the world's forests. Certification ensures forests are managed
in an environmentally sustainable and socially responsible way.
For further information about this scheme, go to
www.annesspublishing.com/trees

A CIP catalogue record for this book is available from
the British Library.

PUBLISHER'S NOTE

Although the advice and information in this book are believed to
be accurate and true at the time of going to press, neither the
authors nor the publisher can accept any legal responsibility or
liability for any errors or omissions that may be made nor for any
inaccuracies nor for any loss, harm or injury that comes about
from following instructions or advice in this book.

NOTES

Bracketed terms are intended for American readers.
For all recipes, quantities are given in both metric and imperial
measures and, where appropriate, in standard cups and spoons.
Follow one set of measures, but not a mixture, because they are
not interchangeable.
Standard spoon and cup measures are level. 1 tsp = 5ml,
1 tbsp = 15ml, 1 cup = 250ml/8fl oz. Australian standard
tablespoons are 20ml. Australian readers should use 3 tsp in
place of 1 tbsp for measuring small quantities.
American pints are 16fl oz/2 cups. American readers should use
20fl oz/2.5 cups in place of 1 pint when measuring liquids.
Electric oven temperatures in this book are for conventional ovens.
When using a fan oven, the temperature will probably need to be
reduced by about 10–20°C/20–40°F. Since ovens vary, you should
check with your manufacturer's instruction book for guidance.
The nutritional analysis given for each recipe is calculated per
portion (i.e. serving or item), unless otherwise stated. If the recipe
gives a range, such as Serves 4–6, then the nutritional analysis will
be for the smaller portion size, i.e. 6 servings. The analysis does not
include optional ingredients, such as salt added to taste.
Medium (US large) eggs are used unless otherwise stated.

Main front cover image shows Sweet and Spicy Chicken – for
recipe, see page 57

Contents

Introduction

Chillies form an important part of many of the world's major cuisines. India is the largest producer and exporter of chillies, with much of the crop used for local consumption. China, Japan, Thailand, Mexico, Turkey, Nigeria, Ethiopia, Uganda, Kenya and Tanzania are also prime producers and consumers of chillies.

The word *chilli* is spelled in several different ways. Sometimes it is chile, sometimes chili, or chilli pepper. This last description is accurate in that it recognizes that chillies are members of the *Capsicum* family, like the sweet (bell) peppers. It also forms a link with all those spicy powders such as chilli, cayenne and paprika, which are an essential part of many national dishes.

The great explorer Columbus was responsible for confusing chillies with peppers. When he set sail in 1492, hoping to find a sea route to the spice islands, it was a source of black pepper (*Piper nigrum*) he was seeking. When he found the hot spice flavouring the local food, he assumed that it was black pepper. When he realized that the fleshy pods of a fruit were responsible, rather than black peppercorns, it was too late. The Spanish called the flavouring *pimiento* (pepper). The name stuck, and it has led to confusion ever since. It was the Aztecs who coined the name *chilli*. They loved the brightly coloured fruit that had originated in the rainforests of South America, and used chillies both as food and for medicinal purposes. Mexico remains a mecca for chilli lovers; it produces about 100 different chillies, with every region having its own special varieties.

There are more than 200 types of chillies, including jalapeños, cayennes, Anaheim chillies and poblanos, as well as sweet peppers. They vary from fairly mild to blisteringly hot. Generally, small chillies are not hotter than large ones and red chillies are not hotter than green. Most chillies are green and ripen to red, but some start yellow and become red, and yet others start yellow and stay yellow. Chillies on the same plant can have

different degrees of heat, and in one type of chilli, the top of the fruit is hotter than the bottom. The chemical capsaicin in the seeds and fibrous white lining provides the heat; either a tingle or a tidal wave of heat, and contributes to the feel-good factor by stimulating the brain to produce endorphins. However, capsaicin is also an irritant, and can cause severe burning to delicate parts of

the face and body, so it is vital to handle chillies with care. Wear gloves or cut them up using a knife and fork. If you do handle chillies, wash your hands in soapy water (capsaicin does not dissolve in water alone) or use vegetable oil to remove any residue. If you bite into a chilli that burns your mouth, don't drink a glass of water; this spreads the discomfort around. Instead, take a mouthful of milk, yogurt or ice cream, hold it in your mouth

for a minute or so, then spit it out. Alternatively, eat a piece of fresh bread, a cooked potato or some rice; these foods absorb the capsaicin oil.

Cooks all over the world value chillies for their heat, for their special flavour and for their ability to pep up the blandest foods. This book celebrates the chilli in all its forms in a collection of recipes that have been sourced from many corners of the globe. Recipes from South-east Asia usually involve complex ingredients such as chillies, shrimp paste and tamarind pulp, as in Red Hot Vegetable and Peanut Soup from Jakarta, and fish sauce and lime leaves in Tomato, Chilli and Egg Drop Soup from Vietnam. From Indonesia comes Spicy Chicken Satay with Chilli Relish, in which the meat is marinated in sambal kecap, a widely used Indonesian sauce and dip made from dark soy sauce, chilli powder and hot chilli peppers that impart an exotic flavour to the dish.

Chillies are also widely used in the Mediterranean in countries such as Turkey, and just two of the delicious meze recipes featured in this book are Stir-fried Spinach with Chilli, Currants and Pine Nuts, and Aubergine and Chilli Pepper Dip. Farther afield, the home of chilli dishes is India, and this book includes many favourites, including Fiery Lamb Pilau, and Spiced Chicken Biryani. Cheese and Chilli Tortillas and Mushrooms with Chipotle Chillies are two popular dishes in Mexico that use their famous dried chillies. With the help of this volume, make a culinary journey around the world and enjoy a wealth of exotic and delicious dishes from the comfort of your own kitchen.

Cucumber Soup with Chilli Salsa and Salmon

The refreshing flavours of cucumber and yogurt in this soup fuse with the cool chilli salsa and a hint of heat from the charred salmon to bring the taste of summer to the table.

Serves 4

3 medium cucumbers
300ml/½ pint/1¼ cups Greek (US strained plain) yogurt
250ml/8fl oz/1 cup vegetable stock, chilled
120ml/4fl oz/½ cup crème fraîche
15ml/1 tbsp chopped fresh chervil
15ml/1 tbsp chopped fresh chives
15ml/1 tbsp chopped fresh flat leaf parsley
1 small red chilli, seeded and very finely chopped
a little oil, for brushing
225g/8oz salmon fillet, skinned and cut into eight thin slices
salt and ground black pepper
fresh chervil or chives, to garnish

1 Peel two of the cucumbers and then cut them in half lengthways. Scoop out and discard the seeds, then roughly chop the flesh.

2 Purée the cucumber in a food processor or blender, then add the Greek yogurt, chilled stock, crème fraîche, chervil and chives, and process until smooth. Season the mixture with a little salt and ground black pepper. Transfer to a bowl and set aside in the refrigerator until needed.

3 Peel, halve and seed the remaining cucumber. Cut the flesh into small neat dice. Mix with the chopped parsley and chilli. Chill until required.

4 Brush a griddle or frying pan with oil and heat until very hot. Sear the salmon slices for 1–2 minutes on each side, until tender and charred.

5 Ladle the chilled soup into individual soup bowls. Top each serving with two slices of the salmon, then pile a portion of salsa into the centre of each. Garnish with the chervil and chives and serve.

Red Hot Vegetable and Peanut Soup

This is a colourful and refreshing soup from Jakarta with more than a hint of sharpness.

Serves 4 or 8 as part of a buffet

For the spice paste

5 shallots or 1 medium red onion, sliced
3 garlic cloves, crushed
2.5cm/1in galangal, peeled and sliced
1–2 fresh red chillies, seeded and sliced
25g/1oz raw peanuts
1cm/½in cube shrimp paste, prepared
1.2 litres/2 pints/5 cups well-flavoured stock
50–75g/2–3oz salted peanuts, lightly crushed
15–30ml/1–2 tbsp soft dark brown sugar
5ml/1 tsp tamarind pulp, soaked in 75ml/5 tbsp warm water for 15 minutes
salt

For the vegetables

1 chayote, thinly peeled, seeds removed, flesh finely sliced
115g/4oz green beans, trimmed and finely sliced
50g/2oz corn kernels (optional)
handful of green leaves, such as watercress, rocket (arugula) or Chinese leaves, finely shredded
1 fresh green chilli, sliced, to garnish

1 Prepare the spice paste by grinding the shallots or onion, garlic, galangal, chillies, raw peanuts and shrimp paste until smooth in a food processor or with a mortar and pestle.

2 Pour in some of the stock to moisten and then pour this mixture into a pan or wok, adding the rest of the stock. Cook for 15 minutes with the peanuts and sugar. Strain the tamarind mixture, discarding the seeds, and reserve the juice.

3 Add the chayote slices, beans and corn, if using, to the soup and cook fairly rapidly for 5 minutes. At the last minute, add the green leaves and salt to taste.

4 Add the tamarind juice, mix well and taste for seasoning. Serve in warmed individual bowls, garnished with the slices of green chilli.

Cucumber Soup Energy 226kcal/942kj; Protein 3.7g; Carbohydrate 64.1g; of which sugars 64.1g; Fat 16.3g; of which saturates 10.3g; Cholesterol 48mg; Calcium 125mg; Fibre 2.3g; Sodium 280mg.
Red Hot Vegetable Soup Energy 80kcal/334kj; Protein 3.8g; Carbohydrate 6.2g; of which sugars 4.9g; Fat 4.7g; of which saturates 0.9g; Cholesterol 0mg; Calcium 46mg; Fibre 1.8g; Sodium 19mg.

Indian Dhal Soup

This is a simple, mildly spiced lentil soup, which is a good accompaniment to heavily spiced meat dishes.

Serves 4 to 6

15ml/1 tbsp ghee
1 large onion, finely chopped
2 garlic cloves, crushed
1 green chilli, chopped
2.5ml/½ tsp ground turmeric
75g/3oz red lentils
250ml/8fl oz/1 cup water
400g/14oz can chopped tomatoes
2.5ml/½ tsp sugar
lemon juice, to taste
200g/7oz/1 cup plain boiled rice or 2 potatoes, boiled (optional)
salt
coriander (cilantro) leaves, chopped, to garnish

1 Heat the ghee in a large pan and fry the onion, garlic, chilli and turmeric together for 4–5 minutes until the onion has softened and turned translucent.

2 Add the lentils and the measured water to the pan and bring to the boil. Reduce the heat, cover and simmer until all the water has been absorbed.

3 Mash the lentils in the pan with the back of a wooden spoon until you have a smooth paste.

4 Add salt to taste and mix well. Add the chopped tomatoes, sugar and lemon juice, to taste, to the pan and stir well until thoroughly combined.

5 Chop the cooked potatoes into cubes, if using, and add to the soup, or add in the plain boiled rice, if you prefer.

6 Heat the soup until it is bubbling and all the ingredients are heated through. Serve immediately, garnished with coriander.

> **Cook's Tip**
> *When using lentils, first rinse in cold water and remove any floating items. Drain them and then carefully pick through the lentils to remove any stones that may be present.*

Tomato, Chilli and Egg Drop Soup

Popular in southern Vietnam and Cambodia, this spicy soup with eggs is probably adapted from the traditional Chinese egg drop soup. Served on its own with chunks of crusty bread, or accompanied by jasmine or ginger rice, this is a tasty dish for a light supper.

Serves 4

30ml/2 tbsp groundnut (peanut) or vegetable oil
3 shallots, finely sliced
2 garlic cloves, finely chopped
2 Thai chillies, seeded and finely sliced
25g/1oz galangal, shredded
8 large, ripe tomatoes, skinned, seeded and finely chopped
15ml/1 tbsp sugar
30ml/2 tbsp Thai fish sauce
4 lime leaves
900ml/1½ pints/3¾ cups chicken stock
15ml/1 tbsp wine vinegar
4 eggs
sea salt and ground black pepper

For the garnish
chilli oil, for drizzling
1 small bunch fresh coriander (cilantro), finely chopped
1 small bunch fresh mint leaves, finely chopped

1 Heat the oil in a wok or heavy pan. Stir in the shallots, garlic, chillies and galangal and cook until golden and fragrant. Add the tomatoes with the sugar, Thai fish sauce and lime leaves. Stir until it resembles a sauce. Pour in the stock and bring to the boil. Reduce the heat and simmer for 30 minutes. Season.

2 Just before serving, bring a wide pan of water to the boil. Add the vinegar and half a teaspoon of salt. Break the eggs into individual cups or small bowls.

3 Stir the water rapidly to create a swirl and drop an egg into the centre of the swirl. Follow immediately with the others, or poach two at a time, and keep the water boiling to throw the whites up over the yolks. Turn off the heat, cover the pan and leave to poach until firm enough to lift. Poached eggs are traditional, but you could use lightly fried eggs instead.

4 Using a slotted spoon, lift the eggs out of the water and slip them into the hot soup. Drizzle a little chilli oil over the eggs, sprinkle with the coriander and mint, and serve.

Indian Dhal Soup Energy 235kcal/991kj; Protein 13g; Carbohydrate 28.4g, of which sugars 3.7g; Fat 8.8g, of which saturates 2.2g; Cholesterol 0mg; Calcium 66mg; Fibre 2.9g; Sodium 40mg.
Tomato and Egg Soup Energy 181kcal/756kj; Protein 8g; Carbohydrate 12.3g, of which sugars 11.5g; Fat 11.7g, of which saturates 2.4g; Cholesterol 190mg; Calcium 52mg; Fibre 2.3g; Sodium 280mg.

Spiced Mango Soup with Yogurt

This delicious, light soup recipe comes from Chutney Mary's, the Anglo-Indian restaurant in London. It is best served lightly chilled.

Serves 4
2 ripe mangoes
15ml/1 tbsp gram flour
120ml/4fl oz/½ cup natural (plain) yogurt
900ml/1½ pints/3¾ cups water
2.5ml/½ tsp grated fresh root ginger
2 red chillies, seeded and finely chopped
30ml/2 tbsp olive oil
2.5ml/½ tsp mustard seeds
2.5ml/½ tsp cumin seeds
8 curry leaves
salt and ground black pepper
fresh mint leaves, shredded, to garnish
natural (plain) yogurt, to serve

1 Peel the mangoes, remove the stones (pits) and cut the flesh into even chunks. Purée the flesh in a food processor or blender until smooth.

2 Pour the puréed mango into a pan and stir in the gram flour, yogurt, water, ginger and chillies. Bring the mixture slowly to the boil, stirring occasionally. Simmer for about 4–5 minutes until the mixture has thickened slightly. Remove the pan from the heat and set aside.

3 Heat the olive oil in a frying pan. Add the mustard seeds and cook for a few seconds until they begin to pop, then add the cumin seeds.

4 Add the curry leaves to the frying pan and then cook for 5 minutes. Stir the spice mixture into the soup, return it to the heat and cook for 10 minutes.

5 Press the soup through a sieve (strainer), if you like, then season to taste.

6 Leave the soup to cool completely, then chill in the refrigerator for at least 1 hour.

7 Ladle the soup into bowls, and top each with a dollop of yogurt. Garnish with shredded mint leaves and serve.

Red-hot Red Lentil Soup with Onion and Parsley

In Istanbul and Izmir, lentil soups are light and subtly spiced, and served as an appetizer or as a snack. In Anatolia, lentil and bean soups are made with chunks of mutton and flavoured with tomato and spices, and are usually served as a meal on their own.

Serves 4 to 6
30–45ml/2–3 tbsp olive or sunflower oil
1 large onion, finely chopped
2 garlic cloves, finely chopped
1 fresh red chilli, seeded and finely chopped
5–10ml/1–2 tsp cumin seeds
5–10ml/1–2 tsp coriander seeds
1 carrot, finely chopped
scant 5ml/1 tsp ground fenugreek
5ml/1 tsp sugar
15ml/1 tbsp tomato purée (paste)
250g/9oz/generous 1 cup split red lentils
1.75 litres/3 pints/7½ cups chicken stock
salt and ground black pepper

To serve
1 small red onion, finely chopped
1 large bunch of fresh flat leaf parsley, finely chopped
4–6 lemon wedges

1 Heat the oil in a heavy pan and stir in the onion, garlic, chilli, cumin and coriander seeds. When the onion begins to colour, toss in the carrot and cook for 2–3 minutes. Add the fenugreek, sugar and tomato purée, and stir in the lentils.

2 Pour in the stock, stir well and bring to the boil. Lower the heat, partially cover the pan and simmer for 30–40 minutes, until the lentils have broken up.

3 If the soup is too thick, thin it down with a little water. Season with salt and pepper to taste.

4 Serve the soup straight from the pan or, if you prefer a smooth texture, whizz it in a blender, then reheat if necessary. Ladle the soup into bowls and sprinkle liberally with the chopped onion and parsley. Serve with a wedge of lemon to squeeze over the soup.

Spiced Mango Soup Energy 121kcal/508kj; Protein 2.8g; Carbohydrate 14.7g, of which sugars 12.7g; Fat 6.2g, of which saturates 1g; Cholesterol 0mg; Calcium 73mg; Fibre 2.4g; Sodium 28mg.
Red-hot Red Lentil Soup Energy 203kcal/354kj; Protein 11.1g; Carbohydrate 31.8g, of which sugars 7.3g; Fat 4.4g, of which saturates 0.6g; Cholesterol 0mg; Calcium 45mg; Fibre 3.5g; Sodium 26mg.

Chilli Noodle Soup with Oyster Mushrooms

Colloquially known as 'marketplace noodles' in Korea, this dish has long been enjoyed as a quick and simple lunch. The oyster mushrooms give the mild broth an appetizing richness, while the noodles have a hint of beef and a dash of chilli.

Serves 2
500ml/17fl oz/2¼ cups water
80g/3oz beef
30ml/2 tbsp light soy sauce
2 eggs, beaten
50ml/3 tbsp vegetable oil
4 oyster mushrooms
80g/3oz courgette (zucchini)
sesame oil, for drizzling
100g/4oz egg noodles
1 spring onion (scallion),
    finely chopped
1 dried red chilli, thinly sliced
2 garlic cloves, crushed
salt and ground white pepper
sesame seeds, to garnish

1 Pour the water into a pan and bring to the boil. Add the beef and cook for 20 minutes, then remove and slice into strips. Strain the stock into a jug (pitcher), and add the soy sauce.

2 Season the eggs with a pinch of salt. Coat a frying pan with 10ml/2 tsp vegetable oil and heat. Add the eggs and make a thin omelette, browning on each side. Cut into thin strips.

3 Cut the mushrooms and courgette into thin strips and sprinkle with salt. Pat the courgette dry with kitchen paper after 5 minutes.

4 Coat a frying pan or wok with the remaining vegetable oil and heat. Stir-fry the mushrooms and drizzle with the sesame oil then set aside. Lightly fry the courgette until it softens, then remove. Stir-fry the beef until lightly browned, and set aside.

5 Boil a pan of water and cook the plain noodles, then drain and rinse in cold water. Quickly reheat the reserved beef stock.

6 Place the noodles in a bowl. Add the mushrooms, courgette and beef. Top with the spring onion, chilli and garlic, then add the stock to cover one-third of the ingredients. Sprinkle with the sesame seeds before serving.

Green Chilli Dumpling Soup

The succulent dumplings taste fantastic in this clear soup. With ready-to-eat dumplings widely available this dish is simple and quick, and the dumpling flavours suffuse the nourishing broth.

Serves 4
750ml/1¼ pints/3 cups
    beef stock
16 frozen dumplings
1 spring onion (scallion),
    finely sliced
¼ green chilli, seeded and
    finely sliced
1 garlic clove, crushed
15ml/1 tbsp light soy sauce
salt and ground black pepper

1 Pour the beef stock into a heavy pan and slowly bring it to the boil.

2 Add the frozen dumplings to the stock, cover the pan, and boil for about 6–8 minutes.

3 Add the spring onion, chilli, garlic and light soy sauce to the pan, and continue to boil the soup, stirring gently, for a further 2–3 minutes.

4 Check that the dumplings are cooked through and then season the soup with salt and black pepper.

5 Spoon the soup into warmed serving bowls, adding four dumplings to each bowl, and serve piping hot. Serve with a dipping sauce, if you wish, for diners to dip their dumplings into.

Cook's Tips
• If you would prefer to use fresh dumplings, they will only need to be cooked for 5 minutes.
• Soy sauce with a drop of vinegar makes a good dipping sauce for the dumplings.
• When cooking dumplings in this way, stir the soup as carefully as you can to avoid causing the dumplings to break apart and lose their fillings in the stock.

Chilli Noodle Soup Energy 492kcal/2059kj; Protein 23.1g; Carbohydrate 40.4g, of which sugars 3.3g; Fat 27.7g, of which saturates 4.9g; Cholesterol 213mg; Calcium 60mg; Fibre 2.3g; Sodium 1167mg.
Green Chilli Dumpling Soup Energy 106kcal/445kj; Protein 2g; Carbohydrate 12.6g, of which sugars 0.6g; Fat 6.1g, of which saturates 3.4g; Cholesterol 5mg; Calcium 30mg; Fibre 0.5g; Sodium 842mg.

Tomato Soup with Chilli Squid and Tarragon

Oriental-style seared squid mingles with the pungent tomato and garlic flavours of the Mediterranean.

Serves 4
4 small squid (or 1–2 large squid)
60ml/4 tbsp olive oil
2 shallots, chopped
1 garlic clove, crushed
1.2kg/2½ lb ripe tomatoes, roughly chopped
15ml/1 tbsp sun-dried tomato paste
450ml/¾ pint/2 scant cups vegetable stock
about 2.5ml/½ tsp sugar
2 red chillies, seeded and chopped
30ml/2 tbsp chopped fresh tarragon
salt and ground black pepper
crusty bread, to serve

1 Wash the squid under cold water. Grasp the head and tentacles and pull the body away with the other hand. Discard the intestines that come away. Cut the tentacles away from the head in one piece and reserve; discard the head. Pull the quills out of the main body and remove any roe. Pull off the fins from the body pouch and rub off the semi-transparent, mottled skin. Wash the squid under cold water. Cut into rings and set these aside with the tentacles.

2 Heat 30ml/2 tbsp of the oil in a heavy pan. Add the shallots and garlic, and cook for 4–5 minutes, until softened. Add the tomatoes and tomato paste. Season, cover and cook for 3 minutes. Add half the stock and simmer for 5 minutes, until the tomatoes are soft. Cool the soup, then rub it through a sieve (strainer) and return it to the rinsed-out pan. Stir in the remaining stock and sugar, and reheat gently.

3 Meanwhile, heat the remaining oil in a frying pan. Add the squid rings and tentacles, and the chillies. Cook for 4–5 minutes, stirring, then remove from the heat and stir in the tarragon.

4 Adjust the seasoning if necessary. If the soup tastes slightly sharp, add a little extra sugar. Ladle the soup into bowls and spoon the chilli squid in the centre. Serve with crusty bread.

Spicy Octopus and Watercress Soup

This refreshing Korean seafood soup has a wonderfully restorative quality. Delicious octopus is cooked in a rich vegetable broth, with mooli and watercress adding an elusive flavour that is quintessentially Korean.

Serves 2 to 3
1 large octopus, cleaned and gutted
150g/5oz mooli (daikon), peeled
½ leek, sliced
20g/¾oz kelp or spinach leaves
3 garlic cloves, crushed
1 fresh red chilli, seeded and finely sliced
15ml/1 tbsp light soy sauce
75g/3oz watercress or rocket (arugula)
salt and ground black pepper

1 Rinse the octopus in salted water and cut into pieces about 2.5cm/1in long. Finely dice the mooli.

2 Pour 750ml/1¼ pints/3 cups water into a large pan and bring to the boil. Reduce the heat and add the mooli, leek, kelp or spinach, and crushed garlic.

3 Simmer over a medium heat until the radish softens and becomes clear. Discard the kelp and leek and then add the sliced chilli.

4 Add the octopus, increase the heat and boil for 5 minutes. Season with soy sauce, salt and pepper, and then add the watercress or rocket.

5 Remove from the heat, cover the pan and leave to stand for 1 minute while the leaves wilt into the liquid. Ladle into bowls and serve immediately.

Variation
If you prefer a little more heat, for a spicier version of this soup try adding a teaspoon of Korean chilli powder. This gives the dish a really tangy kick.

Tomato Soup Energy 186kcal/777kj; Protein 8.1g; Carbohydrate 10.9g; of which sugars 10.2g; Fat 12.6g; of which saturates 2g; Cholesterol 48mg; Calcium 30mg; Fibre 1.7g; Sodium 386mg.
Spicy Octopus Soup Energy 106kcal/449kj; Protein 19.9g; Carbohydrate 2.6g, of which sugars 2.3g; Fat 1.9g, of which saturates 0.5g; Cholesterol 48mg; Calcium 108mg; Fibre 1.7g; Sodium 386mg.

Mackerel and Chilli Tomato Soup

All the ingredients for this unusual soup are cooked in a single pan, so it is not only quick and easy to prepare, there is less to clear up. Smoked mackerel gives the soup a robust flavour, but this is tempered by the citrus tones in the lemon grass and tamarind.

Serves 4
200g/7oz smoked mackerel fillets
4 tomatoes
1 litre/1¾ pints/4 cups
   vegetable stock
1 lemon grass stalk, chopped
5cm/2in piece fresh galangal,
   finely diced
4 shallots, finely chopped
2 garlic cloves, finely chopped
2.5ml/½ tsp dried
   chilli flakes
15ml/1 tbsp Thai fish sauce
5ml/1 tsp palm sugar (jaggery)
   or light muscovado
   (brown) sugar
45ml/3 tbsp thick tamarind juice,
   made by mixing tamarind paste
   with warm water
small bunch fresh chives or spring
   onions (scallions), to garnish

1 Prepare the smoked mackerel fillets. Remove and discard the skin, if necessary, then chop the flesh into large pieces. Remove any stray bones with your fingers or tweezers.

2 Cut the tomatoes in half, squeeze out the seeds with your fingers, then finely dice the flesh with a sharp knife. Set aside.

3 Pour the stock into a pan and add the lemon grass, galangal, shallots and garlic. Bring to the boil, then simmer for 15 minutes.

4 Add the fish, tomatoes, chilli flakes, fish sauce, sugar and tamarind juice. Simmer for 5 minutes, until the fish and tomatoes are heated through. Serve garnished with chives or spring onions.

> **Cook's Tips**
> *Galangal is a rhizome used in Thai and other South-east Asian cuisine. It resembles, and is related to, ginger in appearance. In its raw form, it has a hot, ginger and pepper flavour, with a quite sour taste and pungent aroma.*

Hot and Spicy Fish Soup

This soup is a firm favourite to accompany a glass of rice spirit. Halibut or sea bass work as well as cod. White fish flakes have a bite of red chilli, and the watercress and spring onions add a refreshing zesty quality.

Serves 3 to 4
1 cod, filleted and skinned,
   head separate
225g/8oz Chinese radish, peeled
½ onion, chopped
2 garlic cloves, crushed
22.5ml/4½ tsp Korean
   chilli powder
5ml/1 tsp gochujang
   chilli paste
2 spring onions (scallions),
   roughly sliced
1 block firm tofu, cubed
90g/3½oz watercress or
   rocket (arugula)
salt and ground
   black pepper

1 Slice the cod fillets into three or four large pieces and set the head aside. Cut the white radish into 2cm/¾in cubes.

2 Bring 750ml/1¼ pints/3 cups water to the boil in large pan and add the fish head. Add the radish, onion, crushed garlic and a pinch of salt. Then add the chilli powder and gochujang chilli paste, and boil for 5 minutes more.

3 Remove the fish head and add the sliced fillet to the pan. Simmer until the fish is tender, about 4 minutes, and then add the spring onions, tofu, and watercress or rocket. Simmer the soup without stirring for 2 minutes more.

4 Season with salt and pepper, and serve the soup immediately.

> **Cook's Tips**
> • *Gochujang is a savoury, pungent paste from Korea. Made from chilli powder, rice and soy beans, it is traditionally fermented for long periods in sealed jars. Look out for ready-made versions in Asian stores and food markets.*
> • *For a milder version of this soup omit the chilli powder and gochujang chilli paste. The soup will still be wonderfully hearty and flavoursome.*

Hot and Spicy Fish Soup Energy 132kcal/554kj; Protein 23.4g; Carbohydrate 2.8g, of which sugars 2.3g; Fat 3g, of which saturates 0.5g; Cholesterol 46mg; Calcium 300mg; Fibre 1.1g; Sodium 80mg.
Mackerel and Tomato Soup Energy 209kcal/868kj; Protein 10.3g; Carbohydrate 6.6g; of which sugars 6.5g; Fat 15.9g; of which saturates 3.2g; Cholesterol 53mg; Calcium 19mg; Fibre 0.8g; Sodium 681mg.

Crab and Chilli Soup

Prepared fresh crab is readily available and perfect for creating an exotic soup in minutes.

Serves 4
45ml/3 tbsp olive oil
1 red onion, finely chopped
2 red chillies, seeded and
   finely chopped
1 garlic clove, finely chopped
450g/1lb fresh white crab meat
30ml/2 tbsp chopped
   fresh parsley
30ml/2 tbsp chopped fresh
   coriander (cilantro)
juice of 2 lemons

1 lemon grass stalk
1 litre/1¾ pints/4 cups good fish
   or chicken stock
15ml/1 tbsp Thai fish sauce
150g/5oz vermicelli or angel hair
   pasta, broken into 5–7.5cm/
   2–3in lengths
salt and ground black pepper

For the coriander relish
50g/2oz/1 cup fresh coriander
   (cilantro) leaves
1 green chilli, seeded and chopped
15ml/1 tbsp sunflower oil
25ml/1½ tbsp lemon juice
2.5ml/½ tsp ground roasted
   cumin seeds

1 Heat the oil in a pan and add the onion, chillies and garlic. Cook for 10 minutes until the onion is soft. Transfer to a bowl with the crab meat, parsley, coriander and lemon juice. Set aside.

2 Bruise the lemon grass and add to a pan with the stock and fish sauce. Add the lemon grass and bring to the boil, then stir in the pasta. Simmer, uncovered, for 3–4 minutes or cook for the time suggested on the packet, until the pasta is tender but al dente.

3 Meanwhile, make the coriander relish. Place the coriander, chilli, oil, lemon juice and cumin in a food processor or blender and process to form a coarse paste. Add seasoning to taste.

4 Remove and discard the lemon grass from the soup. Stir the chilli and crab mixture into the soup and season it well. Bring to the boil, then reduce the heat and simmer for 2 minutes.

5 Ladle the soup into four deep, warmed bowls and put a spoonful of the relish in the centre of each. Serve the soup immediately.

Spicy Seafood Noodle Soup

This Korean soup is a spicy, garlic-infused stew.

Serves 2
50g/2oz pork loin
50g/2oz mussels
50g/2oz prawns (shrimp)
90g/3½oz squid
15ml/1 tbsp vegetable oil
1 dried chilli, sliced
½ leek, sliced
2 garlic cloves, finely sliced
5ml/1 tsp grated fresh root ginger

30ml/2 tbsp Korean chilli powder
5ml/1 tsp mirin or rice wine
50g/2oz bamboo shoots, sliced
½ onion, roughly chopped
50g/2oz carrot, roughly chopped
2 Chinese leaves (Chinese
   cabbage), roughly chopped
750ml/1¼ pints/3 cups beef stock
light soy sauce, to taste
300g/11oz udon or flat
   wheat noodles
salt

1 Slice the pork, and set aside. Scrub the mussels' shells and rinse under cold water. Discard any that remain closed after being tapped. Scrape off any barnacles and remove the 'beards'. Rinse well. Gently pull the tail shells from the prawns. Twist off the head. Peel the body shell and the claws. Rinse well.

2 Wash the squid. Hold the body, pull away the head and tentacles. Discard the ink sac. Pull out the innards. Discard the thin purple skin, but keep the two small side fins. Slice the head across just under the eyes, severing the tentacles. Squeeze the tentacles to push out the round beak and discard. Rinse the pouch and tentacles. Score the flesh in a criss-cross pattern, and slice into 2cm/¾in pieces.

3 Heat a pan with the oil. Add the chilli, leek, garlic and ginger. Fry until the garlic has browned and add the pork. Fry quickly, add the chilli powder and mirin or rice wine. Add the bamboo shoots, onion and carrot, and fry until the vegetables are soft.

4 Add the seafood and cabbage and cook for 30 seconds. Pour in the stock and bring to the boil, then cover and simmer for 3 minutes. Season with salt. Discard any closed mussels.

5 Cook the noodles in a pan of boiling water. Place noodles in soup bowls, ladle over the soup and serve immediately.

Crab and Chilli Soup Energy 228kcal/951kj; Protein 23.6g; Carbohydrate 5.4g, of which sugars 5g; Fat 12.6g, of which saturates 6g; Cholesterol 90mg; Calcium 199mg; Fibre 1.1g; Sodium 767mg.
Spicy Seafood Soup Energy 778kcal/3288kj; Protein 39.5g; Carbohydrate 122.8g, of which sugars 9.4g; Fat 17.7g, of which saturates 1.4g; Cholesterol 176mg; Calcium 104mg; Fibre 6.9g; Sodium 734mg.

Chicken, Chilli and Tomato Soup

This delicious, refreshing soup is perfect for a light lunch when you need a lift.

Serves 4

225g/8oz skinless chicken
  breast fillets
1 garlic clove, crushed
pinch of freshly nutmeg
25g/1oz/2 tbsp butter
  or margarine
1/2 onion, finely chopped
15ml/1 tbsp tomato purée (paste)

400g/14oz can tomatoes, puréed
1.2 litres/2 pints/5 cups
  chicken stock
1 fresh chilli, seeded and chopped
1 chayote, peeled and diced,
  about 350g/12oz
5ml/1 tsp dried oregano
2.5ml/1/2 tsp dried thyme
50g/2oz smoked haddock fillet,
  skinned and diced
salt and ground black pepper
fresh chopped chives, to garnish

1 Dice the chicken, place in a bowl and season with salt, pepper, garlic and nutmeg. Mix well to coat the chicken and then set aside for about 30 minutes.

2 Melt the butter or margarine in a large pan, add the chicken and cook over a moderate heat for 5–6 minutes. Stir in the onion and fry gently for a further 5 minutes until the onion is slightly softened.

3 Add the tomato purée, puréed tomatoes, stock, chilli, chayote and herbs. Bring to the boil, cover and simmer gently for 35 minutes until the chayote is tender.

4 Add the smoked fish, simmer for a further 5 minutes or until the fish is cooked through, adjust the seasoning and pour into warmed soup bowls. Garnish with a sprinkling of chopped chives and serve.

Cook's Tip
Chayote, also called christophene, is a member of the gourd family. It is the size and shape of a very large pear, with pale green skin. The flesh has a mild flavour and works well here, where it absorbs the flavours of the other ingredients.

Chicken and Rice Soup with Chilli and Lemon Grass

This tasty soup, known as *shnor chrook*, is Cambodia's answer to the chicken noodle soup that is so popular in the West. Light and refreshing, it is the perfect choice for a hot day, as well as a great pick-me-up when you are feeling low or tired.

Serves 4

2 lemon grass stalks, trimmed, cut
  into three, and lightly bruised
15ml/1 tbsp Thai fish sauce
90g/3 1/2oz/1/2 cup short grain
  rice, rinsed
sea salt

ground black pepper
1 small bunch coriander (cilantro)
  leaves, finely chopped, and
  1 green or red chilli, seeded
  and cut into thin strips,
  to garnish
1 lime, cut in wedges, to serve

For the stock
1 small chicken or 2 meaty
  chicken legs
1 onion, quartered
2 garlic cloves, crushed
25g/1oz fresh root ginger, sliced
2 lemon grass stalks, cut in half
  lengthwise and bruised
2 dried red chillies
30ml/2 tbsp Thai fish sauce

1 Put the chicken into a large pan. Add all the other stock ingredients and pour in 2 litres/3 1/2 pints/8 cups water. Bring to the boil, then reduce the heat and simmer, covered, for 2 hours.

2 Skim any fat from the stock, strain and reserve. Remove the skin from the chicken and shred the meat. Set aside. Pour the stock back into the pan and bring to the boil, then simmer. Stir in the lemon grass, Thai fish sauce and the rice and simmer, uncovered, for 40 minutes. Add the chicken and season to taste.

3 Ladle the hot soup into bowls, garnish with the coriander and strips of chilli and serve with lime wedges to squeeze over.

Cook's Tip
• *Many Vietnamese and Cambodians often spike the soup with additional chillies as a garnish, or served on the side.*

Chicken and Chilli Soup Energy 133kcal/558kj; Protein 16.7g; Carbohydrate 32g; of which sugars 2.4g; Fat 6g; of which saturates 3.5g; Cholesterol 57mg; Calcium 36mg; Fibre 1.1g; Sodium 167mg.
Chicken and Rice Soup Energy 147kcal/615kj; Protein 12.8g; Carbohydrate 19.8g; of which sugars 1.4g; Fat 1.7g; of which saturates 0.4g; Cholesterol 53mg; Calcium 37mg; Fibre 0.8g; Sodium 320mg.

Chicken and Ginger Broth with Papaya

This is a traditional peasant dish that is still cooked every day in rural areas of the Philippines. In some areas, green papaya is added to the broth, which could be regarded as a version of coq au vin. Generally the chicken and broth are served with steamed rice, but the broth is also sipped during the meal to cleanse and stimulate the palate.

Serves 4 to 6
15–30ml/1–2 tbsp palm or
   groundnut (peanut) oil
2 garlic cloves, finely chopped
1 large onion, sliced
40g/1½oz fresh root ginger,
   finely grated
2 whole dried chillies
1 chicken, left whole or jointed,
   trimmed of fat
30ml/2 tbsp patis (fish sauce)
600ml/1 pint/2½ cups
   chicken stock
1.2 litres/2 pints/5 cups water
1 small green papaya, cut into
   fine slices or strips
1 bunch fresh young chilli or
   basil leaves
salt and ground black pepper
cooked rice, to serve

1 Heat the oil in a wok or a large pan that has a lid. Stir in the garlic, onion and ginger and fry gently until they begin to colour. Stir in the chillies, add the chicken and fry, turning often, until the skin is lightly browned all over.

2 Pour in the patis, stock and water, adding more water if necessary so that the whole chicken is completely covered. Bring to the boil, reduce the heat, cover and simmer gently for about 1½ hours, until the chicken is very tender when pierced with a sharp knife.

3 Season the stock with salt and pepper and add the papaya. Continue to simmer for a further 10–15 minutes, then stir in the chilli or basil leaves.

4 Serve the chicken and broth in warmed bowls, and prepare the same number of bowls of steamed rice. Each diner ladles some of the broth over the rice.

Spiced Chicken and Vegetable Soup

This creamy coconut soap, made with chicken and prawns, is substantial enough to serve on its own.

Serves 6 to 8
1 onion, ½ cut in two, ½ sliced
2 garlic cloves, crushed
1 fresh red or green chilli, seeded
   and sliced
1cm/½in cube shrimp paste
3 macadamia nuts or 6 almonds
1cm/½in galangal, peeled
   and sliced, or 5ml/1 tsp
   galangal powder
5ml/1 tsp sugar
vegetable oil, for frying
225g/8oz skinless chicken breast
   fillets, cut into 1cm/½in cubes
300ml/½ pint/1¼ cups
   coconut milk
1.2 litres/2 pints/5 cups
   chicken stock
1 aubergine (eggplant), diced
225g/8oz green beans, chopped
small wedge of crisp white
   cabbage, shredded
1 red (bell) pepper, seeded and
   finely sliced
115g/4oz cooked, peeled
   prawns (shrimp)
salt and ground black pepper

1 Grind the onion quarters, garlic, chilli, shrimp paste, nuts, galangal and sugar to a paste in a processor or in a mortar with a pestle.

2 Heat a wok, add the oil and then fry the paste, without browning, until it gives off a rich aroma.

3 Add the sliced onion and chicken cubes and cook for 3–4 minutes. Stir in the coconut milk and stock. Bring to the boil and simmer for a few minutes.

4 Add the diced aubergine to the soup, with the beans, and cook for a few minutes, until the beans are almost cooked.

5 A few minutes before serving, stir the cabbage, red pepper and prawns into the soup. The vegetables should be cooked so that they are still crunchy and the prawns merely need heating through.

6 Taste the soup and adjust the seasoning if necessary. Ladle the soup into warmed soup bowls and serve immediately.

Chicken and Ginger Broth Energy 290kcal/1219kj; Protein 46.4g; Carbohydrate 9.8g, of which sugars 8.7g; Fat 7.5g, of which saturates 1.5g; Cholesterol 169mg; Calcium 40mg; Fibre 2.2g; Sodium 150mg.
Spiced Chicken Soup Energy 130kcal/544kj; Protein 11.7g; Carbohydrate 7g, of which sugars 6.3g; Fat 6.3g, of which saturates 0.8g; Cholesterol 48mg; Calcium 62mg; Fibre 2g; Sodium 89mg.

Green Chilli, Lamb, Bean and Pumpkin Soup

This spicy, fresh soup combines tender meaty lamb with sweet pumpkin and green bananas.

Serves 4
115g/4oz black-eyed beans (peas), soaked for 2 hours, or overnight
675g/1½lb lamb neck (US shoulder or breast), cut into medium-size chunks
5ml/1 tsp chopped fresh thyme, or 2.5ml/½ tsp dried thyme
2 bay leaves
1.2 litres/2 pints/5 cups stock or water
1 onion, sliced
225g/8oz pumpkin, diced
2 black cardamom pods
7.5ml/1½ tsp ground turmeric
15ml/1 tbsp chopped fresh coriander (cilantro)
2.5ml/½ tsp caraway seeds
1 fresh green chilli, seeded and chopped
2 green bananas
1 carrot
salt and ground black pepper

1 Drain the black-eyed beans, place them in a pan and cover with fresh cold water. Bring to the boil, then boil rapidly for 10 minutes and then reduce the heat and simmer, covered, for 40–50 minutes until tender, adding more water if necessary. Remove from the heat and set aside to cool.

2 Meanwhile, put the lamb in a large pan, add the thyme, bay leaves and stock or water and bring to the boil. Cover and simmer over a moderate heat for 1 hour, until tender.

3 Add the onion, pumpkin, cardamoms, turmeric, coriander, caraway, chilli and seasoning and stir. Bring back to a simmer and then cook, uncovered, for 15 minutes, until the pumpkin is tender, stirring occasionally.

4 When the beans are cool, spoon into a blender or food processor with their liquid and blend to a smooth purée.

5 Cut the bananas into medium slices and the carrot into thin slices. Stir into the soup with the beans and cook for 10–12 minutes, until the vegetables are tender. Adjust the seasoning and serve.

Spicy Vegetable Broth with Minced Beef

This delicious soup is popular throughout Indonesia where it is called *sayur menir*.

Serves 6
30ml/2 tbsp groundnut (peanut) oil
115g/4oz finely minced (ground) beef
1 large onion, grated or finely chopped
1 garlic clove, crushed
1–2 chillies, seeded and chopped
1cm/½in cube shrimp paste
3 macadamia nuts or 6 almonds, finely ground
1 carrot, finely grated
5ml/1 tsp soft light brown sugar
1 litre/1¾ pints/4 cups chicken stock
50g/2oz dried shrimp, soaked in warm water for 10 minutes
225g/8oz spinach, rinsed and finely shredded
8 baby corn, sliced, or 200g/7oz canned corn kernels
1 large tomato, chopped
juice of ½ lemon
salt

1 Heat the oil in a pan. Add the beef, onion and garlic and cook, stirring, until the meat has evenly browned.

2 Add the chillies, shrimp paste, nuts, carrot and sugar to the minced beef. Add salt to taste.

3 Add the stock and bring gently to the boil. Reduce the heat to a simmer and then add the shrimp, with their soaking liquid. Simmer for about 10 minutes.

4 A few minutes before serving, add the spinach, corn, tomato and lemon juice. Simmer for a minute or two, to heat through. Do not overcook at this stage because this will spoil the appearance and the taste of the broth. Ladle into warmed individual bowls and serve immediately.

Cook's Tip
If you prefer a little more heat, to make this soup very hot and spicy simply add the seeds from inside the chillies.

Chilli and Pumpkin Soup Energy 442kcal/1855kJ; Protein 40.8g; Carbohydrate 27.2g, of which sugars 13.1g; Fat 19.7g, of which saturates 9g; Cholesterol 128mg; Calcium 74mg; Fibre 6.4g; Sodium 155mg.
Spicy Vegetable Broth Energy 218kcal/911kJ; Protein 12.6g; Carbohydrate 14.7g, of which sugars 8.4g; Fat 12.5g, of which saturates 2.3g; Cholesterol 54mg; Calcium 199mg; Fibre 3g; Sodium 530mg.

Roasted Coconut Cashew Nuts with Chilli

Serve these hot and sweet cashew nuts in paper or cellophane cones at parties. Not only do they look enticing and taste terrific, but the cones help to keep clothes and hands clean and can simply be thrown away afterwards.

Serves 6 to 8
15ml/1 tbsp groundnut (peanut) oil
30ml/2 tbsp clear honey
250g/8oz/2 cups cashew nuts
115g/4oz/1⅓ cups desiccated
    (dry unsweetened
    shredded) coconut
2 small fresh red chillies,
    seeded and finely chopped
salt and ground black pepper

1 Heat the oil in a wok or large frying pan.

2 Stir the honey into the pan and heat for a few seconds, stirring constantly.

3 Add the nuts and the desiccated coconut and stir-fry until both are golden brown. Stir the mixture constantly to ensure that it does not stick to the base of the pan.

4 Add the chillies to the pan and season with a little salt and ground black pepper to taste. Toss until all the ingredients are well mixed.

5 Serve the nuts warm or cooled in rolled-up paper cones or if you prefer, on saucers.

> **Variations**
> • Almonds would also work well in this recipe. Cashew nuts can be expensive so you could also choose peanuts for a more economical snack.
> • Desiccated coconut is a handy ingredient to have in your pantry as it has many uses, but if you can get hold of a fresh coconut then you can also use that in this recipe. Simply grate the flesh and substitute for the desiccated version.

Hot and Spicy Plantain Snacks

Sweet and crisp, deep-fried slices of plantain make good nibbles with drinks. Make sure the plantains are ripe – the skin should be brown and mottled – otherwise they tend to be woody rather than sweet and fruity. Be liberal with the spices as the starchy plantains can carry strong flavours.

Serves 2 to 4 as a snack
2 large ripe plantains
sunflower oil, for deep-frying
1 dried red chilli, roasted, seeded
    and chopped
15–30ml/1–2 tbsp zahtar
coarse salt

1 To peel the plantains, cut off their ends with a sharp knife and make two to three incisions in the skin from end to end, then peel off the skin. Cut the plantains into thick slices.

2 Heat the oil for deep-frying to 180°C/350°F, or until a cube of day-old bread browns in 30–45 seconds. Fry the plantain slices in batches until golden brown. Drain each batch on a double layer of kitchen paper.

3 While the plantain is still warm, place the pieces in a shallow bowl and sprinkle liberally with the dried roasted chilli, zahtar and salt.

4 Toss the ingredients thoroughly and serve immediately.

> **Cook's Tips**
> • Zahtar is a spice blend popular in North Africa and the Middle East. It is usually composed of toasted sesame seeds, dried thyme, dried marjoram and sumac. It is often sprinkled over meats and vegetables as a seasoning or mixed with olive oil and used as a bread glaze. Look for it in large supermarkets or Middle Eastern food stores.
> • To roast the chilli, place in a small frying pan and cook over a medium heat, stirring constantly, until the chilli darkens and gives off a peppery aroma.

Roasted Nuts Energy 436kcal/1810kJ; Protein 9.7g; Carbohydrate 22.1g, of which sugars 16.6g; Fat 34.9g, of which saturates 14.8g; Cholesterol 0mg; Calcium 20mg; Fibre 4g; Sodium 128mg.
Hot and Spicy Plantain Energy 334kcal/1408kJ; Protein 1.9g; Carbohydrate 59.4g, of which sugars 14.4g; Fat 11.5g, of which saturates 1.3g; Cholesterol 0mg; Calcium 8mg; Fibre 2.9g; Sodium 4mg.

Spiced Walnut and Red Chilli

Made primarily of walnuts, this spicy Turkish dip is usually served with toasted flatbread or chunks of crusty bread. It can also be served as an accompaniment to grilled, broiled or barbecued meats. Arabic in origin, this dish is traditionally made with pomegranate juice, but modern recipes often use lemon juice instead.

Serves 4 to 6
175g/6oz/1 cup broken
   shelled walnuts
5ml/1 tsp cumin seeds, dry-
   roasted and ground
5–10ml/1–2 tsp Turkish red
   pepper, or 1–2 fresh red

chillies, seeded and finely
   chopped, or 5ml/1 tsp
   chilli powder
1–2 garlic cloves (optional)
1 slice of day-old bread, sprinkled
   with water and left for a few
   minutes, then squeezed dry
15–30ml/1–2 tbsp tomato
   purée (paste)
5–10ml/1–2 tsp sugar
30ml/2 tbsp pomegranate syrup
   or juice of 1 lemon
120ml/4fl oz/½ cup olive or
   sunflower oil, plus extra
   for serving
salt and ground black pepper
a few sprigs of fresh flat leaf
   parsley, to garnish
strips of pitta bread, to serve

1 Using a large mortar and pestle, pound the walnuts with the cumin seeds, red pepper or the fresh red chillies and garlic.

2 Add the soaked bread and pound to a paste, then beat in the tomato purée, sugar and pomegranate syrup or the juice of a lemon, if using.

3 Now slowly drizzle in 120ml/4fl oz/½ cup oil, beating all the time until the paste is thick and light. Season with salt and ground black pepper, and spoon into a bowl.

4 Splash a little olive oil over the top to keep it moist, and garnish with parsley leaves. Serve at room temperature.

Cook's Tip
If you have an electric blender, whizz the ingredients together.

Roast Vegetables with Fresh Herbs and Chilli Sauce

Oven roasting brings out all the flavours of these classic Mediterranean vegetables. Serve them hot with grilled or roast meat or fish.

Serves 4
2–3 courgettes (zucchini)
1 large onion

1 red (bell) pepper
16 cherry tomatoes
2 garlic cloves, chopped
pinch of cumin seeds
5ml/1 tsp fresh thyme or
   4–5 torn basil leaves
60ml/4 tbsp olive oil
juice of ½ lemon
5–10ml/1–2 tsp harissa
fresh thyme sprigs, to garnish

1 Preheat the oven to 220°C/425°F/Gas 7. Cut the courgettes into long thin strips. Cut the onion into thin wedges and cut the pepper into fairly large chunks, discarding the seeds and core.

2 Place the vegetables in a roasting pan, add the tomatoes, garlic, cumin seeds and thyme or basil. Sprinkle with oil and toss to coat. Cook in the oven for 25–30 minutes until the vegetables are soft and slightly charred at the edges.

3 Blend the lemon juice and harissa and stir into the vegetables just before serving, garnished with the fresh thyme sprigs.

Variation
Try wedges of red and yellow (bell) peppers in place of one of the courgettes, or add chunks of aubergine (eggplant).

Cook's Tip
Harissa is a spicy paste made from a base of beetroot (beets) and carrots and flavoured with chillies, coriander seeds, caraway, garlic, salt and olive oil. It is a popular ingredient in northern African cooking and is sold in small pots – look out for its distinctive orangey red colour.

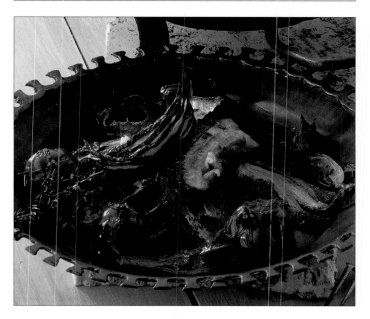

Spiced Walnut Energy 339kcal/1399kJ; Protein 4.8g; Carbohydrate 5.1g, of which sugars 2.8g; Fat 33.4g, of which saturates 3.5g; Cholesterol 0mg; Calcium 34mg; Fibre 1.2g; Sodium 32mg.
Roast Vegetables Energy 154kcal/635kJ; Protein 3.7g; Carbohydrate 8.2g, of which sugars 7.6g; Fat 12g, of which saturates 1.8g; Cholesterol 0mg; Calcium 48mg; Fibre 2.8g; Sodium 8mg.

Stir-fried Spinach with Chilli, Currants and Pine Nuts

There are endless versions of traditional spinach and yogurt meze dishes, ranging from plain steamed spinach served with yogurt, to this sweet and tangy Anatolian creation tamed with garlic-flavoured yogurt. Serve while still warm, with flatbread or chunks of a crusty loaf to accompany it.

Serves 3 to 4
350g/12oz fresh spinach leaves, thoroughly washed and drained
about 200g/7oz/scant 1 cup thick and natural (plain) yogurt
2 garlic cloves, crushed
30–45ml/2–3 tbsp olive oil
1 red onion, cut in half lengthways, in half again crossways, and sliced along the grain
5ml/1 tsp sugar
15–30ml/1–2 tbsp currants, soaked in warm water for 5–10 minutes and drained
30ml/2 tbsp pine nuts
5–10ml/1–2 tsp Turkish red pepper, or 1 fresh red chilli, seeded and finely chopped
juice of 1 lemon
salt and ground black pepper
a pinch of paprika, to garnish

1 Steam the spinach for 3–4 minutes, until wilted and soft. Drain off any excess water and chop the spinach.

2 In a medium bowl, beat the yogurt with the garlic. Season the mixture and set aside.

3 Heat the oil in a heavy pan and fry the onion and sugar, stirring, until the onion begins to colour. Add the currants, pine nuts and red pepper or chilli and fry until the nuts begin to darken slightly.

4 Add the spinach, tossing it around the pan until well mixed, then pour in the lemon juice and season with salt and pepper.

5 Serve the spinach straight from the pan with the yogurt spooned on top, or tip into a serving dish and make a well in the middle, then spoon the yogurt into the well, drizzling some of it over the spinach. Serve hot, garnished with a sprinkling of paprika.

Spicy Pumpkin Dip

This spicy dip is great to serve at a buffet or picnic. It can be stored in an airtight container for at least a week in the refrigerator. Serve it with chunks of bread or raw vegetables to dip into it.

Serves 6 to 8
45–60ml/3–4 tbsp olive oil
1 onion, finely chopped
5–8 garlic cloves, roughly chopped
675g/1½lb pumpkin, peeled and diced
5–10ml/1–2 tsp ground cumin
5ml/1 tsp paprika
1.5–2.5ml/¼–½ tsp ground ginger
1.5–2.5ml/¼–½ tsp curry powder
75g/3oz chopped canned tomatoes or diced fresh tomatoes and 15–30ml/1–2 tbsp tomato purée (paste)
½–1 red jalapeño or serrano chilli, chopped, or cayenne pepper, to taste
pinch of sugar, if necessary
juice of ½ lemon, or to taste
salt
30ml/2 tbsp chopped fresh coriander (cilantro) leaves, to garnish

1 Heat the oil in a frying pan, add the onion and half the garlic and fry until softened. Add the pumpkin, then cover the pan and cook for about 10 minutes, or until half-tender.

2 Add the spices to the pan and cook for 1–2 minutes. Stir in the tomatoes, chilli, sugar and salt and cook over a medium-high heat until the liquid has evaporated.

3 When the pumpkin is tender, mash to a paste. Add the remaining garlic and season, then stir in the lemon juice. Serve the dip at room temperature, sprinkled with the chopped fresh coriander.

Variation
• Use butternut squash, or any other winter squash, or sweet potato, in place of the pumpkin, if you prefer.
• To use as dippers, try strips of pitta bread or bread sticks, celery, carrot or cucumber sticks, or vegetables such as whole radishes or chicory (Belgian endive) spears.

Stir-fried Spinach Energy 145kcal/603kJ; Protein 5.8g; Carbohydrate 10.2g, of which sugars 9.8g; Fat 9.3g, of which saturates 1.3g; Cholesterol 1mg; Calcium 252mg; Fibre 2.2g; Sodium 165mg.
Spicy Pumpkin Dip Energy 54kcal/224kJ; Protein 0.9g; Carbohydrate 2.9g; of which sugars 2.3g; Fat 4.4g; of which saturates 0.7g; Cholesterol 1mg; Calcium 37mg; Fibre 1.3g; Sodium 3mg.

Aubergine and Chilli Pepper Dip

This is a lovely Anatolian meze dish of smoked aubergine and peppers with a refreshing lemon and chilli tang. Arabic in origin, it is traditionally served warm with lemon wedges to squeeze over it. Increase the quantities and serve it as a main dish with yogurt and bread, or serve it as an accompaniment to a barbecue spread.

Serves 4
2 red (bell) peppers
1 large aubergine (eggplant)
30–45ml/2–3 tbsp olive oil
1 red onion, cut in half lengthways and finely sliced along the grain
1 fresh red chilli, seeded and finely sliced
2 garlic cloves, chopped
5–10ml/1–2 tsp sugar
juice of 1 lemon
dash of white wine vinegar
a big handful of fresh flat leaf parsley, roughly chopped
salt and ground black pepper
lemon wedges and toasted pitta bread, to serve

1 Place the peppers under a conventional grill (broiler), or on a rack over the hot coals of a barbecue. Turn them from time to time until the skin is charred on all sides and the flesh feels soft. Place in a plastic bag and leave for a few minutes.

2 One at a time, hold the charred vegetables under cold running water and, using a small vegetable knife, peel off the skins of the charred vegetables. Place them on a chopping board and remove the stalks. Halve the peppers lengthways and scoop out the seeds, then chop the flesh to a pulp. Chop the aubergine flesh to a pulp too.

3 Pour the oil into a wide, heavy pan and toss in the onion, chilli, garlic and sugar. Cook over a medium heat for 2–3 minutes, until they begin to colour.

4 Add the pulped peppers and aubergine, stir in the lemon juice and vinegar and season with salt and pepper. Toss in the parsley and serve with lemon wedges and toasted pitta bread.

Herby Tomato and Chilli Dip

This Turkish meze dish is a mixture of chopped fresh vegetables. Along with cubes of honey-sweet melon and feta, or plump, juicy olives spiked with red pepper and oregano, this is meze at its simplest and best. Popular in kebab houses throughout Turkey, it makes a tasty snack or appetizer, and tastes great served with chunks of warm, crusty bread or toasted pitta to dip into the meze.

Serves 4
2 large tomatoes, skinned, seeded and finely chopped
2 Turkish green peppers or 1 green (bell) pepper, seeded and finely chopped
1 onion, finely chopped
1 green chilli, seeded and finely chopped
1 small bunch of fresh flat leaf parsley, finely chopped
a few fresh mint leaves, finely chopped
15–30ml/1–2 tbsp olive oil
salt and ground black pepper

1 Put all the finely chopped ingredients in a large bowl and mix well together until thoroughly combined.

2 Bind the mixture with the olive oil and season generously with salt and pepper.

3 Serve at room temperature, in individual bowls or a large dish.

> **Cook's Tip**
> To skin tomatoes, place in a bowl, cover with boiling water and leave for about 1 minute. The skin should peel off easily.

> **Variation**
> When you bind the chopped vegetables with the olive oil, add 15–30ml/1–2 tbsp tomato purée (paste) with a little extra chilli and 5–10ml/1–2 tsp sugar. The mixture will become a tangy paste to spread on fresh, crusty bread or toasted pitta, and it can also be used as a sauce for grilled (broiled) or barbecued meats.

Aubergine Dip Energy 102kcal/425kJ; Protein 1.8g; Carbohydrate 10.5g, of which sugars 9.8g; Fat 6.2g, of which saturates 1g; Cholesterol 0mg; Calcium 19mg; Fibre 3.1g; Sodium 6mg.
Herby Tomato and Chilli Dip Energy 101kcal/420kJ; Protein 2.3g; Carbohydrate 9.3g, of which sugars 8g; Fat 6.3g, of which saturates 0.9g; Cholesterol 0mg; Calcium 66mg; Fibre 2.7g; Sodium 15mg.

Italian Bread with Spicy Aromatic Tomatoes

This is a great way to keep hunger pangs at bay while you wait for the main course to come off the barbecue. As soon as the coals are hot enough, simply grill the sliced bread, heap on the sauce and drizzle over plenty of good quality extra virgin olive oil.
To accompany the breads, put out little bowls of pine nuts, lightly toasted in a pan over the barbecue.

Serves 6
2 sfilatino (Italian bread sticks),
  sliced lengthways into 3 pieces

1 garlic clove, cut in half
leaves from 4 fresh
  oregano sprigs
18 kalamata olives, pitted
  and sliced
extra virgin olive oil, for drizzling
ground black pepper

For the aromatic tomatoes
800g/1¾lb ripe
  plum tomatoes
30ml/2 tbsp extra virgin
  olive oil
2 garlic cloves, crushed to a paste
  with a pinch of salt
1 small piece of dried chilli, seeds
  removed, finely chopped

1 Prepare the barbecue. Plunge the tomatoes into boiling water for 30 seconds, then refresh in cold water. Peel away the skins, remove the seeds and core and roughly chop the flesh. Mix the oil and crushed garlic in a large frying pan. Place on the stove over a high heat. When the garlic sizzles, add the tomatoes and the chilli. Cook for 2 minutes. The aim is to evaporate the liquid not to pulp the tomatoes, which should keep their shape.

2 Once the flames have died down, position a lightly oiled grill rack over the hot coals. When the coals are medium-hot, or with a moderate coating of ash, toast the bread on both sides. Generously rub each slice with the cut side of a piece of garlic.

3 Roughly chop all but a few of the oregano leaves and mix them into the tomato sauce. Pile the mixture on to the toasted sfilatino. Scatter over the whole oregano leaves and the olive slices. Sprinkle with plenty of pepper, drizzle with lots of extra virgin olive oil and serve immediately.

Cheese and Chilli Tortillas

These cheese-filled tortillas are the Mexican equivalent of toasted sandwiches. Serve them as soon as they are cooked, or they will become chewy. If you are making them for a crowd, fill and fold the tortillas ahead of time, but only cook them to order.

Serves 4
200g/7oz mozzarella,
  Monterey Jack or mild
  Cheddar cheese
1 fresh whole fresno
  chilli (optional)
8 wheat flour tortillas, about
  15cm/6in across
onion chutney or relish,
  to serve

1 If using mozzarella cheese, it must be drained thoroughly and then patted dry and sliced into thin strips. Monterey Jack and Cheddar should both be coarsely grated, as finely grated cheese will melt and ooze away when cooking. Set the cheese aside in a bowl.

2 If using the chilli, spear it on a long-handled metal skewer and roast it over the flame of a gas burner until the skin blisters and darkens. Do not let the flesh burn. Alternatively, dry fry it in a griddle pan until the skin is scorched. Place the roasted chilli in a strong plastic bag and tie the top to keep the steam in. Set aside for 20 minutes.

3 Remove the chilli from the bag and peel off the skin. Cut off the stalk, then slit the chilli and scrape out the seeds. Cut the flesh into eight thin strips.

4 Warm a large frying pan or griddle. Place one tortilla on the pan or griddle at a time, sprinkle about an eighth of the cheese on to one half and add a strip of chilli, if using. Fold the tortilla over the cheese and press the edges together gently to seal. Cook the filled tortilla for about 1 minute until the cheese is beginning to melt, then carefully turn over and cook the other side for 1 minute.

5 Remove the filled tortilla from the pan or griddle, cut it into three triangles or four strips and serve immediately, with the onion chutney or relish.

Italian Bread Energy 473kcal/2000kJ; Protein 13.7g; Carbohydrate 80.3g, of which sugars 8g; Fat 13.1g, of which saturates 2.1g; Cholesterol 0mg; Calcium 177mg; Fibre 5.1g; Sodium 1021mg.
Cheese and Chilli Tortillas Energy 418kcal/1764kJ; Protein 17g; Carbohydrate 66g, of which sugars 7g; Fat 11g, of which saturates 7g; Cholesterol 29mg; Calcium 303mg; Fibre 2.6g; Sodium 0.5mg.

Spicy Omelette

Eggs are packed with nutritional value and make wholesome and delicious dishes. This omelette, cooked with potato, onion and a touch of spices, can be put together quickly for a quick snack.

Serves 4 to 6
30ml/2 tbsp vegetable oil
1 medium onion, finely chopped
2.5ml/½ tsp cumin powder

1 clove garlic, finely crushed
1 or 2 green chillies,
   finely chopped
a few sprigs fresh coriander
   (cilantro), chopped
1 firm tomato, chopped
1 small potato, cubed
   and boiled
25g/1oz cooked peas
25g/1oz cooked corn
salt and pepper, to taste
2 eggs, beaten
25g/1oz grated cheese

1 Heat the oil in a pan and fry the onion for 5 minutes until softened and beginning to colour.

2 Add the cumin powder, crushed garlic and chopped chillies and cook for 1–2 minutes, stirring until well combined.

3 Add the coriander, tomato, potato cubes, peas and corn to the pan, stir until thoroughly mixed and cook until hot but the potato and tomato are still firm. Season to taste.

4 Increase the heat and pour in the beaten eggs. Shake the pan until the eggs are evenly spread around the pan and well combined with the other ingredients.

5 Reduce the heat, cover the pan and cook until the bottom of the omelette is a golden brown colour. Turn the omelette and sprinkle with the grated cheese. Place under a hot grill (broiler) and cook until the egg sets and the cheese has melted.

Variation
Other vegetables will work well here: try using a thinly sliced red (bell) pepper in place of the potato, or substitute a few chopped mushrooms instead of peas or corn.

Steamed Tofu Dumplings with Chilli and Chives

The slight spiciness and delicate texture of Korean chives make them a wonderful ingredient to add to these stuffed paper-thin steamed dumplings, called *mandu* in Korea. Here the succulent filling of tofu is combined with beef and rice wine.

Serves 4
30 dumpling skins
1 egg, beaten

For the filling
3 spring onions (scallions),
   finely chopped
3 garlic cloves, crushed

5ml/1 tsp finely grated fresh
   root ginger
5ml/1 tsp mirin or rice wine
90g/3½oz/scant ½ cup minced
   (ground) beef
90g/3½oz firm tofu
90g/3½oz Korean chives,
   finely chopped
½ onion, finely chopped
30ml/2 tbsp soy sauce
30ml/2 tbsp sesame oil
15ml/1 tbsp sugar
15ml/1 tbsp salt
10ml/2 tsp ground black pepper

For the dipping sauce
60ml/4 tbsp dark soy sauce
30ml/2 tbsp rice vinegar
5ml/1 tsp Korean chilli powder

1 To make the dipping sauce, mix the soy sauce, rice vinegar and chilli powder in a small serving bowl.

2 For the filling, put the spring onions, garlic, ginger, mirin or rice wine and beef into a bowl and mix well. Marinate for 15 minutes.

3 Meanwhile, drain off any excess liquid from the tofu, then crumble into a bowl. Add the chives to the seasoned beef, with the tofu and remaining filling ingredients. Mix together thoroughly.

4 Take a dumpling skin and brush with a little beaten egg. Place a spoonful of the stuffing in the middle and fold into a half-moon shape, crimping the edges firmly to seal. Repeat with the other dumpling skins. Place them in a steamer over a pan of boiling water and cook for 6 minutes. Or, you can just cook the dumplings in boiling water for about 3 minutes. Arrange on a serving dish and serve with the soy dipping sauce.

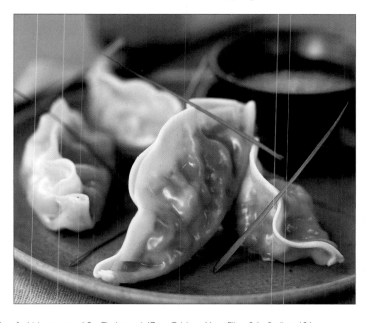

Spicy Omelette Energy 93kcal/388kJ; Protein 4g; Carbohydrate 3.7g, of which sugars 1.2g; Fat 7.1g, of which saturates 1.9g; Cholesterol 67mg; Calcium 46mg; Fibre 0.6g; Sodium 104mg.
Steamed Dumplings Energy 235kcal/982kJ; Protein 9.9g; Carbohydrate 26.1g, of which sugars 6.5g; Fat 10.8g, of which saturates 2.5g; Cholesterol 14mg; Calcium 208mg; Fibre 2.2g; Sodium 1054mg.

Hot Spring Rolls

These Thai spring rolls are filled with a tasty garlic, pork and noodle mixture.

Makes 24
24 x 15cm/6in square spring roll
  wrappers, thawed if frozen
30ml/2 tbsp plain
  (all-purpose) flour
vegetable oil, for deep-frying
sweet chilli dipping sauce, to serve

For the filling
6 Chinese dried mushrooms, soaked
  for 30 minutes in warm water
50g/2oz cellophane noodles
30ml/2 tbsp vegetable oil

2 garlic cloves, chopped
2 fresh red chillies, seeded
  and chopped
225g/8oz minced (ground) pork
50g/2oz peeled cooked prawns
  (shrimp), thawed if frozen
30ml/2 tbsp Thai fish sauce
5ml/1 tsp sugar
1 carrot, grated
50g/2oz piece of canned bamboo
  shoot, drained and chopped
50g/2oz/⅔ cup beansprouts
2 spring onions (scallions),
  finely chopped
15ml/1 tbsp chopped fresh
  coriander (cilantro)
ground black pepper

1 Drain the mushrooms. Cut off and discard the stems. Chop the caps finely. Cover the noodles with boiling water and soak for 10 minutes. Drain and snip them into 5cm/2in lengths. Heat the oil in a wok, add the garlic and chillies and stir-fry for 30 seconds. Transfer to a plate.

2 Stir-fry the pork until browned. Add the mushrooms, noodles and prawns. Stir in the fish sauce and sugar. Season with pepper. Pour into a bowl. Stir in the carrot, bamboo, beansprouts, spring onions and coriander. Mix in the reserved chilli mixture.

3 Stir a little water into the flour in a small bowl to make a paste. Place a spoonful of the filling in the centre of a wrapper. Turn the bottom edge over to cover the filling, then fold in the sides. Roll up almost to the top, then brush the top edge with the flour paste and seal. Fill the remaining wrappers.

4 Heat the oil in a deep-fryer or wok to 190°C/375°F, or until a cube of bread browns in about 45 seconds. Fry the spring rolls, in batches, until crisp and golden. Drain on kitchen paper and serve hot with sweet chilli sauce.

Fiery Potato Cakes

Only a few communities in India make these unusual appetizers. They can also be served as a main meal accompanied with a salad.

Makes 8 to 10
15ml/1 tbsp vegetable oil
1 large onion, finely chopped
2 garlic cloves, finely crushed
5cm/2in piece fresh root ginger,
  finely crushed
5ml/1 tsp ground coriander
5ml/1 tsp ground cumin

2 green chillies, finely chopped
30ml/2 tbsp each chopped fresh
  coriander (cilantro) and mint
225g/8oz lean minced (ground)
  beef or lamb
50g/2oz frozen peas, thawed
juice of 1 lemon
900g/2lb potatoes, boiled
  and mashed
2 eggs, beaten
breadcrumbs, for coating
vegetable oil, for shallow-frying
salt
lemon wedges, to serve

1 Heat the vegetable oil in a wok or frying pan and fry the onion for 5 minutes until it begins to turn translucent. Add the garlic, ginger, coriander, cumin, chillies and fresh herbs, and cook, stirring frequently, for another 5 minutes.

2 Add the minced meat and the peas and fry until the meat is cooked, then season with salt and lemon juice to taste. The mixture should be very dry.

3 Divide the mashed potato into about eight or ten portions. Take one portion and flatten it into a pancake shape in the palm of your hand.

4 Place a spoonful of the meat mixture into the centre of the potato and gather the sides together to enclose the meat. Flatten it slightly to make a round shape. Repeat until the remaining potato portions are filled.

5 Place the beaten egg and breadcrumbs on separate small plates. Dip each potato cake first in the egg and then in the breadcrumbs, ensuring they are evenly coated. Chill for 1 hour.

6 Heat the oil in a frying pan and shallow-fry the cakes until brown and crisp all over. Serve hot, with lemon wedges.

Hot Spring Rolls Energy 135kcal/562kJ; Protein 3.1g; Carbohydrate 7.8g, of which sugars 0.5g; Fat 10.3g, of which saturates 1.4g; Cholesterol 10mg; Calcium 15mg; Fibre 0.4g; Sodium 41g.
Fiery Potato Cakes Energy 207kcal/864kJ; Protein 8.1g; Carbohydrate 18g, of which sugars 3g; Fat 12g, of which saturates 2.8g; Cholesterol 52mg; Calcium 24mg; Fibre 1.6g; Sodium 43mg.

Onion Bhajias

Bhajias are a classic Indian snack. Gram flour is used to make the batter, which can also be used with a variety of other vegetables, meat or seafood to make pakoras.

Makes 20 to 25

225g/8oz/2 cups gram flour, or
　channa atta
2.5ml/¹/₂ tsp chilli powder
5ml/1 tsp turmeric powder
5ml/1 tsp baking powder
1.5ml/¹/₄ tsp asafoetida
salt, to taste
¹/₂ tsp each nigella, fennel,
　cumin and onion seeds,
　coarsely crushed
2 large onions, finely sliced
2 green chillies,
　finely chopped
50g/2oz coriander (cilantro)
　leaves, chopped
cold water, to mix
vegetable oil, for deep-frying

1 In a bowl, mix together the flour, chilli, turmeric, baking powder, asafoetida and salt to taste. Pass the mixture through a sieve (strainer) into a large mixing bowl.

2 Add the coarsely crushed seeds, onion, green chillies and coriander leaves and toss together well. Very gradually mix in enough cold water until a thick batter forms and surrounds all the ingredients.

3 Heat enough oil in a wok for deep-frying. Drop spoonfuls of the mixture into the hot oil and fry until they are golden brown. Leave enough space to turn the fritters. Drain well and serve hot.

> **Cook's Tips**
> • Gram flour, also known as besan, is a pale-yellow flour made from ground chickpeas. More aromatic and with less starch content and higher protein than wheat flour, it is used widely in Indian cookery for doughs, batters and for thickening sauces. Look for it in large supermarkets or Indian and Asian food stores.
> • Asafoetida is a pungent spice obtained from the resin of a fennel-like plant. It has a very strong odour of garlic and onion and should only be used sparingly.

Spicy Split Pea or Lentil Fritters

These delicious spicy fritters, called *piaju*, come from India.

Serves 4 to 6

250g/9oz/generous 1 cup yellow
　split peas or red lentils,
　soaked overnight
3–5 garlic cloves, chopped
30ml/2 tbsp roughly chopped
　fresh root ginger
120ml/4fl oz/¹/₂ cup chopped
　fresh coriander (cilantro) leaves
2.5–5ml/¹/₂–1 tsp ground cumin
1.5–2.5ml/¹/₄–¹/₂ tsp
　ground turmeric
large pinch of cayenne pepper or
　¹/₂–1 fresh green chilli, chopped
120ml/4fl oz/¹/₂ cup gram flour
5ml/1 tsp baking powder
30ml/2 tbsp couscous
2 large or 3 small
　onions, chopped
vegetable oil, for frying
salt and ground black pepper
lemon and fresh chilli, to serve

1 Drain the split peas or lentils, reserving a little of the soaking water. Put the chopped garlic and ginger in a food processor or blender and process until finely minced (ground). Add the drained peas or lentils, 15–30ml/1–2 tbsp of the reserved soaking water and the coriander, and process to form a paste.

2 Add the cumin, turmeric, cayenne or chilli, 2.5ml/¹/₂ tsp salt, 2.5ml/¹/₂ tsp pepper, the gram flour, baking powder and couscous to the mixture and combine. The mixture should form a thick batter. If it seems too thick, add a spoonful of the soaking water. Add a little more flour or couscous if it is too watery. Mix in the onions.

3 Heat the oil in a wide, deep frying pan, to a depth of about 5cm/2in, until it is hot enough to brown a cube of bread in 30 seconds. Using two spoons, form the mixture into two-bitesize balls and slip each one gently into the hot oil. Cook until golden brown on the underside, then turn and cook the second side until golden brown.

4 Remove the fritters from the hot oil with a slotted spoon and drain well on kitchen paper. Transfer the fritters to a baking sheet and keep them warm in the oven until all the mixture is cooked. Serve the fritters hot or at room temperature with lemon wedges and chopped fresh chilli.

Onion Bhajias Energy 72kcal/301kJ; Protein 1.2g; Carbohydrate 8.8g, of which sugars 1.3g; Fat 3.8g, of which saturates 0.4g; Cholesterol 0mg; Calcium 23mg; Fibre 0.7g; Sodium 2mg.
Split Pea Fritters Energy 360kcal/1511kJ; Protein 14.1g; Carbohydrate 51.3g, of which sugars 8.3g; Fat 12.3g, of which saturates 1.4g; Cholesterol 0mg; Calcium 119mg; Fibre 5.3g; Sodium 26g.

Spiced Samosas

Traditional samosa pastry requires a lot of time and hard work but spring roll pastry makes an excellent substitute and is readily available from supermarkets and Asian stores.
One packet will generally make about 30 samosas. They can be frozen either before or after frying.

Makes 30
I packet spring roll pastry, thawed and wrapped in a damp dish towel
vegetable oil, for deep-frying

For the filling
3 large potatoes, boiled and coarsely mashed
85g/3oz/¾ cup frozen peas, boiled and drained
50g/2oz/⅓ cup canned corn, drained
5ml/I tsp ground coriander
5ml/I tsp ground cumin
5ml/I tsp amchur (dry mango powder)
I small onion (red if available), finely chopped
2 green chillies, seeded and finely chopped
30ml/2 tbsp each chopped coriander (cilantro) and mint leaves
juice of I lemon
salt

I Toss all the ingredients together for the samosa filling in a large mixing bowl. Mix together with a wooden spoon or your hands until thoroughly blended. Adjust the seasoning with salt and lemon juice, to taste.

2 To make the samosas, use one strip of the spring roll pastry at a time, keeping the rest under the dish towel to prevent them from drying out. Place I tbsp of the filling mixture at one end of the strip of pastry and diagonally fold it so that it forms a triangle.

3 Put the vegetable oil in a wide, deep frying pan or wok, so you have enough for deep-frying. Heat the oil until it is hot enough to brown a cube of bread in 30 seconds.

4 Fry the samosas in small batches of about five until they are golden brown all over. Serve hot with a fruity chutney or a sweet chilli sauce.

Fried Yam Balls

Yam balls are a popular snack in many African countries. They are traditionally made quite plain, but can be flavoured with chopped vegetables and herbs, as in this recipe, or with cooked meat or fish, or spices.

Makes about 24 balls
450g/1lb white yam, diced

30ml/2 tbsp finely chopped onion
45ml/3 tbsp chopped tomatoes
2.5ml/½ tsp chopped fresh thyme
I green chilli, seeded and finely chopped
15ml/I tbsp finely chopped spring onion (scallion)
I garlic clove, crushed
I egg, beaten
salt and ground black pepper
vegetable oil, for shallow frying
seasoned flour, for dusting

I Boil the yam in salted water for about 30 minutes until tender. Drain and mash the yam. Add the onion, tomatoes, thyme, chilli, spring onion and garlic, then stir in the egg and seasoning and mix well.

2 Using a dessertspoon, scoop a little of the mixture at a time and, using your fingers, mould into small balls. Heat a little oil in a large frying pan, roll the yam balls in the seasoned flour and then fry for a few minutes until golden brown. Drain the yam balls on kitchen paper and keep them warm while cooking the rest of the mixture. Serve the balls immediately.

Cook's Tip
Yam is a tropical-vine tuber, similar in many ways to a sweet potato – although they are in fact from different plant species. You can use sweet potatoes instead if yams are hard to find.

Variation
Try adding fresh chopped herbs to the yam mixture; parsley and chives make a good combination. Mix in 30ml/2 tbsp with the egg and seasoning.

Spiced Samosas Energy 86kcal/359kJ; Protein 1g; Carbohydrate 7g, of which sugars 1g; Fat 6g, of which saturates 1g; Cholesterol 0mg; Calcium 4mg; Fibre 0.5g; Sodium 0.1mg.
Fried Yam Balls Energy 179kcal/754kJ Protein 1.7g; Carbohydrate 31.8g, of which sugars 5.9g; Fat 5.9g, of which saturates 0.8g; Cholesterol 0mg; Calcium 21mg; Fibre 1.6g; Sodium 4mg.

Popcorn with Lime and Chilli

If the only popcorn you've had came out of a carton at the movies, try this Mexican speciality. The lime juice and chilli powder are inspired additions, and the snack is quite a healthy choice to serve with drinks.

Makes 1 large bowl
30ml/2 tbsp vegetable oil
225g/8oz/1¼ cups corn
  kernels for popcorn
10ml/2 tsp chilli powder
juice of 2 limes

1 Heat the oil in a large, heavy frying pan until it is very hot. Add the popcorn and immediately cover the pan with a lid and reduce the heat.

2 After a few minutes the corn should start to pop. Resist the temptation to lift the lid to check. Shake the pan occasionally so that all corn will be cooked and browned.

3 When the sound of popping corn has stopped, quickly remove the pan from the heat and allow to cool slightly.

4 Take off the pan lid and with a spoon lift out and discard any corn kernels that have not popped. The uncooked corn will have fallen to the bottom of the pan and is completely inedible.

5 Add the chilli powder. Shake the pan again and again to make sure that all of the corn is covered with a colourful dusting of chilli.

6 Transfer the popcorn to a large bowl and keep warm. Add a squeeze of lime juice immediately before serving.

> **Variation**
> Give your popcorn an Indian flavour by replacing the chilli powder with curry powder. Omit the lime juice and add 5ml/½ tsp salt and 5ml/½ tsp sugar to the popcorn. You can also add in some flaked (sliced) almonds and sultanas (golden raisins), if you like.

Rice Cakes with Spicy Dipping Sauce

Prepare these rice cakes at least a day before you plan to serve them, as the rice needs to dry out overnight.

Serves 4 to 6
175g/6oz/1 cup Thai jasmine rice
350ml/12fl oz/1½ cups water
oil, for deep-frying and greasing

For the spicy dipping sauce
6 dried chillies, halved and seeded
2.5ml/½ tsp salt
2 shallots, chopped
2 garlic cloves, chopped
4 coriander (cilantro) roots
10 white peppercorns
250ml/8fl oz/1 cup coconut milk
5ml/1 tsp shrimp paste
115g/4oz minced (ground) pork
115g/4oz cherry tomatoes, chopped
15ml/1 tbsp Thai fish sauce
15ml/1 tbsp palm sugar (jaggery)
  or light muscovado (brown) sugar
30ml/2 tbsp tamarind juice
  (tamarind paste mixed with
  warm water)
30ml/2 tbsp coarsely chopped
  roasted peanuts
2 spring onions (scallions), chopped

1 For the sauce, soak the chillies in warm water for 20 minutes. Drain and crush in a mortar with the salt. Add the shallots, garlic, coriander and peppercorns. Pound to a coarse paste.

2 Boil the coconut milk in a pan until it separates. Add the chilli paste and cook for 2–3 minutes. Stir in the shrimp paste.

3 Add the pork and cook for 5–10 minutes. Stir in the tomatoes, fish sauce, sugar and tamarind juice. Simmer, stirring until thickened, then stir in the peanuts and spring onions. Leave to cool.

4 Preheat the oven to the lowest setting. Wash the rice in several changes of water. Put it in a pan, add the water, cover and bring to the boil. Reduce the heat and simmer for 15 minutes.

5 Fluff up the rice. Spoon on to a greased baking sheet and press down. Leave in the oven to dry out overnight.

6 Break the rice into cake-size pieces. Heat the oil in a wok or deep-fryer. Deep-fry the cakes, in batches, for about 1 minute, until they puff up. Remove and drain well. Serve with the sauce.

Popcorn with Lime and Chilli Energy 484kcal/2021kJ; Protein 8g; Carbohydrate 39g,of which sugars 5g; Fat 34g, of which saturates 4g; Cholesterol 0mg; Calcium 12mg; Fibre 3.4g; Sodium 0.4mg.
Rice Cakes Energy 316kcal/1508kJ; Protein 11.7g; Carbohydrate 42g, of which sugars 8.8g; Fat 16g, of which saturates 2.9g; Cholesterol 19mg; Calcium 38mg; Fibre 0.8g; Sodium 359mg.

Seafood Fritters with a Fiery Pear and Chilli Dip

Succulent seafood is battered and lightly fried to create these golden fritters.

Serves 4

2 eggs, beaten
45ml/3 tbsp vegetable oil, for frying
75g/3oz/²⁄₃ cup plain (all-purpose) flour for dusting
salt and ground black pepper

For the dipping sauce

45ml/3 tbsp light soy sauce
45ml/3 tbsp sugar
1 garlic clove, crushed
10ml/2 tsp pear juice
2.5ml/½ tsp lemon juice
1.5ml/½ tsp Korean chilli powder

For the prawn fritters

5 medium-size prawns (shrimp), peeled

juice of ½ lemon
30ml/2 tbsp white wine
2.5ml/½ tsp sesame oil
1 dried shiitake mushroom, soaked in warm water for about 30 minutes until soft
1 green chilli, finely chopped

For the crab fritters

75g/3oz crab meat
3 oyster mushrooms, finely sliced
¼ green (bell) pepper, chopped
25g/1oz Korean chives, finely sliced
1 garlic clove, thinly sliced
2 eggs, beaten
45ml/3 tbsp plain (all-purpose) flour

For the cod fritters

300g/11oz cod fillet
7.5ml/1½ tsp dark soy sauce
5ml/1 tsp white wine
2.5ml/½ tsp sesame oil

1 Combine all the ingredients for the sauce in a small bowl. For the prawn fritters, season the prawns with salt, pepper, lemon juice, white wine and sesame oil. Chop the mushroom and mix with the chilli, season with sesame oil, and dust with flour. Set aside. Dust the prawns with flour. Coat with egg and set aside.

2 To make the crab fritters, season the crab meat and place in a bowl. Add the remaining ingredients, mix well and set aside. For the cod fritters, cut into bitesize pieces and mix with the other ingredients. Dust with flour, coat with egg and set aside.

3 Heat the oil in a frying pan. Fry the fritters until browned and then add mushroom mixture to the prawn fritters. Continue frying until all are golden brown. Serve with the dipping sauce.

Hot Spicy Prawns with Coriander

This is a quick and easy way of preparing prawns for a snack or appetizer. If you increase the quantities, this dish can also be served as a main course, and is simple enough to make for a tasty midweek dinner. Select a variety of mushrooms and add them to the pan with the sauce ingredients, if you like. Serve the prawns with bread to mop up the tasty juices.

Serves 2 to 4

450g/1lb uncooked king prawns (jumbo shrimp)
60ml/4 tbsp olive oil
2–3 garlic cloves, chopped
25g/1oz fresh root ginger, peeled and shredded
1 chilli, seeded and chopped
5ml/1 tsp cumin seeds
5ml/1 tsp paprika
bunch of fresh coriander (cilantro), chopped
salt
1 lemon, cut into wedges, to serve

1 To prepare the prawns, hold each one between two fingers and gently pull off the tail shell. Twist off the head. Peel away the soft body shell and the small claws beneath and rinse thoroughly under cold water.

2 Pour the olive oil into a large, heavy frying pan, and heat the oil over a medium heat. Add the chopped garlic, stirring to ensure it does not burn, or it will taste bitter.

3 Stir in the ginger, chilli and cumin seeds. Cook the mixture briefly, stirring constantly, until the ingredients give off a lovely fragrant aroma. Add the paprika and stir in well.

4 Add the prawns to the pan. Fry them over a fairly high heat, turning them frequently, for 3–5 minutes, until just cooked.

5 Season to taste with salt and add the coriander. Serve immediately, with lemon wedges for squeezing over the prawns.

> **Variation**
> This dish is also delicious made with scallops or mussels in place of the prawns.

Seafood Fritters Energy 294kcal/1227kJ; Protein 29.3g; Carbohydrate 9.1g, of which sugars 6.1g; Fat 15.3g, of which saturates 2.8g; Cholesterol 287mg; Calcium 103mg; Fibre 1.1g; Sodium 671mg.
Hot Spicy Prawns Energy 382kcal/1591kJ; Protein 40.8g; Carbohydrate 1.1g; of which sugars 0.9g; Fat 23.9g; of which saturates 3.4g; Cholesterol 439mg; Calcium 254mg; Fibre 1.9g; Sodium 440mg.

Prawns in Chilli-chocolate Sauce

There is a long tradition in Spain, which originates in Mexico, of cooking savoury food – even shellfish – with chocolate. Known as *langostinos en chocolate* in Spanish, this is just the kind of culinary adventure that Spanish chefs love.

Serves 4
8 large raw prawns (shrimp),
　in the shell
15ml/1 tbsp seasoned plain
　(all-purpose) flour
15ml/1 tbsp pale dry sherry
juice of 1 large orange
15g/½oz dark (bittersweet)
　chocolate, chopped
30ml/2 tbsp olive oil
2 garlic cloves, finely chopped
2.5cm/1in piece fresh root ginger,
　finely chopped
1 small dried chilli, seeded
　and chopped
salt and ground black pepper

1 Peel the prawns, leaving just the tail sections intact. Make a shallow cut down the back of each one and carefully pull out and discard the dark intestinal tract.

2 Turn the prawns over so that the undersides are uppermost, and then carefully slit them open from tail to top, using a small sharp knife, cutting them almost, but not quite, through to the central back line.

3 Press the prawns down firmly to flatten them out. Coat with the seasoned flour and set aside.

4 Gently heat the sherry and orange juice in a small pan. When warm, remove from the heat and stir in the chopped chocolate until melted.

5 Heat the oil in a frying pan. Add the garlic, ginger and chilli and cook for 2 minutes until golden. Remove with a slotted spoon and reserve. Add the prawns, cut side down, and cook for 2–3 minutes until golden brown with pink edges. Turn the prawns and cook for a further 2 minutes.

6 Return the garlic mixture to the pan and pour the chocolate sauce over. Cook for 1 minute, turning the prawns to coat them in the glossy sauce. Season to taste and serve hot.

Seafood and Spring Onion Pancake with Mixed Chillies

This pancake combines the silky texture of squid and scallops with the crunch and piquancy of spring onions.

Serves 4
90g/3½oz squid, trimmed,
　cleaned, skinned and sliced
2 oysters, removed from the shell
5 clams, removed from the shell
5 small prawns (shrimp), shelled
3 scallops, removed from the shell
15ml/1 tbsp vegetable oil
5 spring onions (scallions), sliced
　into thin strips
½ red chilli, seeded and cut into
　thin strips
½ green chilli, seeded and cut
　into thin strips
50g/2oz enoki mushrooms
1 garlic clove, thinly sliced
salt and ground black pepper

For the batter
115g/4oz/1 cup plain
　(all-purpose) flour
40g/1½oz/⅓ cup cornflour
　(cornstarch)
2 eggs, beaten
5ml/1 tsp salt
5ml/1 tsp sugar

For the dipping sauce
90ml/6 tbsp light soy sauce
22.5ml/4½ tsp rice vinegar
1 spring onion (scallion), shredded
1 red chilli, finely shredded
1 garlic clove, crushed
5ml/1 tsp sesame oil
5ml/1 tsp sesame seeds

1 For the batter, sift the flour into a large bowl. Add the rest of the batter ingredients with 200ml/7fl oz/scant 1 cup iced water and whisk until smooth. Set aside. Put the seafood into another large bowl. Season, and leave to stand for 10 minutes.

2 Meanwhile, make the dipping sauce. Put all the ingredients in a small bowl, mixing well until combined.

3 Heat the vegetable oil in a large frying pan. Pour one-third of the batter in, spreading it evenly in the pan. Place the spring onions, chillies, mushrooms and garlic on to the pancake and then add the seafood. Pour over the remaining batter and cook, turning once, until the pancake is golden brown on both sides.

4 Slice the pancake into bitesize pieces and serve on a large plate with the dipping sauce.

Prawns Energy 133kcal/554kJ; Protein 9.5g; Carbohydrate 7.4g, of which sugars 3.6g; Fat 6.9g, of which saturates 1.5g; Cholesterol 98mg; Calcium 49mg; Fibre 0.3g; Sodium 97mg.
Seafood Pancake Energy 255kcal/1077kJ; Protein 16.5g; Carbohydrate 33.7g, of which sugars 1.9g; Fat 7.1g, of which saturates 1.4g; Cholesterol 232mg; Calcium 80mg; Fibre 1.4g; Sodium 613mg.

Steamed Mussels with Chilli and Lemon Grass

This dish, called *so hap xa*, is Vietnam's version of the French classic, *moules marinière*. In this recipe, the mussels are steamed open in a herby stock with lemon grass and chilli instead of wine and parsley. Both versions are delicious, and, as in France, this one can be served with chunks of baguette to mop up the cooking liquid. This is also a popular Vietnamese method of steaming clams and snails. Beer is sometimes used instead of stock and it makes a rich, fragrant sauce.

Serves 4
1kg/2¼lb fresh mussels
600ml/1 pint/2½ cups chicken
  stock or beer, or a mixture
1 green or red Thai chilli, seeded
  and finely chopped
2 shallots, finely chopped
2–3 lemon grass stalks,
  finely chopped
1 bunch of ginger leaves
salt and ground black pepper
baguette, to serve (optional)

1 Scrub the mussels, removing any barnacles and pull away any 'beards'. Discard any mussels that do not close when tapped sharply. Place the prepared mussels in a bowl in the refrigerator until ready to use.

2 Pour the stock into a deep pan. Add the chilli, shallots, lemon grass and ginger leaves and bring it to the boil. Cover and simmer for 10–15 minutes to let the flavours mingle, then season to taste with salt and pepper.

3 Tip the mussels into the stock. Give the pan a good shake, cover tightly and cook for about 2 minutes, or until the mussels have opened.

4 Discard any mussels that remain closed. Ladle the remaining mussels into individual bowls, making sure everyone gets some of the cooking liquid.

5 Serve the mussels decorated with ginger leaves and with a chunk of baguette, if using, so each diner can mop up the juices.

Scallops in Hot Chilli Sauce

Shellfish are often cooked very simply in Mexico. Hot chilli sauce and lime are popular ingredients in many fish recipes.

Serves 4
20 scallops
2 courgettes (zucchini)
75g/3oz/6 tbsp butter
15ml/1 tbsp vegetable oil
4 garlic cloves, chopped
30ml/2 tbsp hot chilli sauce
juice of 1 lime
small bunch of fresh coriander
  (cilantro), finely chopped

1 If you have bought scallops in their shells, open them. Hold a scallop shell in the palm of your hand, with the flat side uppermost. Insert the blade of a knife close to the hinge that joins the shells and prise them apart. Run the blade of the knife across the inside of the flat shell to cut away the scallop. Only the white adductor muscle and the orange coral are eaten, so pull away and discard all other parts. Rinse the scallops under cold running water.

2 Cut the courgettes in half, then into four pieces. Melt the butter in the vegetable oil in a large frying pan. Add the courgettes to the pand and fry for about 5 minutes, or until soft. Remove from the pan.

3 Add the garlic to the frying pan and fry until golden. Stir in the hot chilli sauce.

4 Add the scallops to the sauce. Cook, stirring constantly, for 1–2 minutes only.

5 Stir in the lime juice, chopped coriander and the courgette pieces. Serve immediately on heated plates.

Cook's Tip
Oil is capable of withstanding higher temperatures than butter, but butter gives fried food added flavour. Using a mixture of both ingredients, as here, provides the perfect compromise because the oil prevents the butter from burning.

Steamed Mussels Energy 73kcal/311kJ; Protein 11g; Carbohydrate 3g, of which sugars 1g; Fat 2g, of which saturates 0g; Cholesterol 36mg; Calcium 37mg; Fibre 0.7g; Sodium 0.7mg.
Scallops in Chilli Sauce Energy 291kcal/1213kJ; Protein 24.2g; Carbohydrate 4.4g of which sugars 1g; Fat 19.8g of which saturates 10.6g; Cholesterol 87mg; Calcium 45mg; Fibre 0.5g; Sodium 294mg.

Rice Seaweed Roll with Spicy Squid

This Korean favourite is cooked rice, wrapped in seaweed, and then served with spicy squid and mooli. This delicious snack is perfect when accompanied by a bowl of clear soup.

Serves 2
400g/14oz/4 cups cooked rice
rice vinegar, for drizzling
sesame oil, for drizzling
150g/5oz squid, trimmed,
 cleaned, and skinned
90g/3½oz mooli (daikon), peeled
 and diced
3 large sheets dried seaweed
 or nori

For the squid seasoning
22.5ml/4½ tsp Korean
 chilli powder
7.5ml/1½ tsp sugar
1 garlic clove, crushed
5ml/1 tsp sesame oil
2.5ml/½ tsp sesame seeds

For the mooli seasoning
15ml/1 tbsp sugar
30ml/2 tbsp rice vinegar
22.5ml/4½ tsp Korean
 chilli powder
15ml/1 tbsp Thai fish sauce
1 garlic clove, crushed
1 spring onion (scallion),
 finely chopped

1 Put the cooked rice in a bowl and drizzle over some rice vinegar and sesame oil. Mix well, then set aside. Use a sharp knife to score the squid with a criss-cross pattern, and slice into pieces about 5cm/2in long and 1cm/½in wide.

2 Bring a pan of water to the boil over high heat. Blanch the squid for 3 minutes, then drain under cold running water. Combine all the squid seasoning ingredients in a bowl, and then coat the squid. Set aside to absorb the flavours.

3 Put the mooli in a bowl, then drizzle over some rice vinegar. Leave for 15 minutes and then drain the mooli and transfer to a bowl. Add the mooli seasoning ingredients, mix well and chill in the refrigerator.

4 Place the rice evenly on each of the three seaweed sheets, roll each into a cylinder and slice into bitesize pieces.

5 Arrange the rolls on a serving plate and serve with the seasoned squid and mooli.

Grilled Squid in Serrano Chilli Dressing

This is a lovely dish – sweet, charred squid served in a tangy dressing made with tamarind, lime and the intensely flavoured Thai fish sauce. It is best made with baby squid because they are tender and sweet. Traditionally, the squid are steamed for this dish, but their flavour is enhanced if they are cooked on a griddle, as here, or lightly charred on a grill over a barbecue. Serve immediately while the squid is still warm.

Serves 4
2 large tomatoes, skinned, halved
 and seeded
500g/1¼lb fresh baby squid
1 bunch each of fresh basil,
 coriander (cilantro) and mint,
 stalks removed, leaves chopped

For the dressing
15ml/1 tbsp tamarind paste
juice of half a lime
30ml/2 tbsp Thai fish sauce
15ml/1 tbsp raw cane sugar
1 garlic clove, crushed
2 shallots, halved and finely sliced
1–2 Serrano chillies, seeded and
 finely sliced

1 Put the ingredients for the dressing in a bowl and stir until thoroughly mixed. Set aside.

2 Heat a ridged griddle, wiping with oil. Cook the tomatoes until lightly charred. Chop into bitesize chunks, and put in a bowl.

3 Clean the griddle, then heat it up again and wipe with a little more oil. Cook the squid for 2–3 minutes each side until browned. Add to the tomatoes, add the herbs and the dressing and toss well. Serve immediately.

> **Cook's Tip**
> *To prepare squid yourself, firm grasp the head and pull it from the body. Reach inside the body sac and remove the transparent back bone, as well as any stringy parts. Rinse the sac inside and out and pat dry. Cut the tentacles off and add to the pile of squid. Discard everything else.*

Rice Seaweed Roll Energy 195kcal/830kJ; Protein 8.8g; Carbohydrate 36.2g, of which sugars 4.8g; Fat 2.8g, of which saturates 0.6g; Cholesterol 84mg; Calcium 32mg; Fibre 0.4g; Sodium 312mg.
Grilled Squid Energy 165kcal/701kJ; Protein 22g; Carbohydrate 15g, of which sugars 10g; Fat 3g, of which saturates 1g; Cholesterol 281mg; Calcium 105mg; Fibre 1g; Sodium 0.5mg.

Herring Cured with Chilli and Ginger

Generally served as an appetizer or snack in the Philippines, the herring is not cooked but cured and eaten raw. As with sushi or any other raw fish dish, the fish has to be absolutely fresh. Cured in coconut vinegar and lime juice, and flavoured with ginger and chillies, this is a delicious and refreshing snack.

Serves 4
150ml/¼ pint/⅔ cup
  coconut vinegar
juice of 2 limes
40g/1½oz fresh root ginger, grated
2 red chillies, seeded and
  finely sliced
8–10 herring fillets, cut into
  bitesize pieces
2 shallots, finely sliced
1 green mango, cut into
  julienne strips
salt and ground black pepper
fresh coriander (cilantro) sprigs,
  lime wedges, shredded red
  chillies and shredded fresh
  ginger, to garnish

1 Put the coconut vinegar, lime juice, ginger and chillies in a bowl and mix together. Season the mixture with salt and pepper, to taste

2 Place the herring fillets in a shallow dish, sprinkle the shallots and green mango over, and pour in the vinegar mixture.

3 Cover with clear film (plastic wrap) and leave to marinate in the refrigerator for 1–2 hours or overnight, turning the fish several times.

4 Serve the fish garnished with coriander, lime wedges to squeeze over, shredded chillies and shredded ginger.

> **Variation**
> This dish can be made with many types of seafood, including octopus, halibut and salmon, although mackerel and herring are particularly suitable.

Fried Whitebait in Spicy Dressing

Serve these tangy morsels as an appetizer with drinks or as a main course with a salad of cold mashed potatoes dressed with onions, chillies, olive oil and lemon juice.

Serves 4
800g/1¾lb whitebait or tiny
  white fish
juice of 2 lemons
5ml/1 tsp salt
plain (all-purpose) flour,
  for dusting
vegetable oil, for frying
2 onions, chopped or thinly sliced
2.5–5ml/½–1 tsp cumin seeds
2 carrots, thinly sliced
2 jalapeño chillies, chopped
8 garlic cloves, roughly chopped
120ml/4fl oz/½ cup white wine
  or cider vinegar
2–3 large pinches of
  dried oregano
15–30ml/1–2 tbsp chopped fresh
  coriander (cilantro) leaves
slices of corn on the cob, black
  olives and coriander (cilantro),
  to serve

1 Put the fish in a bowl, add the lemon juice and salt and leave for 30–60 minutes. Remove the fish and dust with flour.

2 Heat the oil in a deep-frying pan until hot enough to turn a cube of bread golden brown in 30 seconds. Fry the fish, in small batches, until crisp, then put in a dish and set aside.

3 In a separate pan, heat 30ml/2 tbsp of oil. Add the onions, cumin seeds, carrots, chillies and garlic and fry for 5 minutes. Stir in the vinegar, oregano and coriander and cook for 1–2 minutes.

4 Pour the onion mixture over the fried fish and leave to cool. Serve the fish at room temperature, with slices of corn on the cob, black olives and coriander leaves.

> **Cook's Tips**
> • When selecting whitebait or any other smelt, make sure the fish are very tiny as they are eaten whole.
> • If you prefer, use chunks of any firm white fish such as cod or halibut instead of tiny whole fish. Simply flour the chunks of fish and fry as above.

Herring Energy 408kcal/1699kJ; Protein 36.4g; Carbohydrate 5.9g, of which sugars 5.7g; Fat 26.7g, of which saturates 6.6g; Cholesterol 100mg; Calcium 160mg; Fibre 1.9g; Sodium 260mg.
Whitebait Energy 1087kcal/4504kJ; Protein 40.3g; Carbohydrate 18.5g, of which sugars 5.9g; Fat 95.3g, of which saturates 8.9g; Cholesterol 0mg; Calcium 1734mg; Fibre 2.3g; Sodium 471mg.

Chilli-marinated Sardines

The Arabs invented marinades as a means of preserving poultry, meat and game. In Spain this method was enthusiastically adopted as a means of keeping fish fresh and they created this dish, called *escabeche*. The fish are always fried first and then stored in vinegar.

Serves 2 to 4
12–16 sardines, cleaned
seasoned plain (all-purpose) flour,
  for dusting
30ml/2 tbsp olive oil
roasted red onion, green (bell)
  pepper and tomatoes, to garnish

For the marinade
90ml/6 tbsp olive oil
1 onion, sliced
1 garlic clove, crushed
3–4 bay leaves
2 cloves
1 dried red chilli, seeded
  and chopped
5ml/1 tsp paprika
120ml/4fl oz/½ cup wine
  or sherry vinegar
120ml/4fl oz/½ cup white wine
salt and ground black pepper

1 Using a sharp knife, cut the heads off the sardines and split each of them along the belly. Turn the fish over so that the backbone is uppermost. Press down along the backbone to loosen it, then carefully lift out the backbone and as many of the remaining little bones as possible. Close the sardines up again and dust them with seasoned flour.

2 Heat the olive oil in a frying pan and fry the sardines for 2–3 minutes on each side. With a metal spatula, remove the fish from the pan to a plate and allow to cool, then pack them in a single layer in a large shallow dish.

3 To make the marinade, add the olive oil to the oil remaining in the frying pan. Fry the onion and garlic for 5–10 minutes until soft, stirring occasionally. Add the bay leaves, cloves, chilli and paprika, with pepper to taste. Fry, stirring, for 1–2 minutes.

4 Stir in the vinegar, wine and a little salt. Allow to bubble up, then pour over the sardines. The marinade should cover the fish completely. When the fish is cool, cover then chill overnight or for up to three days. Serve the sardines and their marinade, garnished with the onion, pepper and tomatoes.

Chilli Hot Salt Fish Fritters

These delicious fish fritters combine salt cod with crispy spring onion in a light batter spiked with fresh chilli.

Makes 15
115g/4oz/1 cup self-raising
  (self-rising) flour
115g/4oz/1 cup plain
  (all-purpose) flour
2.5ml/½ tsp baking powder
175g/6oz soaked salt
  cod, shredded
1 egg, whisked
15ml/1 tbsp chopped spring
  onion (scallion)
1 garlic clove, crushed
2.5ml/½ tsp ground black pepper
½ hot chilli pepper, seeded and
  finely chopped
1.5ml/¼ tsp turmeric
45ml/3 tbsp milk
vegetable oil, for shallow frying
sprig of dill, to garnish

1 Sift the self-raising and plain flours together into a bowl. Sift the baking powder into the flour and mix together.

2 Add the salt cod, egg, spring onion, garlic, pepper, hot pepper and turmeric. Add a little of the milk and mix well.

3 Gradually stir in the remaining milk, adding just enough to make a thick batter. Stir thoroughly so that all ingredients are completely combined.

4 Heat a little vegetable oil in a large frying pan until very hot. Add spoonfuls of the mixture then fry for a few minutes on each side until golden brown and puffy.

5 Lift out the fritters from the pan, drain on kitchen paper and keep warm while cooking the remainder of the mixture in the same way. Serve the fritters garnished with the dill sprig.

Cook's Tip
Salt cod is popular in Mediterranean countries as well as in tropical countries where it keeps well in the heat. It is called bacalhau in Portugal and is the national dish. Salt cod needs soaking in three changes of water for about a day before use.

Chilli Hot Saltfish Fritters Energy 109kcal/458kJ; Protein 5.8g; Carbohydrate 12.3g, of which sugars 0.8g; Fat 4.4g, of which saturates 0.6g; Cholesterol 20mg; Calcium 30mg; Fibre 0.6g; Sodium 53mg.
Chilli-marinated Sardines Energy 242kcal/1004kJ Protein 15.8g; Carbohydrate 1.7g; of which sugars 0.9g; Fat 18.1g; of which saturates 3.6g; Cholesterol 0mg; Calcium 70mg; Fibre 0.2g; Sodium 92mg.

Prawn and Fish Spikes with Chilli Dip

Tolee molee are Burmese bits and pieces that accompany a main course. For this dish, bowls of herbs, crispy fried onions and *balachaung*, a wonderful chilli and prawn paste that comes in a jar, make ideal choices.

Makes 12

400g/14oz Mediterranean
  prawns (jumbo shrimp), peeled
225g/8oz skinned cod or halibut
  fillet, roughly cut into pieces
pinch of ground turmeric
1.5ml/¼ tsp ground white pepper
1.5ml/¼ tsp salt
60ml/4 tbsp chopped fresh
  coriander (cilantro)
1 red chilli, seeded and
  finely chopped
30ml/2 tbsp sunflower oil
a piece of sugar cane cut into 12
  spikes or 12 wooden skewers

For the tolee molee

25g/1oz coriander (cilantro) leaves
45ml/3 tbsp olive oil
300g/11oz sweet onions, halved
  and finely sliced
90ml/6 tbsp balachaung
15ml/1 tbsp sugar
juice of ½ lime
30ml/2 tbsp water

1 Soak the sugar cane spikes or wooden skewers in water for 30 minutes. Make a shallow cut down the centre of the curved back of each prawn. Pull out the black vein and slice the prawns roughly. Place in a food processor with the fish, turmeric, pepper and salt. Blend the mixture to a paste. Add the coriander and chilli and blend. Spoon into a bowl and chill for 30 minutes.

2 Make the tolee molee. Place the coriander in a bowl filled with cold water. Chill. Heat the olive oil in a large frying pan and fry the onion for 10 minutes, stirring occasionally and increasing the heat for the last few minutes so that the onions become golden and crisp. Pile them into a serving bowl. Place the balachaung in a serving bowl. Mix the sugar, lime juice and measured water, stir into the balachaung and set aside.

3 Prepare the barbecue. Mould the seafood mixture around the sugar cane spikes or skewers into an oval sausage shape. Once the flames have died down, position a grill rack over the coals. When the coals are medium-hot, brush the seafood with the oil and grill for 3 minutes each side until cooked through. Serve with the tolee molee.

Chillied Prawns in Almond Sauce

Succulent spicy prawns are served on a bed of vegetables with a nutty, creamy sauce that has a delicious hint of fresh chilli.

Serves 4

450g/1lb raw king prawns
  (jumbo shrimp)
600ml/1 pint/2½ cups water
3 thin slices fresh root ginger
10ml/2 tsp curry powder
2 garlic cloves, crushed
15g/½ oz/1 tbsp butter
  or margarine
60ml/4 tbsp ground almonds
1 green chilli, seeded and
  finely chopped
45ml/3 tbsp single (light) cream
salt and ground black pepper

For the vegetables

15ml/1 tbsp mustard oil
15ml/1 tbsp vegetable oil
1 onion, sliced
½ red (bell) pepper, thinly sliced
½ green (bell) pepper, thinly sliced
1 chayote, peeled, stoned (pitted)
  and cut into strips
salt and ground black pepper

1 Shell the prawns and place the shells in a pan with the water and ginger. Simmer, uncovered, for 15 minutes until the liquid is reduced by half. Strain into a jug (pitcher) and discard the shells.

2 Devein the prawns, place in a bowl and season with the curry powder, garlic and salt and pepper and set aside.

3 Heat the mustard and vegetable oils in a large frying pan, add all the vegetables and cook for 5 minutes, stirring constantly. Season with salt and pepper, spoon into a serving dish and keep warm.

4 Wipe out the frying pan, then melt the butter or margarine and sauté the prawns for about 5 minutes until pink. Spoon over the bed of vegetables, cover and keep warm.

5 Add the ground almonds and chilli to the pan, stir-fry for a few seconds and then add the reserved stock and bring to the boil. Reduce the heat, stir in the cream and simmer for a few minutes, without boiling.

6 Pour the creamy sauce over the vegetables and prawns before serving.

Prawn and Fish Spikes Energy 98kcal/409kJ; Protein 9.8g; Carbohydrate 3.5g, of which sugars 2.9g; Fat 5.1g, of which saturates 0.7g; Cholesterol 74mg; Calcium 51mg; Fibre 0.7g; Sodium 78mg.
Chillied Prawns Energy 301kcal/125kJ; Protein 24.3g; Carbohydrate 6.1g; of which sugars 5.1g; Fat 20.1g; of which saturates 4.8g; Cholesterol 234mg; Calcium 154mg; Fibre 2.4g; Sodium 244mg.

Prawns and Courgettes in Turmeric and Chilli Sauce

This delicious, attractively coloured dish is popular in Indonesia and combines creamy coconut milk with vegetables and chilli.

Serves 4

1–2 chayotes or 2–3
  courgettes (zucchini)
2 fresh red chillies, seeded
1 onion, quartered
5mm/¼in piece galangal, sliced
1 lemon grass stalk, lower
  5cm/2in sliced, top bruised
2.5cm/1in piece fresh
  turmeric, peeled
200ml/7fl oz/scant 1 cup water
lemon juice
400ml/14fl oz can coconut milk
450g/1lb cooked, peeled
  prawns (shrimp)
salt
red chilli shreds, to garnish (optional)
boiled rice, to serve

1 Peel the chayotes, remove the seeds and cut into strips. If using courgettes, cut them into 5cm/2in strips.

2 Grind the fresh red chillies, onion, galangal, sliced lemon grass and the fresh turmeric to a paste in a food processor or with a mortar and pestle. Add the water to the paste mixture, with a squeeze of lemon juice and salt to taste.

3 Pour into a pan. Add the top of the lemon grass stem. Bring to the boil and cook for 1–2 minutes. Add the chayote or courgette pieces and cook for 2 minutes. Stir in the coconut milk. Taste and adjust the seasoning.

4 Stir in the prawns and cook gently for 2–3 minutes. Remove the lemon grass stem. Garnish with shreds of chilli, if using, and serve with rice.

Cook's Tip
Galangal belongs to the same family as root ginger and is prepared in the same way. In its raw form, it has a soapy, earthy aroma and a pine-like flavour with a faint hint of citrus. Look for it in Asian stores.

Marinated Octopus with Fiery Sauce

The red pipian sauce is made with ancho chilli, which is sweet and hot with a fruity aroma when cooked.

Serves 8

1kg/2¼lb whole octopus, cleaned
  and gutted
1 onion, quartered
2 bay leaves
30ml/2 tbsp olive oil
grated rind and juice of 1 lemon
15ml/1 tbsp chopped fresh
  coriander (cilantro)
fresh coriander (cilantro) sprigs,
  to garnish

For the red pipian
1 ancho chilli (dried poblano)
4 whole garlic cloves, peeled
1 small pink onion, chopped
500g/1¼lb plum tomatoes,
  cored and seeded
30ml/2 tbsp olive oil
5ml/1 tsp sugar
30ml/2 tbsp pine nuts
30ml/2 tbsp pumpkin seeds
pinch of ground cinnamon
15ml/1 tbsp smoky chilli sauce
45ml/3 tbsp vegetable stock
leaves from 4 large fresh thyme
  sprigs, finely chopped
salt

1 Preheat the oven to 200°C/400°F/Gas 6. Make the red pipian. Cover the chilli with hot water in a bowl. Leave for 20 minutes. Place the garlic, onion and tomatoes in a roasting pan and drizzle with oil, sprinkle over sugar and a little salt. Roast for 15 minutes.

2 Add the pine nuts, pumpkin seeds and cinnamon to the pan and roast for a further 5 minutes. Meanwhile, drain the chilli, discard the seeds and chop. Transfer the roasted mixture and the chilli to a food processor. Add the chilli sauce, stock and thyme. Blend to a paste, transfer to a bowl and leave to cool.

3 Place the octopus tentacles in a large pan, cover with cold water and add the onion and bay leaves. Bring to the boil, then simmer for up to 2 hours, checking frequently, until tender.

4 Drain and rinse the tentacles, then thread on to metal skewers and place in a dish. Add the olive oil, lemon rind and juice, and coriander. Mix well and marinate for 1 hour or overnight.

5 Prepare the barbecue. When the coals are medium-hot, grill the octopus skewers for 2–4 minutes on each side, or until golden. Serve with the red pipian, garnished with the coriander.

Prawns and Courgettes Energy 162kcal/658kj; Protein 28g; Carbohydrate 10g; of which sugars 9g; Fat 2g; of which saturates 1g; Cholesterol 10mg; Calcium 182mg; Fibre 1.2g; Sodium 1.9mg.
Marinated Octopus Energy 149kcal/627kj; Protein 23.2g; Carbohydrate 3.8g, of which sugars 3.4g; Fat 4.7g, of which saturates 0.8g; Cholesterol 60mg; Calcium 62mg; Fibre 1.2g; Sodium 8mg.

Chargrilled Squid with Red Chilli and White Wine

The squid in this Spanish recipe, known as *calamares a la plancha* are traditionally cooked on the hot griddle that is an essential part of every Spanish kitchen. The method is fast and simple and really brings out the flavour of the squid. This dish is an ideal first course for four people, or can be served on a bed of rice as a main dish for two.

Serves 2 to 4

2 whole cleaned squid, with
   tentacles, about 275g/10oz each
75ml/5 tbsp olive oil
30ml/2 tbsp sherry vinegar
2 fresh red chillies, finely chopped
60ml/4 tbsp dry white wine
salt and ground black pepper
hot cooked rice, to
   serve (optional)
15–30ml/1–2 tbsp chopped
   parsley, to garnish

1 Make a lengthways cut down the side of the body of each squid, then open it out flat. Score the flesh on both sides of the bodies in a criss-cross pattern with the tip of a sharp knife. Chop the tentacles into short lengths. Place all the squid pieces in a non-metallic dish.

2 Whisk together the oil and vinegar in a small bowl until well combined. Season with salt and pepper to taste, pour over the squid and toss to mix. Cover the bowl and set aside to marinate for about 1 hour.

3 Heat a ridged griddle pan until hot. Add the body of one of the squid and cook over a medium heat for 2–3 minutes, pressing the squid down on to the ridges with a metal spatula to keep it flat. Repeat on the other side. Cook the other squid body in the same way.

4 Slice the bodies of the squid into diagonal strips. If serving with rice, arrange the strips over the rice and keep warm.

5 Add the chopped tentacles and chillies to the pan and toss over a medium heat for about 2–3 minutes. Stir in the white wine, then drizzle over the squid. Garnish with the parsley.

Saigon Shellfish Curry

There are many variations of this tasty curry all over the south of Vietnam. This recipe is made with prawns, squid and scallops but you could use any combination of shellfish, or even add chunks of filleted fish.

Serves 4

4cm/1½in fresh root ginger,
   peeled and roughly chopped
2–3 garlic cloves, roughly chopped
45ml/3 tbsp groundnut (peanut) oil
1 onion, finely sliced
2 lemon grass stalks, finely sliced
2 green or red Thai chillies,
   seeded and finely sliced

15ml/1 tbsp raw cane sugar
10ml/2 tsp shrimp paste
15ml/1 tbsp Thai fish sauce
30ml/2 tbsp curry powder or
   garam masala
550ml/18fl oz can coconut milk
juice and rind of 1 lime
4 medium squid, cleaned and cut
   diagonally into 3 or 4 pieces
12 king or queen scallops, shelled
20 raw prawns (shrimp), shelled
   and deveined
1 small bunch of fresh basil,
   stalks removed
1 small bunch of fresh coriander
   (cilantro), stalks removed, leaves
   finely chopped, to garnish
salt

1 Using a mortar and pestle, grind the ginger with the garlic until it almost resembles a paste. Heat the oil in a traditional clay pot, wok or heavy pan and stir in the onion. Cook until it begins to turn brown, then stir in the garlic and ginger paste.

2 Once the aromas begin to lift from the pot, add the lemon grass, chillies and sugar. Cook for 2 minutes before adding the shrimp paste, fish sauce and curry powder or garam masala. Stir the mixture well and allow the flavours to mingle and combine over the heat for 1–2 minutes.

3 Add the coconut milk, lime juice and rind. Mix well and bring the liquid to the boil. Simmer for 2–3 minutes. Season to taste with salt.

4 Gently stir in the squid, scallops and prawns. Bring the liquid to the boil once more. Reduce the heat and cook gently until the shellfish turns opaque. Add the basil leaves and sprinkle the coriander over the top. Serve immediately from the pot into individual bowls.

Squid with Chilli Energy 258kcal/1076kJ; Protein 23.5g; Carbohydrate 2g; of which sugars 0.2g; Fat 16.4g; of which saturates 2.6g; Cholesterol 338mg; Calcium 25mg; Fibre 0g; Sodium 167mg.
Saigon Shellfish Curry Energy 528kcal/2225kJ; Protein 68g; Carbohydrate 24g, of which sugars 14g; Fat 18g, of which saturates 4g; Cholesterol 699mg; Calcium 250mg; Fibre 2.5g; Sodium 1.3mg.

Chilli Crab and Tofu Stir-fry

For a light healthy meal, this speedy stir-fry is an ideal choice. The silken tofu has a fairly bland taste on its own but is excellent for absorbing all the delicious flavours of this dish – the crab meat, garlic, chillies, spring onions and soy sauce.

Serves 2
250g/9oz silken tofu
60ml/4 tbsp vegetable oil
2 garlic cloves, finely chopped
115g/4oz white crab meat
130g/4¹⁄₂oz/generous 1 cup baby
  corn, halved lengthways
2 spring onions (scallions),
  finely chopped
1 fresh red chilli, seeded and
  finely chopped
30ml/2 tbsp soy sauce
15ml/1 tbsp Thai fish sauce
5ml/1 tsp palm sugar (jaggery) or
  light muscovado (brown) sugar
juice of 1 lime
small bunch fresh coriander
  (cilantro), chopped, to garnish

1 Using a sharp knife, cut the silken tofu into 1cm/½in cubes.

2 Heat the oil in a wok or large, heavy frying pan. Add the tofu cubes and stir-fry until they are golden all over, taking care not to break them up while cooking. Remove from the pan with a slotted spoon and set aside.

3 Add the garlic to the wok or pan and stir-fry until just golden. Ensure that it doesn't burn otherwise it will have a slightly bitter taste.

4 Add the crab meat, tofu, corn, spring onions, chilli, soy sauce, fish sauce and sugar to the pan. Cook, stirring constantly, until the vegetables are just tender.

5 Stir in the lime juice, transfer to warmed bowls, sprinkle with the coriander and serve immediately.

Cook's Tip
This is a very economical dish to prepare as you only need a small amount of crab meat. The canned variety could also be used in this recipe, which would make it even cheaper.

Lobster and Crab Steamed in Beer and Hot Spices

Depending on the size and availability of the lobsters and crabs, you can make this delicious spicy dish for as many people as you like, because the quantities are simple to adjust.

Serves 4
4 uncooked lobsters, about
  450g/1lb each
4–8 uncooked crabs, about
  225g/8oz each
about 600ml/1 pint/2½ cups beer
4 spring onions (scallions),
  trimmed and chopped into
  long pieces
4cm/1½in fresh root ginger,
  peeled and finely sliced
2 green or red Thai chillies,
  seeded and finely sliced
3 lemon grass stalks,
  finely sliced
1 bunch of fresh dill,
  fronds chopped
1 bunch each of fresh basil
  and coriander (cilantro),
  stalks removed, leaves
  finely chopped
about 30ml/2 tbsp Thai fish
  sauce, plus extra for serving
juice of 1 lemon
salt and ground black
  pepper

1 Clean the lobsters and crabs well and rub them with salt and pepper. Place half of them in a large steamer and pour the beer into the base. Sprinkle half the spring onions, ginger, chillies, lemon grass and herbs over the lobsters and crabs, and steam for 10 minutes, or until the lobsters turn red. Lift them on to a serving dish. Cook the remaining half in the same way.

2 Add the lemon grass, herbs and fish sauce to the simmering beer, stir in the lemon juice, then pour into a dipping bowl. Serve the shellfish hot, dipping the lobster and crab meat into the broth and adding extra splashes of fish sauce, if you like.

Cook's Tip
Whether you cook the lobsters and crabs at the same time depends on the number of people you are cooking for and the size of your steamer. However, they don't take long to cook so it is easy to steam them in batches.

Crab Stir-fry Energy 370kcal/1532kJ; Protein 23.3g; Carbohydrate 6.2g, of which sugars 5.1g; Fat 28.1g, of which saturates 1g; Cholesterol 210mg; Calcium 185mg; Fibre 1.2g; Sodium 2487mg.
Lobster and Crab Energy 264kcal/1112kJ; Protein 48g; Carbohydrate 4g, of which sugars 1g; Fat 7g, of which saturates 1g; Cholesterol 210mg; Calcium 185mg; Fibre 0.5g; Sodium 1.3mg.

Seared Tuna with Ginger, Chilli and Watercress Salad

Tuna steaks are wonderful seared and served slightly rare with a punchy, spicy sauce or salad. In this recipe the salad is served just warm as a bed for the tender tuna. Add a dab of harissa as a condiment to create a dish that will transport you to the warmth of the North African coastline.

Serves 4
30ml/2 tbsp olive oil
5ml/1 tsp harissa

5ml/1 tsp clear honey
4 X 200g/7oz tuna steaks
salt and ground black pepper
lemon wedges, to serve

For the salad
30ml/2 tbsp olive oil
a little butter
25g/1oz fresh root ginger, peeled
   and finely sliced
2 garlic cloves, finely sliced
2 green chillies, seeded and sliced
6 spring onions (scallions), cut into
   bitesize pieces
2 large handfuls of watercress
juice of ½ lemon

1 Mix the olive oil, harissa, honey and salt, and rub it over the tuna. Heat a little oil in a frying pan and sear the tuna steaks for 2 minutes on each side. They should still be pink inside.

2 Keep the tuna warm while you prepare the salad: heat the olive oil and butter in a pan. Add the ginger, garlic, chillies and spring onions, cook for a few minutes, then add the watercress. When the watercress begins to wilt, toss in the lemon juice and season well with salt and black pepper.

3 Tip the warm salad on to a serving dish or individual plates. Slice the tuna steaks and arrange on top of the salad. Serve immediately with lemon wedges for squeezing over.

> **Variation**
> Prawns (shrimp) and scallops can be cooked in the same way. The shellfish just need to be cooked through briefly – if they are cooked too long, they will become rubbery.

Spicy Swordfish and Green Chilli Tacos

It is important not to overcook swordfish, or it can be tough and dry. Cooked correctly, however, it is absolutely delicious and makes a great change from beef or chicken as a spicy filling for a taco.

Serves 6
3 swordfish steaks
30ml/2 tbsp vegetable oil

2 garlic cloves, crushed
1 small onion, chopped
3 fresh green chillies, seeded
   and chopped
3 tomatoes
small bunch of fresh coriander
   (cilantro), chopped
6 fresh corn tortillas
½ iceberg lettuce, shredded
salt and ground black pepper
lemon wedges, to serve
   (optional)

1 Preheat the grill (broiler). Put the swordfish on an oiled rack over a grill pan and grill (broil) for 2–3 minutes on each side. When cool enough to handle, remove the skin and flake the fish into a bowl.

2 Heat the vegetable oil in a pan. Add the garlic, onion and chillies and fry for 5 minutes, or until the onion has turned soft and translucent.

3 Cut a cross in the base of each tomato, place in a heatproof bowl and pour over boiling water. After 3 minutes plunge the tomatoes into another bowl of cold water. Drain the tomatoes. Their skins will have begun to peel back from the crosses. Remove the skins, halve the tomatoes and cut out the seeds. Chop the flesh into 1cm/½in dice.

4 Add the tomatoes and swordfish to the onion mixture. Cook for 5 minutes over a low heat. Add the coriander and cook for 1–2 minutes. Season to taste.

5 Wrap the tortillas in foil and steam on a plate over a pan of boiling water until they are heated through and pliable. Place some shredded lettuce and fish mixture on to each tortilla. Fold in half, covering the filling, and serve with lemon wedges, if liked.

Seared Tuna Energy 383kcal/1604kJ; Protein 48.1g; Carbohydrate 2g, of which sugars 2g; Fat 20.4g, of which saturates 4g; Cholesterol 56mg; Calcium 59mg; Fibre 0.4g; Sodium 102mg.
Swordfish Tacos Energy 357kcal/1507kJ; Protein 32g; Carbohydrate 36g, of which sugars 3g; Fat 11g, of which saturates 2g; Cholesterol 105mg; Calcium 80mg; Fibre 2.1g; Sodium 400mg.

Fried Cod with Spiced Tomato Sauce

The cod is lightly dusted with spices and cornflour before being added to the tomato sauce. Mashed potatoes are the perfect accompaniment, although roast potatoes and rice are also good.

Serves 4
30ml/2 tbsp cornflour (cornstarch)
5ml/1 tsp salt
5ml/1 tsp garlic powder
5ml/1 tsp chilli powder
5ml/1 tsp ginger powder
5ml/1 tsp ground fennel seeds
5ml/1 tsp ground coriander
2 medium cod fillets, each cut into 2 pieces

15ml/1 tbsp corn oil
mashed potatoes, to serve

For the sauce
30ml/2 tbsp tomato purée (paste)
5ml/1 tsp garam masala
5ml/1 tsp chilli powder
5ml/1 tsp crushed garlic
5ml/1 tsp crushed ginger
2.5ml/½ tsp salt
175ml/6 fl oz/⅔ cup water
15ml/1 tbsp corn oil
1 bay leaf
3–4 black peppercorns
1 cm/½ in cinnamon bark
15ml/1 tbsp chopped fresh fresh coriander (cilantro)
15ml/1 tbsp chopped fresh mint

1 Mix together the cornflour, salt, garlic powder, chilli powder, ginger powder, ground fennel seeds and ground coriander. Pour over the cod fillets and ensure that they are well coated.

2 Preheat the grill (broiler) to hot, reduce the heat to medium and place the fish under the grill. After 5 minutes, brush the cod with the oil. Turn the cod over and repeat the process. Grill (broil) for a further 5 minutes. When cooked, set aside.

3 Make the sauce by mixing together the tomato purée, garam masala, chilli powder, garlic, ginger, salt and water. Set aside.

4 Heat the oil in a non-stick wok. Add the bay leaf, peppercorns and cinnamon. Pour the sauce into the wok and reduce the heat to low. Bring to the boil and simmer for 5 minutes. Add the fish and cook for a further 2 minutes. Add the coriander and mint and serve with mashed potatoes.

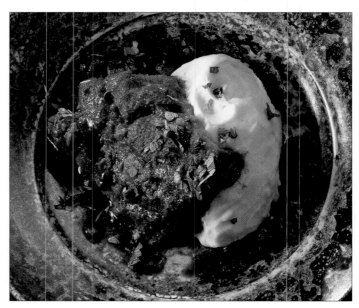

Grilled Fish with Spiced Mushrooms

This tasty spicy dish originates in India. The cod is grilled before it is added to the spicy mushroom sauce to prevent it from breaking up during cooking. Serve as an appetizer, or increase the portions slightly to make a delicious main course.

Serves 4
4 small cod fillets
15ml/1 tbsp lemon juice
15ml/1 tbsp olive oil

1 medium onion, chopped
1 bay leaf
4 black peppercorns, crushed
115g/4oz mushrooms
175ml/6fl oz/⅔ cup natural (plain) low-fat yogurt
5ml/1 tsp crushed ginger
5ml/1 tsp crushed garlic
2.5ml/½ tsp garam masala
2.5ml/½ tsp chilli powder
5ml/1 tsp salt
15ml/1 tbsp fresh coriander (cilantro) leaves, to garnish
lightly cooked green beans, to serve

1 Remove the skin and any bones from the cod fillets. Sprinkle with lemon juice, then grill (broil) under a preheated grill (broiler) for about 5 minutes on each side. Remove from the heat and set aside.

2 Heat the oil in a non-stick wok or frying pan and fry the onion with the bay leaf and peppercorns for 2–3 minutes. Lower the heat, then add the mushrooms and stir-fry for 4–5 minutes.

3 In a bowl mix together the yogurt, ginger and garlic, garam masala, chilli powder and salt. Pour over the onions and stir-fry for 3 minutes.

4 Add the cod to the sauce and cook for a further 2 minutes. Serve garnished with coriander leaves and accompanied by lightly cooked green beans.

> **Cook's Tip**
> Jars of ready-to-use crushed ginger and garlic, also called pulp, are very useful to the busy cook. They are widely available in supermarkets and Asian food stores.

Grilled Fish Energy 149kcal/626kJ; Protein 21.8g; Carbohydrate 5.9g, of which sugars 4.2g; Fat 4.6g, of which saturates 0.8g; Cholesterol 47mg; Calcium 104mg; Fibre 0.5g; Sodium 100mg.
Fried Cod Energy 294kcal/1229kJ; Protein 41.8g; Carbohydrate 2.7g, of which sugars 2.7g; Fat 12.8g, of which saturates 1.9g; Cholesterol 104mg; Calcium 26mg; Fibre 0.9g; Sodium 143mg.

Red Snapper with Tomato and Green Chilli Sauce

This dish is quick and easy to prepare, perfect for a mid-week treat.

Serves 3 to 4
1 large red snapper, cleaned
juice of 1 lemon
2.5ml/½ tsp paprika
2.5ml/½ tsp garlic granules
2.5ml/½ tsp dried thyme
2.5ml/½ tsp ground black pepper

For the sauce
30ml/2 tbsp palm or vegetable oil
1 onion
400g/14oz can chopped tomatoes
2 garlic cloves
1 thyme sprig or 2.5ml/½ tsp dried thyme
1 green chilli, seeded and chopped
½ green (bell) pepper, chopped
300ml/½ pint/1¼ cups fish stock
boiled rice, to serve

1 Preheat the oven to 200°C/400°F/Gas 6 and then prepare the sauce. Heat the oil in a pan, fry the onion for 5 minutes, then add the tomatoes, garlic, thyme and chilli.

2 Add the pepper and stock or water. Bring to the boil, stirring, then reduce the heat and simmer, covered, for about 10 minutes until the vegetables are soft.

3 Remove the pan from the heat and leave to cool. Place the mixture in a blender or food processor and blend to a purée.

4 Wash the fish well and then score the skin with a sharp knife in a criss-cross pattern. Mix together the lemon juice, paprika, garlic, thyme and black pepper, then spoon over the fish, to cover it, and rub in well.

5 Place the fish in a greased baking dish and pour over the sauce. Cover with foil and bake for about 30–40 minutes, or until the fish is cooked. Serve with boiled rice.

Cook's Tip
If you prefer less sauce, remove the foil after 20 minutes and continue baking uncovered, until cooked.

Salmon in Coconut Chilli Sauce

This is an ideal dish to serve as an appetizer at dinner parties. The salmon is first marinated in a spicy coating before being cooked in a delicious coconut sauce.

Serves 4
10ml/2 tsp ground cumin
10ml/2 tsp chilli powder
2.5ml/½ tsp ground turmeric
30ml/2 tbsp white wine vinegar
1.5ml/¼ tsp salt
4 salmon steaks, about
    175g/6oz each

45 ml/3 tbsp oil
1 onion, chopped
2 green chillies, seeded
    and chopped
2 garlic cloves, crushed
2.5cm/1in piece fresh root
    ginger, grated
5 ml/1 tsp ground coriander
175 ml/6 fl oz/¾ cup
    coconut milk
spring onion rice, to serve
fresh coriander (cilantro) sprigs,
    to garnish

1 In a small bowl, mix 5ml/1 tsp of the ground cumin together with the chilli powder, turmeric, vinegar and salt.

2 Rub the paste over the salmon steaks and leave to marinate for about 15 minutes.

3 Heat the oil in a large frying pan and fry the onion, chillies, garlic and ginger for 5–6 minutes. Put into a food processor or blender and process to a paste.

4 Return the paste to the pan. Add the remaining cumin, coriander and coconut milk. Bring the mixture to the boil and simmer, stirring occasionally, for 5 minutes.

5 Add the salmon steaks to the sauce. Cover the pan and cook for 15 minutes until the fish is tender. Serve with spring onion rice and garnish with coriander sprigs.

Cook's Tip
If coconut milk is unavailable, substitute coconut cream diluted with water to get the desired consistency.

Red Snapper Energy 198kcal/837kJ; Protein 33.1g; Carbohydrate 7.4g, of which sugars 6.6g; Fat 4.3g, of which saturates 0.8g; Cholesterol 58mg; Calcium 91mg; Fibre 1.7g; Sodium 201mg.
Salmon in Coconut Sauce Energy 417kcal/1740kJ; Protein 37g; Carbohydrate 6g, of which sugars 4g; Fat 28g, of which saturates 4g; Cholesterol 88mg; Calcium 73mg; Fibre 0.6g; Sodium 200mg.

Whole Fish with Sweet and Sour Chilli Sauce

Cooking fish whole will make an impressive appetizer for dinner guests – and the spicy sauce is sure to please.

Serves 4
1 whole fish, such as red snapper
    or carp, about 1kg/2¼lb
30–45ml/2–3 tbsp
    cornflour (cornstarch)
oil for frying
salt and ground black pepper
boiled rice, to serve

For the spice paste
5 macadamia nuts or 10 almonds
2 garlic cloves
2 lemon grass stems, sliced
2.5cm/1in fresh galangal, peeled
2.5cm/1in fresh root ginger, peeled
2cm/¾in fresh turmeric, peeled, or
    2.5ml/½ tsp ground turmeric

For the sauce
15ml/1 tbsp brown sugar
45ml/3 tbsp cider vinegar
350ml/12fl oz/1½ cups water
2 lime leaves, torn
4 shallots, quartered
3 tomatoes, skinned and chopped
3 spring onions (scallions),
    finely shredded
1 fresh red chilli, seeded
    and shredded

1 Ask the fishmonger to gut and scale the fish, leaving on the head and tail. Wash and dry the fish and sprinkle inside and out with salt. Set aside for 15 minutes.

2 Grind the nuts, garlic, lemon grass, galangal, ginger and turmeric to a fine paste in a food processor or with a pestle and mortar. Scrape the paste into a bowl. Stir in the sugar, cider vinegar, seasoning to taste and the water. Add the lime leaves.

3 Dust the fish with the cornflour and fry on both sides in hot oil for about 8–9 minutes, or until cooked through. Drain the fish and transfer to a serving dish. Keep warm.

4 Pour the spicy liquid into the pan and bring to the boil, then simmer for 3–4 minutes. Add the shallots and tomatoes, followed by the spring onions and chilli and simmer for 2–3 minutes.

5 Pour the sauce over the fish. Serve immediately, with plenty of boiled rice.

Indonesian Spiced Fish

If you make this tasty appetizer a day ahead, put it straight on to a serving dish after cooking and then pour over the sauce, cover and chill until required.

Serves 3 to 4
450g/1lb fish fillets, such as
    mackerel, cod or haddock
30ml/2 tbsp plain
    (all-purpose) flour
groundnut (peanut) oil for frying
1 onion, roughly chopped
1 small garlic clove, crushed
4cm/1½in fresh root ginger,
    peeled and grated
1–2 red chillies, seeded and sliced
1cm/½in cube shrimp
    paste, prepared
60ml/4 tbsp water
juice of ½ lemon
15ml/1 tbsp soft light brown sugar
30ml/2 tbsp dark soy sauce
salt
roughly torn lettuce leaves, to serve

1 Rinse the fish fillets under cold water and dry well on absorbent kitchen paper. Cut into serving portions and remove any bones.

2 Season the flour with salt and use it to dust the fish. Heat the oil in a large frying pan and fry the fish on both sides for 3–4 minutes, or until cooked. Lift on to a plate and set aside.

3 Rinse out and dry the pan. Heat a little more oil and fry the onion, garlic, ginger and chillies just to bring out the flavour. Do not brown.

4 Blend the shrimp paste with a little water. Add it to the onion mixture, with a little extra water if necessary. Cook for 2 minutes and then stir in the lemon juice, brown sugar and soy sauce.

5 Pour the sauce over the fish and serve either hot or cold, with roughly torn lettuce.

> **Cook's Tip**
> This will make an ideal dish for a buffet. Simply cut the fish into bitesize pieces or small serving portions.

Whole Fish Energy 1103kcal/4200kJ; Protein 21g; Carbohydrate 210g; of which sugars 9g; Fat 7g; of which saturates 0g; Cholesterol 0mg; Calcium 83mg; Fibre 1.9g; Sodium 0mg.
Indonesian Fish Energy 218kcal/917kJ; Protein 22.8g; Carbohydrate 11.4g, of which sugars 4.3g; Fat 9.5g, of which saturates 1.2g; Cholesterol 41mg; Calcium 36mg; Fibre 0.2g; Sodium 344mg.

Salmon in Red Chilli Stock

This recipe is an Asian interpretation of gravadlax, a Scandinavian speciality. Use very fresh salmon. The raw fish is marinated for several days in a brine flavoured with Thai spices, which effectively 'cooks' it.

Serves 4 to 6

tail piece of 1 salmon, weighing about 675g/1½lb, cleaned, scaled and filleted
20ml/4 tsp coarse sea salt
20ml/4 tsp sugar
2.5cm/1in piece fresh root ginger, peeled and grated
2 lemon grass stalks, coarse outer leaves removed, thinly sliced
4 kaffir lime leaves, finely chopped or shredded
grated rind of 1 lime
1 fresh red chilli, seeded and finely chopped
5ml/1 tsp black peppercorns, coarsely crushed
30ml/2 tbsp chopped fresh coriander (cilantro)
fresh coriander (cilantro) sprigs and quartered kaffir limes, to garnish

For the dressing

150ml/¼ pint/⅔ cup mayonnaise
juice of ½ lime
10ml/2 tsp chopped fresh coriander (cilantro)

1 Remove any remaining bones from the salmon. Put the sea salt, sugar, ginger, lemon grass, lime leaves, lime rind, chilli, black peppercorns and coriander in a bowl and mix together.

2 Sprinkle one-quarter of the spice mixture in a shallow dish. Place one salmon fillet, skin down, on top. Spread two-thirds of the remaining mixture over the flesh, then place the remaining fillet on top, flesh side down. Sprinkle the rest of the spice mixture over the fish.

3 Cover with foil, then place a board on top. Add some weights, such as clean cans of food. Chill for 2–5 days, turning the fish daily in the spicy brine.

4 Make the dressing by mixing the mayonnaise, lime juice and chopped coriander in a bowl.

5 Scrape the spices off the fish. Slice it as thin as possible. Garnish with coriander and kaffir limes, and serve with the lime dressing.

Mackerel Fillets with Chilli and Coconut

Delicious fish fillets are smothered in a spicy coconut sauce. Serve with rice for a more substantial meal. Haddock or cod fillet may be substituted in this recipe if you prefer.

Serves 6 to 8

1kg/2¼lb fresh mackerel fillets, skinned
30ml/2 tbsp tamarind pulp, soaked in 200ml/7fl oz/scant 1 cup water
1 onion
1cm/½in fresh lengkuas
2 garlic cloves
1–2 fresh red chillies, seeded, or 5ml/1 tsp chilli powder
5ml/1 tsp ground coriander
5ml/1 tsp ground turmeric
2.5ml/½ tsp ground fennel seeds
15ml/1 tbsp dark brown sugar
90–105ml/6–7 tbsp oil
200ml/7fl oz/scant 1 cup coconut cream
salt and ground black pepper
fresh chilli shreds, to garnish
cooked rice, to serve (optional)

1 Rinse the fish fillets in cold water and dry them well on kitchen paper. Put into a shallow dish and sprinkle with a little salt. Strain the tamarind and pour the juice over the fish fillets. Leave for 30 minutes.

2 Quarter the onion, peel and slice the lengkuas and peel the garlic. Grind the onion, lengkuas, garlic and chillies or chilli powder to a paste in a food processor or with a mortar and pestle. Add the ground coriander, turmeric, fennel seeds and sugar and mix well.

3 Heat half of the oil in a frying pan. Drain the fish fillets and fry them for 3–4 minutes on each side, or until cooked. Set aside.

4 Wipe out the pan and heat the remaining oil. Fry the spice paste, stirring all the time, until it gives off a spicy aroma. Do not let it turn brown. Add the coconut cream and simmer for a few minutes. Add the fish fillets and gently heat through.

5 Taste the sauce for seasoning, adjusting if necessary and serve on a bed of rice, if using, sprinkled with shredded chilli.

Salmon in Red Chilli Stock Energy 509kcal/2108kJ; Protein 26g; Carbohydrate 7g; of which sugars 6g; Fat 42g; of which saturates 7g; Cholesterol 91mg; Calcium 44mg; Fibre 0g; Sodium 1700mg.
Mackerel Fillets Energy 717kcal/297kJ; Protein 34g; Carbohydrate 9g; of which sugars 8g; Fat 61g; of which saturates 27g; Cholesterol 90mg; Calcium 47mg; Fibre 0.4g; Sodium 200mg.

Grilled Spiced Bream

This whole fish is simply grilled after being marinated in a delicious spicy paste. The fish can be cooked on an oiled rack over a barbecue if you prefer.

Serves 6

1kg/2¼lb bream, carp or pomfret (porgy), cleaned and scaled if necessary
1 fresh red chilli, seeded, or 5ml/1 tsp of chilli powder
4 garlic cloves, crushed
2.5cm/1in fresh root ginger, peeled and sliced
4 spring onions (scallions), chopped
juice of ½ lemon
30ml/2 tbsp sunflower oil
salt
boiled rice, to serve

1 Rinse the fish and dry it well inside and out with absorbent kitchen paper. Slash two or three times through the fleshy part on each side of the fish.

2 Place the chilli, garlic, ginger and spring onions in a food processor and blend to a paste, or grind the mixture together with a mortar and pestle. Add the lemon juice and salt, then stir in the oil.

3 Spoon a little of the mixture inside the fish and pour the rest over the top. Coat it completely in the spice mixture and leave to marinate for at least an hour.

4 Preheat the grill (broiler). Place a long strip of double foil under the fish to support it and to make turning it over easier.

5 Cook under the hot grill for about 5 minutes on one side. Turn the fish over and cook for a further 8 minutes on the second side, basting with the marinade during cooking. Serve with boiled rice.

> **Cook's Tip**
> There are many other fish that will work well in this dish, allowing you to use whatever is available locally. Try making it with red snapper, pompano or butterfish.

Hot Smoked Salmon with Sweet Chilli Sauce

This is a fantastic way of smoking fish on a charcoal barbecue, using soaked hickory wood chips. Mojo, a spicy sauce popular in Cuba, cuts the richness of the hot smoked salmon.

Serves 6

6 salmon fillets, about 175g/6oz each, with skin
15ml/1 tbsp sunflower oil
salt and ground black pepper
2 handfuls hickory wood chips, soaked in cold water for at least 30 minutes

For the mojo
1 ripe mango, diced
4 drained canned pineapple slices, diced
1 small red onion, finely chopped
1 fresh long mild red chilli, seeded and finely chopped
15ml/1 tbsp good quality sweet chilli sauce
grated rind and juice of 1 lime
leaves from 1 small basil plant or 45ml/3 tbsp fresh coriander (cilantro) leaves, chopped

1 Place the salmon fillets, skin side down, on a platter. Sprinkle the flesh lightly with salt. Cover and leave for about 30 minutes.

2 Make the mojo by putting the mango, pineapple slices, onion and chilli in a bowl. Add the chilli sauce, lime rind and juice, and the herb leaves. Mix well. Cover and set aside until needed.

3 Prepare the barbecue. Pat the salmon fillets with kitchen paper, then brush with a little oil. When the coals are medium-hot, and with a moderate coating of ash, add the salmon fillets, placing them on an oiled rack skin side down. Cover with a lid or tented heavy-duty foil and cook the fish for about 3 minutes.

4 Drain the hickory chips into a colander and sprinkle a third of them over the coals. Carefully drop them through the grill racks, taking care not to sprinkle the ash as you do so.

5 Replace the barbecue cover and continue cooking for a further 8 minutes, adding a small handful of hickory chips twice more during this time. Serve the salmon hot or cold, with the mojo.

Grilled Spiced Bream Energy 211kcal/887kj; Protein 30g; Carbohydrate 1g; of which sugars 0g; Fat 10g; of which saturates 1g; Cholesterol 63mg; Calcium 60mg; Fibre 0.2g; Sodium 224mg.
Hot Smoked Salmon Energy 365kcal/1522kj; Protein 36g; Carbohydrate 7.8g, of which sugars 7.5g; Fat 21.3g; of which saturates 3.6g; Cholesterol 88mg; Calcium 61mg; Fibre 1.3g; Sodium 83mg.

Trout with Tamarind Chilli Sauce

Sometimes trout can taste rather bland, but this spicy sauce really gives it a zing. If you like your food very spicy, add an extra chilli.

Serves 4

4 trout, cleaned
6 spring onions (scallions), sliced
60ml/4 tbsp soy sauce
15ml/1 tbsp vegetable oil
30ml/2 tbsp chopped fresh
  coriander (cilantro) and strips
  of fresh red chilli, to garnish

For the sauce
50g/2oz tamarind pulp
105ml/7 tbsp boiling water
2 shallots, coarsely chopped
1 fresh red chilli, seeded and
  finely chopped
1cm/½in piece fresh root ginger,
  peeled and chopped
5ml/1 tsp soft light brown sugar
45ml/3 tbsp Thai fish sauce

1 Slash each trout diagonally four or five times on each side. Place them in a shallow dish that is large enough to hold them all in a single layer.

2 Fill the cavities with spring onions and douse each fish with soy sauce. Carefully turn the fish over to coat both sides with the sauce. Sprinkle any remaining spring onions over the top.

3 Make the sauce. Put the tamarind pulp in a small bowl and pour on the boiling water. Mash well with a fork until the pulp is thoroughly softened. Transfer the tamarind mixture to a food processor or blender. Add the shallots, fresh chilli, fresh root ginger, sugar and fish sauce. Process to a coarse pulp. Scrape into a bowl.

4 Heat the oil in a large heavy frying pan or wok and cook the trout, one at a time if necessary, for about 5 minutes on each side, until the skin is crisp and browned and the flesh cooked.

5 Put the fish on warmed plates and spoon over some of the chilli sauce. Sprinkle with the coriander and chilli and serve with the remaining sauce.

Fragrant Trout with Hot Spices

Cooking doesn't get much simpler than this. The beauty of this paste is that it is easy to make in a food processor. The deliciously-spiced paste is then smeared over the fish, which are briefly cooked on the grill.

Serves 4
2 large fresh green chillies, seeded
  and coarsely chopped
5 shallots, peeled

5 garlic cloves, peeled
30ml/2 tbsp fresh lime juice
30ml/2 tbsp Thai fish sauce
15ml/1 tbsp palm sugar
  (jaggery) or light muscovado
  (brown) sugar
4 kaffir lime leaves, rolled
  into cylinders and thinly sliced
2 trout or similar firm-fleshed
  fish, about 350g/12oz
  each, cleaned
fresh garlic chives, to garnish
boiled rice, to serve

1 Wrap the chillies, shallots and garlic in a foil package. Place the package under a hot grill (broiler) for about 10 minutes, until the contents have softened.

2 When the package is cool enough to handle, pour the contents into a mortar or food processor and pound with a pestle or process to a paste.

3 Add the lime juice, fish sauce, sugar and lime leaves to the spice paste and mix well.

4 With a teaspoon, stuff the paste inside each fish. Smear a little over the skin as well.

5 Grill (broil) the fish for about 5 minutes on each side, until just cooked. The flesh should flake easily when tested with a knife.

6 Lift each fish on to a platter, garnish with garlic chives and serve with rice.

> **Cook's Tip**
> This hot paste can be used as a marinade for any fish or meat. It also makes a wonderful spicy dip for grilled (broiled) meat.

Trout with Tamarind Energy 247kcal/1038kJ; Protein 36.6g; Carbohydrate 3.5g, of which sugars 3.3g; Fat 9.7g, of which saturates 2g; Cholesterol 147mg; Calcium 65mg; Fibre 0.2g; Sodium 1736mg.
Fragrant Trout Energy 117kcal/490kJ; Protein 14.8g; Carbohydrate 7.9g, of which sugars 6.7g; Fat 3.1g, of which saturates 0.7g; Cholesterol 59mg; Calcium 36mg; Fibre 0.7g; Sodium 57mg.

Lime and Pasilla Chilli Baked Trout

Lime juice, chillies and leeks are perfect partners for the oily trout.

Serves 4
2 fresh chillies

4 rainbow trout, cleaned
4 garlic cloves
10ml/2 tsp dried oregano
juice of 2 limes
50g/2oz/½ cup slivered almonds
salt and ground black pepper

1 Roast the chillies in a dry frying pan until the skins blister. Put them in a strong plastic bag and tie the top to keep the steam in. Set aside for 20 minutes.

2 Meanwhile, rub a little salt into the cavities in the trout, to ensure they are completely clean, then rinse them under cold running water. Drain and pat dry with kitchen paper.

3 Remove the chillies from the bag and peel off the skins. Cut off the stalks, then slit the chillies and scrape out the seeds. Chop the flesh roughly and put it in a mortar. Crush with a pestle until the mixture forms a paste.

4 Place the paste in a shallow dish that will hold all the trout in a single layer. Slice the garlic lengthways and add to the dish. Add the oregano and 10ml/2 tsp salt, then stir in the lime juice and pepper to taste. Add the trout, turning to coat them in the mixture. Cover the dish and set aside for at least 30 minutes, turning the trout again halfway through.

5 Preheat the oven to 200°C/400°F/Gas 6. Have ready four pieces of foil, large enough to wrap a fish. Top each with a sheet of baking parchment of the same size.

6 Place a trout on each piece of parchment, moisten with the marinade. Sprinkle a quarter of the almonds over. Bring up the sides of the paper and fold to seal, then fold the foil to make a parcel. Repeat with the other fish, then place in a single layer in a roasting pan. Bake the parcels in the oven for 25 minutes.

7 Serve each parcel on an individual plate, or unwrap before serving. This dish goes well with new potatoes and vegetables.

Sea Trout with Chilli and Lime

Sea trout is best served with strong flavours such as chillies and lime that cut the richness of the flesh.

Serves 6
6 sea trout cutlets, about 115g/4oz each, or wild or farmed salmon
2 garlic cloves, chopped

1 fresh long red chilli, seeded and chopped
45ml/3 tbsp chopped Thai basil
15ml/1 tbsp palm sugar (jaggery) or granulated (white) sugar
3 limes
400ml/14fl oz/1⅔ cups coconut milk
15ml/1 tbsp Thai fish sauce

1 Place the fish in a dish. Using a pestle, pound the garlic and chilli in a large mortar to break it up. Add 30ml/2 tbsp of the Thai basil with the sugar and continue to pound to a paste. Grate the rind from one lime and squeeze it. Mix the rind and juice into the paste, with the coconut milk. Pour over the fish, cover and chill for 1 hour. Cut the remaining limes into wedges.

2 Prepare the barbecue. Remove the fish from the refrigerator. Once the flames have died down, position a lightly oiled grill rack over the coals to heat. When the coals are cool to medium-hot, or with a thick to moderate coating of ash, remove the cutlets from the marinade. Place them in an oiled hinged wire fish basket or directly on the grill rack. Cook the fish for 4 minutes on each side, trying not to move them. They may stick to the grill rack if not seared first.

3 Strain the remaining marinade into a pan, and reserve the contents of the sieve (strainer). Bring the marinade to the boil, then simmer for 5 minutes. Stir in the contents of the sieve and cook for 1 minute more. Add the Thai fish sauce and the remaining Thai basil. Lift each fish cutlet on to a plate, pour over the sauce and serve with the lime wedges.

> **Variation**
> If sea trout is not in season, use good quality environmentally sound farmed salmon or, if your budget can stretch to it, buy wild salmon.

Lime Baked Trout Energy 257kcal/1077kJ; Protein 31.1g; Carbohydrate 1.5g, of which sugars 1.1g; Fat 14.1g, of which saturates 2g; Cholesterol 92mg; Calcium 59mg; Fibre 1.3g; Sodium 75mg.
Sea Trout with Chilli Energy 139kcal/587kJ; Protein 21.3g; Carbohydrate 4.1g, of which sugars 4.1g; Fat 4.3g, of which saturates 0.1g; Cholesterol 0mg; Calcium 30mg; Fibre 0g; Sodium 253g.

Baked Spicy Cod Steaks

Serve this delicious dish with a large fresh salad, or some little boiled potatoes and garlicky green beans, for a main course if you wish.

Serves 4

4 cod or hake steaks
2 or 3 sprigs of fresh flat leaf parsley
4 slices white bread, toasted, then
    crumbed in a food processor
salt and ground black pepper

For the sauce

75–90ml/5–6 tbsp extra virgin
    olive oil
175ml/6fl oz/³⁄₄ cup white wine
2 garlic cloves, crushed
60ml/4 tbsp finely chopped flat
    leaf parsley
1 fresh red or green chilli, seeded
    and finely chopped
400g/14oz ripe tomatoes, peeled
    and finely diced
salt and ground black pepper

1 Mix all the sauce ingredients in a bowl, and add some salt and pepper. Set the mixture aside.

2 Preheat the oven to 190°C/375°F/Gas 5. Rinse the fish steaks then pat them dry with kitchen paper. Arrange them in a single layer in an oiled baking dish and sprinkle over the parsley. Season with salt and pepper.

3 Spoon the sauce over the fish, distributing it evenly over each steak. Then sprinkle over half of the breadcrumbs, again evenly covering each steak. Bake for 10 minutes, then baste with the juices in the dish, trying not to disturb the breadcrumbs.

4 Sprinkle the remaining breadcrumbs over the top of the dish. Return to the oven and bake for a further 10–15 minutes, until the fish are cooked and the breadcrumbs are crisp and have turned golden brown.

Variation

If you like, use two whole fish, such as sea bass or grey mullet, total weight about 1kg/2¼lb. Rinse thoroughly inside and out, pat dry, then tuck the parsley sprigs inside. Add the sauce and breadcumbs as above. Bake the fish for about 15 minutes, then turn them over carefully, and bake for 20–25 minutes more.

Fish in a Spicy Turmeric, Mango and Tomato Sauce

Tilapia is widely used in African cooking, but can be found in most fishmongers.

Serves 4

4 tilapia
½ lemon
2 garlic cloves, crushed
2.5ml/½ tsp dried thyme
30ml/2 tbsp chopped spring
    onions (scallions)
vegetable oil, for shallow frying
flour, for dusting
30ml/2 tbsp groundnut (peanut) oil

15g/½oz/1 tbsp butter
1 onion, finely chopped
3 tomatoes, peeled and chopped
5ml/1 tsp ground turmeric
60ml/4 tbsp white wine
1 green chilli, seeded
    and chopped
600ml/1 pint/2½ cups fish stock
5ml/1 tsp sugar
1 medium underripe mango,
    peeled and diced
15ml/1 tbsp chopped fresh parsley
salt and ground black pepper

1 Place the fish in a shallow bowl, squeeze the lemon juice all over the fish and gently rub in the garlic, thyme and salt and pepper. Place the spring onions in the cavity of each fish, cover loosely with clear film (plastic wrap) and leave to marinate for a few hours or overnight in the refrigerator.

2 Heat a little vegetable oil in a large frying pan, coat the fish with a little flour, then fry on both sides for a few minutes until golden brown. Transfer to a plate and set aside.

3 Heat the groundnut oil and butter in a pan and fry the onion for 5 minutes, until soft. Add the tomatoes and cook for a few minutes. Add the turmeric, white wine, chilli, stock and sugar, stir well and bring to the boil, then simmer, covered, for 10 minutes.

4 Add the fish and cook gently for about 15–20 minutes, until cooked through. Add the mango, arranging it around the fish, and cook briefly for 1–2 minutes to heat through.

5 Arrange the fish on a serving plate with the mango and tomato sauce poured over. Garnish with parsley and serve.

Baked Spicy Cod Energy 362kcal/1,510kJ; Protein 31g; Carbohydrate 13.1g, of which sugars 3.7g; Fat 17.9g, of which saturates 2.7g; Cholesterol 36mg; Calcium 49mg; Fibre 1.3g; Sodium 274mg.
Fish in a Spicy Sauce Energy 238kcal/998kJ; Protein 23.4g; Carbohydrate 10.1g, of which sugars 9.6g; Fat 10.8g, of which saturates 3.1g; Cholesterol 8mg; Calcium 168mg; Fibre 2g; Sodium 97mg.

Fried Fish in Chilli Coconut Sauce

This tasty dish is easy to make and diners will enjoy the partnership of succulent fish with a creamy ginger and coconut sauce that has a nice kick from the chillies.

Serves 4
4 medium pomfret, porgy
    or butterfish
juice of 1 lemon
5ml/1 tsp garlic granules
salt and ground black pepper
vegetable oil, for shallow frying

For the coconut sauce
450ml/³⁄₄ pint/scant 2 cups water
    2 thin slices fresh root ginger
150ml/¹⁄₄ pint/²⁄₃ cup
    coconut cream
30ml/2 tbsp vegetable oil
1 red onion, sliced
2 garlic cloves, crushed
1 green chilli, seeded and
    thinly sliced
15ml/1 tbsp chopped fresh
    coriander (cilantro)

1 Cut the fish in half and sprinkle inside and out with the lemon juice. Season with the garlic granules and salt and pepper and set aside to marinate for a few hours.

2 Heat a little oil in a frying pan. Pat away the excess lemon juice from the fish. Fry for 10 minutes, turning once. Set aside.

3 To make the sauce, place the water in a pan with the slices of ginger, bring to the boil and simmer until the liquid is reduced to just over 300ml/½ pint/1¼ cups.

4 Take out the slices of ginger from the pan and reserve. Add the coconut cream to the pan and stir well.

5 Heat the oil in a wok or large frying pan and fry the onion and garlic for 4–5 minutes until the onions are beginning to soften and turn translucent.

6 Add the reserved ginger and coconut stock, the chilli and coriander, stir well and then gently add the fish. Simmer for 10 minutes, until the fish is cooked through.

7 Transfer the fish to a serving plate, adjust the seasoning for the sauce and pour over the fish. Serve immediately.

Chilli-coated Fish in Banana Leaves

Cooking fish in banana leaves is a delightful method that can be found throughout South-east Asia. The banana leaves impart their own flavour and the fish remains beautifully succulent, with a wonderful fragrance from the spices inside the leaf.

Serves 4
500g/1¼lb fresh fish fillets, cut
    into chunks
juice of 2 limes
4–6 shallots, chopped

2 red chillies, seeded
    and chopped
25g/1oz fresh root
    ginger, chopped
15g/½oz fresh turmeric, chopped
2 lemon grass stalks, chopped
3–4 candlenuts, ground
10ml/2 tsp palm sugar (jaggery)
1–2 banana leaves, cut into
    4 big squares
salt

To serve
cooked rice
chilli sambal

1 In a large bowl, toss the fish fillets in the lime juice then leave to marinate at room temperature for 10–15 minutes.

2 Meanwhile, using a mortar and pestle, pound the shallots, chillies, ginger, turmeric and lemon grass to a coarse paste. Add the ground candlenuts with the sugar and season with salt. Transfer the paste to the bowl with the fish and toss to coat the fish in it.

3 Place the banana leaves on a flat surface and divide the fish mixture equally among them. Tuck in the sides and fold over the ends to form a neat parcel. Secure with string.

4 Place the banana leaf parcels in a steamer and steam for 25–30 minutes until tender. Serve hot with rice and a sambal.

> **Cook's Tip**
> Banana leaves are available in South-east Asian, Chinese and African food shops but, if you cannot find them, you can use foil instead and bake the fish in the oven at 180°C/350°F/Gas 4 rather than steaming them.

Fried Fish in Coconut Sauce Energy 325kcal/1356kJ; Protein 33g; Carbohydrate 4g, of which sugars 3g; Fat 20g, of which saturates 6g; Cholesterol 0mg; Calcium 142mg; Fibre 0.6g; Sodium 400mg.
Chilli-coated Fish Energy 225kcal/943kJ; Protein 27.6g; Carbohydrate 14.1g, of which sugars 10.4g; Fat 6.9g, of which saturates 1.2g; Cholesterol 58mg; Calcium 51mg; Fibre 2.5g; Sodium 79mg.

Red-hot Red Snapper Burritos

Fish makes a great filling for a tortilla, especially when it is succulent red snapper mixed with rice, chilli and tomatoes.

Serves 6

3 red snapper fillets
90g/3¹/₂oz/¹/₂ cup long grain
    white rice
30ml/2 tbsp vegetable oil
I small onion, finely chopped
5ml/I tsp ground achiote seed
    (annatto powder)
I pasilla or similar dried chilli,
    seeded and ground
75g/3oz/³/₄ cup slivered
    almonds
200g/7oz can chopped
    tomatoes in tomato juice
150g/5oz/1¹/₄ cups grated
    Monterey Jack or mild
    Cheddar cheese
8 X 20cm/8in wheat
    flour tortillas
fresh flat-leaved parsley to garnish
lime wedges (optional)

I Preheat the grill (broiler). Cook the fish fillets on an oiled rack for about 5 minutes, turning once. When cool, remove the skin and flake the fish into a bowl. Set it aside.

2 Meanwhile, put the rice in a pan, cover with cold water, cover and bring to the boil. Drain, rinse and drain again.

3 Heat the oil in a pan and fry the onion until soft and translucent. Stir in the ground achiote and the chilli and cook for 5 minutes.

4 Add the rice, stir well, then stir in the fish and almonds. Add the tomatoes, with their juice. Cook over a moderate heat until all the juice is absorbed and the rice is tender. Stir in the cheese and remove from the heat. Warm the tortillas.

5 Divide the filling among the tortillas and fold them as shown, to make neat parcels. Garnish with fresh parsley and serve with lime wedges, if liked. A green salad makes a good accompaniment.

Cook's Tip
If red snapper is not available this dish will also be delicious with other fish such as grey mullet, pompano or butterfish.

Monkfish Stir-fry with Spices

Monkfish is a rather expensive fish these days, but it is ideal to use in a stir-fry recipe as it is a robust fish and will not break up easily.

Serves 4

30ml/2 tbsp corn oil
2 medium onions, sliced
5ml/I tsp crushed garlic
5ml/I tsp ground cumin
5ml/I tsp ground coriander
5ml/I tsp chilli powder
175g/6oz monkfish, cut into
    bitesize cubes
30ml/2 tbsp fresh fenugreek leaves
2 tomatoes, seeded and sliced
    into wedges
I courgette (zucchini), sliced
15ml/I tbsp lime juice
salt

I Heat the oil in a non-stick wok or heavy frying pan and fry the onions over a low heat until they are soft and have turned slightly translucent.

2 Meanwhile, in a small bowl mix together the garlic, cumin, coriander and chilli powder, stirring until thoroughly combined.

3 Add this spice mixture to the onions in the pan and stir for about 1–2 minutes, until the mixture starts to release a fragrant spicy aroma.

4 Add the fish to the wok or pan and continue to stir-fry the mixture for 3–5 minutes, until the fish pieces are well cooked through and tender.

5 Add the fenugreek leaves, tomatoes and courgette to the pan. Season with salt to taste, and stir-fry for a further 2–3 minutes until all the ingredients are well heated. Sprinkle with lime juice before serving.

Variation
Try to use monkfish for this recipe, but if it is not available, or your budget won't stretch that far, then either cod or prawns (shrimp) will make a suitable substitute. You can even use a mixture of seafood if that is what you have to hand.

Snapper Burritos Energy 519kcal/2177kj; Protein 30g; Carbohydrate 54.4g; of which sugars 2.9g; Fat 20.7g; of which saturates 6.7g; Cholesterol 52mg; Calcium 326mg; Fibre 3g; Sodium 430mg.
Monkfish Stir-fry Energy 86kcals/360kj; Protein 9.18g; Carbohydrate 8.30g, of which sugars 2.3g; Fat 2.38g, of which saturates 0.35g; Cholesterol 16mg; Calcium 98mg; Fibre 1.87g; Sodium 270mg.

Halibut Steaks with Lemon, Red Chilli and Coriander

Succulent fish steaks are first marinated in herbs and spices then cooked in a tasty stock with chillies and coriander, and served with a red onion topping.

Serves 4
4 halibut or cod steaks, about 175g/6oz each
juice of 1 lemon
5ml/1 tsp garlic granules
5ml/1 tsp paprika
5ml/1 tsp ground cumin
5ml/1 tsp dried tarragon
about 60ml/4 tbsp olive oil
flour, for dusting
300ml/½ pint/1¼ cups fish stock
2 red chillies, seeded and finely chopped
30ml/2 tbsp chopped fresh coriander (cilantro)
1 red onion, cut into rings
salt and ground black pepper

1 Place the fish in a shallow bowl. Mix together the lemon juice, garlic, paprika, cumin, tarragon and a little salt and pepper.

2 Spoon the lemon mixture over the fish, cover loosely with clear film (plastic wrap) and set aside to marinate for a few hours or overnight in the fridge.

3 Gently heat all of the oil in a large non-stick frying pan, dust the fish with flour and then fry the fish for a few minutes each side, until golden brown all over.

4 Pour the fish stock around the fish, and then simmer gently, covered, for about 5 minutes, stirring occasionally until the fish is thoroughly cooked through.

5 Add the chopped red chillies and 15ml/1 tbsp of the coriander to the pan. Simmer for 5 minutes.

6 Carefully transfer the fish steaks to a serving plate. Spoon the sauce over the fish and keep warm.

7 Wipe the pan, heat some olive oil and stir fry the onion rings until speckled brown. Sprinkle over the fish with the remaining chopped coriander and serve immediately.

Sea Bass Steamed in Coconut Milk with Ginger and Red Chilli

This is a delicious spicy recipe for any whole white fish, such as sea bass or cod, or for large chunks of trout or salmon.

Serves 4
200ml/7fl oz coconut milk
10ml/2 tsp raw cane or muscovado (molasses) sugar
about 15ml/1 tbsp sesame or vegetable oil
2 garlic cloves, finely chopped
1 red Thai chilli, seeded and finely chopped
4cm/1½in fresh root ginger, peeled and grated
750g/1⅔lb sea bass, gutted and skinned on one side
1 star anise, ground
1 bunch of fresh basil, stalks removed
30ml/2 tbsp cashew nuts
sea salt and ground black pepper

1 Heat the coconut milk with the sugar in a small pan, stirring until the sugar dissolves, then remove from the heat. Add the oil to a small frying pan and stir in the garlic, chilli and ginger. Cook until they begin to brown, then add the mixture to the coconut milk and mix well to combine.

2 Place the fish, skin side down, on a wide piece of foil and tuck up the sides to form a boat-shaped container. Using a sharp knife, cut several diagonal slashes into the flesh on the top and rub with the ground star anise. Season with salt and pepper and spoon the coconut milk over the top.

3 Sprinkle about half the basil leaves over the top of the fish and pull the sides of the foil over the top, so that it is almost enclosed. Gently lay the foil packet in a steamer. Cover the steamer, bring the water to the boil, then reduce the heat and simmer for 20–25 minutes, or until just cooked.

4 Meanwhile, roast the cashew nuts in the small frying pan, adding a little extra oil if necessary. Drain the nuts on kitchen paper, then grind them to crumbs. When cooked, lift the fish out of the foil and transfer it to a serving dish. Spoon the cooking juices over, sprinkle with the cashew nut crumbs and garnish with the remaining basil leaves. Serve immediately.

Halibut Steaks Energy 265kcal/1106kJ; Protein 33g; Carbohydrate 5.4g, of which sugars 1.2g; Fat 12.5g, of which saturates 1.8g; Cholesterol 81mg; Calcium 47mg; Fibre 0.9g; Sodium 109mg.
Sea Bass Energy 235kcal/983kJ; Protein 26g; Carbohydrate 8g, of which sugars 6g; Fat 11g, of which saturates 2g; Cholesterol 100mg; Calcium 217mg; Fibre 0.3g; Sodium 300mg.

Chicken Fillets with a Chilli Marmalade

The aji amarillo is a hot yellowy-orange Peruvian chilli. It is best to make the marmalade a day ahead so the flavours can mellow.

Serves 4
500g/1¼lb skinless chicken breast fillets each cut into 4 long strips
2 garlic cloves, crushed to a paste with 2.5ml/½ tsp salt
30ml/2 tbsp olive oil
ground black pepper
flat bread, to serve

For the chilli marmalade
50g/2oz dried aji amarillo chillies
120ml/4fl oz/½ cup water
20ml/4 tsp olive oil
2 onions, finely chopped
3 garlic cloves, crushed
5ml/1 tsp ground cumin
10ml/2 tsp Mexican oregano
130g/4½oz/scant ¾ cup sugar
200ml/7fl oz/scant 1 cup cider or white wine vinegar
2 small orange (bell) peppers, quartered and seeded

1 Make the marmalade. Heat a frying pan, add the dried chillies and roast, stirring, for 1½ minutes. Put them in a bowl with enough hot water to cover. Rehydrate for about 2 hours.

2 Discard the chilli seeds and dice the flesh. Place in a food processor, add the water and process to a purée. Heat the oil in a heavy pan. Cook the onions and garlic for 5 minutes. Add the cumin, oregano and chilli purée. Add the sugar and stir until turning syrupy. Add the vinegar. Boil, then simmer for 30 minutes.

3 Heat a griddle. Roast the peppers, skin side down to char the skins. Place in a bowl and cover. When cool, rub off the skins and dice the flesh. Add to the chilli mixture. Simmer for 25 minutes, or until the marmalade thickens. Transfer to a bowl. When cool, cover and chill until needed.

4 Spread the chicken pieces in a shallow dish and coat with the garlic, oil and pepper. Cover and set aside for 30–45 minutes.

5 Prepare the barbecue. When the coals are medium-hot, and with a covering of ash, grill the chicken pieces for 2½–3 minutes on each side. Serve with the marmalade and toasted flat bread.

Spiced Chicken Wings

Fresh crushed ginger is used in the marinade and this spicy dish is also garnished with shredded ginger. Try to buy chicken wings that are already skinned, as it is very hard to skin them yourself.

Serves 4
10–12 chicken wings, skinned
175ml/6fl oz/⅔ cup natural (plain) low-fat yogurt
7.5ml/1½ tsp crushed ginger

5ml/1 tsp salt
5ml/1 tsp Tabasco sauce
15ml/1 tbsp tomato ketchup
5ml/1 tsp crushed garlic
15ml/1 tbsp lemon juice
15ml/1 tbsp fresh coriander (cilantro) leaves
15ml/1 tbsp corn oil
2 medium onions, sliced
15ml/1 tbsp grated fresh root ginger
salt and ground black pepper

1 Place the chicken wings in a large mixing bowl, season and set aside while making the marinade.

2 Pour the yogurt into another bowl along with the crushed ginger, salt, Tabasco, tomato ketchup, crushed garlic, lemon juice and half the coriander.

3 Whisk all the ingredients together, pour over the chicken wings and mix well until the chicken is thoroughly coated.

4 Heat the oil in a non-stick wok or frying pan and fry the onions until they begin to soften and turn translucent.

5 Add the chicken wings to the pan. Cook over a medium heat, stirring occasionally, for 10–15 minutes. Add the remaining coriander and the shredded ginger and cook for 1–2 minutes. Serve immediately, garnished with the rest of the coriander.

Variation
This dish will work just as well with other cuts of chicken. You can substitute drumsticks or chicken breast portions for the wings in this recipe. Remember to increase the cooking time depending on what part of the chicken you are using.

Chicken with Marmalade Energy 348kcal/1467kJ; Protein 31.4g; Carbohydrate 41.6g, of which sugars 40.9g; Fat 7.3g, of which saturates 1.3g; Cholesterol 88mg; Calcium 35mg; Fibre 1.8g; Sodium 82mg.
Chicken Wings Energy 224kcals/936kJ; Protein 24.33g; Carbohydrate 12.07g, of which sugars; 10g; Fat 9.00g, of which saturates 2.2g; Cholesterol 124mg; Calcium 50g; Fibre 1.24g; Sodium 0.66mg.

East African-spiced Roast Chicken

A delicious, and impressive whole roast chicken stuffed with a tasty African paste.

Serves 6
1.8kg/4lb chicken
30ml/2 tbsp softened butter, plus extra for basting
3 garlic cloves, crushed
5ml/1 tsp ground black pepper
5ml/1 tsp ground turmeric
2.5ml/½ tsp ground cumin
5ml/1 tsp dried thyme
15ml/1 tbsp finely chopped fresh coriander (cilantro)
60ml/4 tbsp thick coconut milk
60ml/4 tbsp medium-dry sherry
5ml/1 tsp tomato purée (paste)
salt and chilli powder
coriander (cilantro) leaves, to garnish

1 Remove the giblets from the chicken, if necessary, rinse out the cavity and pat the skin dry.

2 Put the softened butter together with all the remaining ingredients in a large bowl and mix together well to form a thick paste.

3 Gently ease the skin of the chicken away from the flesh and rub generously with the herb and butter mixture. Rub more of the mixture over the skin, legs and wings of the chicken and into the neck cavity.

4 Place the chicken in a roasting pan, cover loosely with foil and leave to marinate for about 4 hours or overnight in the refrigerator, if possible.

5 Preheat the oven to 190°C/375°F/Gas 5. Cover the chicken with clean foil and roast for 1 hour.

6 Take the chicken out of the oven, turn the chicken over and baste thoroughly with the pan juices. Cover again with foil, and cook for a further 30 minutes.

7 Remove the foil and place the chicken breast side up. Rub all over with a little extra butter and roast for a further 10–15 minutes until the skin is golden brown and the juices run clear when the thickest part of the chicken is pierced with a skewer. Serve with a rice dish or a salad, garnished with coriander.

Spicy Chicken Satay with Chilli Relish

This spicy marinade quickly gives an exotic flavour to tender chicken. The satays can be cooked on a barbecue or under the grill.

Serves 4
4 skinless chicken breast fillets, about 175g/6oz each
60ml/4 tbsp sambal kecap

1 Cut the chicken breast fillets into 2.5cm/1in cubes and place in a bowl with the sambal kecap. Mix thoroughly so the chicken is well coated. Cover and leave in a cool place to marinate for at least 1 hour.

2 Soak eight bamboo skewers in cold water for 30 minutes so they don't burn while cooking the chicken.

3 Pour the chicken and the marinade into a sieve (strainer) placed over a pan and leave to drain for a few minutes. Set the sieve aside.

4 Add 30ml/2 tbsp hot water to the marinade and bring to the boil. Lower the heat and simmer for 2 minutes, then pour into a bowl and leave to cool.

5 Drain the skewers, thread them with the chicken and cook under a grill (broiler) or on a barbecue for about 10 minutes, turning regularly until the chicken is golden brown and cooked through. Serve with the sambal kecap as a dip.

Cook's Tip
Sambal kecap is a popular Indonesian sauce. Look for it in Asian food stores or, if unavailable, try making your own version. In a bowl, mix together 30ml/2 tbsp dark soy sauce; juice of ½ a lemon or 1 lime; 2 hot chilli peppers, crushed, or 5ml/1 tsp chilli powder; 2 shallots, sliced very thin; 1 clove of garlic, crushed (optional); 15ml/1 tbsp hot water. Leave to stand for 30 minutes before serving to let the flavours mingle.

African-spiced Chicken Energy 439kcal/1824kJ; Protein 43.3g; Carbohydrate 1.2g, of which sugars 1.2g; Fat 27.9g, of which saturates 10.7g; Cholesterol 2.6mg; Calcium 23mg; Fibre 0g; Sodium 211mg.
Spicy Chicken Satay Energy 265kcal/1120kJ; Protein 55.2g; Carbohydrate 3.5g, of which sugars 2g; Fat 3.4g, of which saturates 1g; Cholesterol 158mg; Calcium 19mg; Fibre 0.6g; Sodium 1204mg.

Chicken Chilli Parcels

These fried burritos are a common sight on street stalls and in cafés along the Mexican border with Texas, but are not so well known farther south.

Serves 4
2 skinless chicken breast fillets
1 chipotle chilli, seeded
15ml/1 tbsp vegetable oil
oil, for frying
2 onions, finely chopped

4 garlic cloves, crushed
2.5ml/½ tsp ground cumin
2.5ml/½ tsp ground coriander
2.5ml/½ tsp ground cinnamon
2.5ml/½ tsp ground cloves
300g/11oz/scant 2 cups drained canned tomatillos
400g/14oz/2¾ cups cooked pinto beans
8 X 20–25cm/8–10in fresh wheat flour tortillas
salt and ground black pepper

1 Put the chicken in a large pan, pour over water to cover and add the chilli. Bring to the boil, and then simmer for 10 minutes or until the chicken is cooked and the chilli has softened. Remove the chilli and chop finely. Transfer the chicken on to a plate. Leave to cool slightly, then shred with two forks.

2 Heat the oil in a frying pan. Fry the onions until translucent, then add the garlic and ground spices and cook for 3 minutes. Add the tomatillos and pinto beans. Cook over a moderate heat for 5 minutes, stirring to break up the tomatillos and some of the beans. Simmer for 5 minutes. Add the chicken and season.

3 Wrap the tortillas in foil and place them on a plate. Stand the plate over boiling water for about 5 minutes until they become pliable. Alternatively, wrap them in microwave-safe film and heat them in a microwave on full power for 1 minute.

4 Spoon one-eighth of the bean filling into the centre of a tortilla, fold in both sides, then fold the bottom of the tortilla up and the top down to form a neat parcel. Secure with a cocktail stick (toothpick).

5 Heat the oil in a large frying pan and fry the tortilla parcels in batches until crisp, turning once. Remove them from the oil with a slotted spoon and drain on kitchen paper. Serve hot.

Hot Caribbean Peanut Chicken

Peanut butter is used in many Caribbean dishes. It adds a richness to this spicy dish, as well as a delicious nutty flavour all of its own.

Serves 4
4 skinless chicken breast fillets, cut into thin strips
225g/8oz/generous 1 cup white long grain rice
30ml/2 tbsp groundnut oil
15g/½oz/1 tbsp butter, plus extra for greasing
1 onion, finely chopped
2 tomatoes, peeled, seeded and chopped

1 green chilli, seeded and sliced
60ml/4 tbsp smooth peanut butter
450ml/¾ pint/scant 2 cups chicken stock
lemon juice, to taste
salt and ground black pepper
lime wedges and sprigs of fresh flat leaf parsley, to garnish

For the marinade
15ml/1 tbsp sunflower oil
1–2 garlic cloves, crushed
5ml/1 tsp chopped fresh thyme
25ml/1½ tbsp medium curry powder
juice of half a lemon

1 Mix all the marinade ingredients in a large bowl and stir in the chicken. Cover loosely with clear film (plastic wrap) and set aside in a cool place for 2–3 hours.

2 Meanwhile, cook the rice in boiling water until tender. Drain well and turn into a generously buttered casserole.

3 Preheat the oven to 180°C/350°F/Gas 4. Heat 15ml/1 tbsp of the oil and butter in a flameproof casserole and fry the chicken for 4–5 minutes until evenly brown. Transfer to a plate. Add the onion to the casserole and fry for 5–6 minutes until lightly browned. Stir in the tomatoes and chilli. Cook for 3–4 minutes, stirring occasionally.

4 Mix the peanut butter with the stock. Mix into the tomato and onion mixture, then add the chicken. Stir in the lemon juice, season, then spoon the mixture into the casserole over the rice.

5 Cover the casserole. Cook in the oven for 15–20 minutes or until hot. Toss the rice with the chicken. Serve immediately, garnished with the lime wedges and parsley sprigs.

Chicken Parcels Energy 468kcal/1968kJ; Protein 27.5g; Carbohydrate 51.1g, of which sugars 6g; Fat 18.5g, of which saturates 2.3g; Cholesterol 61mg; Calcium 105mg; Fibre 3.3g; Sodium 271mg.
Hot Caribbean Peanut Chicken Energy 574kcal/2412kJ; Protein 39g; Carbohydrate 56g, of which sugars 5g; Fat 23g, of which saturates 6g; Cholesterol 95mg; Calcium 73mg; Fibre 2.6g; Sodium 600mg.

Ginger Chicken with Spiced Lentils

This delicious tangy chicken stew comes from Kenya. The amount of lemon juice can be reduced, if you would prefer a less sharp sauce.

Serves 4 to 6
6 chicken thighs or pieces
2.5–4ml/½–¾ tsp ground ginger
50g/2oz mung beans
60ml/4 tbsp corn oil
2 onions, finely chopped
2 garlic cloves, crushed
5 tomatoes, peeled and chopped
1 green chilli, seeded and finely chopped
30ml/2 tbsp lemon juice
300ml/½ pint/1¼ cups coconut milk
300ml/½ pint/1¼ cups water
15ml/1 tbsp chopped fresh coriander (cilantro)
salt and ground black pepper
green vegetable, to serve

1 Place the chicken pieces in a large bowl, season with the ginger and a little salt and pepper and set aside in a cool place to marinate.

2 Meanwhile, boil the mung beans in a pan with plenty of water for 35 minutes until soft, then mash well.

3 Heat the oil in a large pan over a moderate heat and fry the chicken pieces, in batches if necessary, until evenly browned. Transfer to a plate and set aside, reserving the oil and chicken juices in the pan.

4 Add the onions to the same pan and cook them with the garlic for 5 minutes. Add the tomatoes and chilli and cook for a further 1–2 minutes, stirring well.

5 Add the mashed mung beans, lemon juice and coconut milk to the pan. Simmer for 5 minutes, then add the chicken pieces and a little water if the sauce is too thick.

6 Stir in the chopped coriander to the pan and simmer for about 35 minutes until the chicken is cooked through. Season with salt and pepper, if necessary. Serve with a green vegetable and rice or chapatis, if you like.

Chicken in Spicy Onions

This is one of the few dishes of India in which onions appear prominently. Chunky onion slices infused with toasted cumin seeds, shredded ginger and green chillies add a delicious contrast to the flavour of the chicken.

Serves 4 to 6
1.3kg/3lb chicken, jointed and skinned
2.5ml/½ tsp ground turmeric
2.5ml/½ tsp chilli powder
salt, to taste
60ml/4 tbsp vegetable oil
4 small onions, finely chopped
175g/6oz coriander (cilantro) leaves, coarsely chopped
5cm/2in piece fresh root ginger, finely shredded
2 green chillies, finely chopped
10ml/2 tsp cumin seeds, dry-roasted
75ml/5 tbsp/⅓ cup natural (plain) yogurt
75ml/5 tbsp/⅓ cup double (heavy) cream
2.5ml/½ tsp cornflour (cornstarch)

1 Rub the chicken joints with the turmeric, chilli powder and salt and leave to marinate for 1 hour.

2 Heat the oil in a frying pan and fry the chicken pieces without overlapping until both sides are sealed. Remove and keep warm.

3 Reheat the oil and fry three of the chopped onions, 150g/5oz of the coriander leaves, half the ginger, the green chillies and the cumin seeds until the onions are beginning to soften and turn translucent.

4 Return the chicken to the pan with any juices and mix well. Cover and cook gently for 15 minutes.

5 Remove the pan from the heat and allow to cool a little. In a bowl, mix together the natural yogurt, cream and cornflour until well combined. Gradually fold the mixture into the chicken pieces, mixing well.

6 Return the pan to the heat and gently cook until the chicken is tender and cooked through. Just before serving, stir in the reserved onion, coriander and ginger. Serve hot.

Ginger Chicken Energy 221kcal/928kJ; Protein 20g; Carbohydrate 16.5g, of which sugars 10.1g; Fat 8.9g, of which saturates 1.3g; Cholesterol 47mg; Calcium 66mg; Fibre 2.8g; Sodium 111mg.
Chicken in Spicy Onions Energy 439kcal/1840kJ; Protein 62.8g; Carbohydrate 7.8g, of which sugars 5.6g; Fat 17.7g, of which saturates 5.9g; Cholesterol 192mg; Calcium 120mg; Fibre 2.4g; Sodium 175mg.

Chilli Lemon Chicken Energy 462kcal/1918kJ; Protein 37g; Carbohydrate 8.9g, of which sugars 6.3g; Fat 31g, of which saturates 8g; Cholesterol 163mg; Calcium 43mg; Fibre 1.6g; Sodium 141mg.

Duck Sausages with Chilli Sauce

Rich duck sausages are best baked in their own juices for 30 minutes. Creamy mashed sweet potatoes and spicy plum sauce complement and contrast with the richness of the sausages.

Serves 4

8–12 duck sausages

For the sweet potato mash
1.5kg/3¼lb sweet potatoes, cut
   into chunks

25g/1oz/2 tbsp butter
60ml/4 tbsp milk
salt and ground
   black pepper

For the plum sauce
30ml/2 tbsp olive oil
1 small onion, chopped
1 small red chilli, seeded and
   finely chopped
450g/1lb plums, stoned
   and chopped
30ml/2 tbsp red wine vinegar
45ml/3 tbsp clear honey

1 Preheat the oven to 190°C/375°F/Gas 5. Arrange the duck sausages in a single layer in a large, shallow ovenproof dish and bake, uncovered, for 25–30 minutes, turning the sausages two or three times during cooking, to ensure that they brown and cook evenly.

2 Meanwhile, put the sweet potatoes in a pan and pour in enough water to cover them. Bring to the boil, reduce the heat and simmer for 20 minutes, or until tender.

3 Drain and mash the sweet potatoes, then place the pan over a low heat. Stir frequently for about 5 minutes to dry out the mashed potatoes. Beat in the butter and milk, and season with salt and pepper.

4 Heat the oil in a frying pan and fry the onion and chilli gently for about 5 minutes until the onion is soft and translucent. Stir in the plums, vinegar and honey, then simmer gently for about 10 minutes.

5 Divide the freshly cooked sausages among four plates and serve immediately with the sweet potato mash and piquant plum sauce.

Balinese Spiced Duck

This delicious recipe is popular in Bali. Slow-cooked pieces of duck are enlivened by fragrant herbs and spices.

Serves 4

8 duck portions, fat trimmed
   and reserved
50g/2oz desiccated (dry
   unsweetened shredded) coconut
175ml/6fl oz/¾ cup coconut milk
salt and ground black pepper
fried onions, salad leaves or fresh
   herb sprigs, to garnish

For the spice paste
1 small onion or
   4–6 shallots, sliced
2 garlic cloves, sliced
2.5cm/1in fresh root ginger,
   peeled and sliced
1cm/½in fresh galangal, peeled
   and sliced
2.5cm/1in fresh turmeric or
   2.5ml/½ tsp ground turmeric
1–2 red chillies, seeded and sliced
4 macadamia nuts or 8 almonds
5ml/1 tsp coriander seeds,
   dry-fried

1 Place the duck fat trimmings in a heated frying pan, without oil, to render. Reserve the fat. Dry-fry the desiccated coconut in a preheated pan until it turns crisp and brown in colour.

2 To make the paste, blend the onion or shallots, garlic, ginger, galangal, fresh or ground turmeric, chillies, nuts and coriander seeds to a paste in a food processor or with a mortar and pestle.

3 Spread the spice paste over the duck portions and leave to marinate in a cool place for 3–4 hours. Preheat the oven to 160°C/325°F/Gas 3. Shake off the spice paste and transfer the duck pieces to an oiled roasting pan. Cover with a double layer of foil and cook the duck in the oven for 2 hours.

4 Turn the oven temperature up to 190°C/375°F/Gas 5. Heat the reserved duck fat in a pan, add the spice paste and fry for 1–2 minutes. Stir in the coconut milk and simmer for 2 minutes. Discard the duck juices then cover the duck with the spice mixture and sprinkle with the toasted coconut. Cook in the oven for 20–30 minutes.

5 Arrange the duck on a warm serving platter and sprinkle with the fried onions. Season to taste and serve with the salad leaves or fresh herb sprigs of your choice.

Duck Sausages Energy 894kcal/3755kJ; Protein 17.8g; Carbohydrate 110.8g, of which sugars 42.9g; Fat 45.5g, of which saturates 17.9g; Cholesterol 67mg; Calcium 170mg; Fibre 11.6g; Sodium 1052mg.
Balinese Spiced Duck Energy 305kcal/1270kJ; Protein 18.7g; Carbohydrate 9.2g, of which sugars 4.2g; Fat 22g, of which saturates 9.3g; Cholesterol 63mg; Calcium 79mg; Fibre 2.8g; Sodium 108mg.

Jungle Spiced Curry of Guinea Fowl

A traditional spicy curry from Thailand.

Serves 4
1 guinea fowl or similar game bird
15ml/1 tbsp vegetable oil
10ml/2 tsp green curry paste
15ml/1 tbsp Thai fish sauce
2.5cm/1in piece fresh galangal, peeled and finely chopped
15ml/1 tbsp fresh green peppercorns
3 kaffir lime leaves, torn
15ml/1 tbsp whisky, preferably Mekhong
300ml/¹⁄₂ pint/1¹⁄₄ cups chicken stock
50g/2oz yard-long beans, cut into 2.5cm/1in lengths (about ¹⁄₂ cup)
225g/8oz/3¹⁄₄ cups chestnut mushrooms, sliced
1 piece drained canned bamboo shoot, about 50g/2oz, shredded
5ml/1 tsp dried chilli flakes, to garnish (optional)

1 Cut up the guinea fowl, remove the skin, then strip the meat off the bones. Chop into bitesize pieces and set aside.

2 Heat the oil in a wok or frying pan and add the paste. Stir-fry over a medium heat for 30 seconds, until it gives off its aroma.

3 Add the fish sauce and the guinea fowl meat and stir-fry until the meat is browned all over. Add the galangal, peppercorns, lime leaves and whisky, then pour in the stock.

4 Bring to the boil. Add the vegetables, return to a simmer and cook gently for 2–3 minutes, until they are just cooked. Spoon into a dish, sprinkle with chilli flakes, if you like, and serve.

Cook's Tips
• Guinea fowl originated in West Africa and was regarded as a game bird, but has been domesticated in Europe for over 500 years. Their average size is about 1.2kg/2¹⁄₂lb. American readers could substitute two or three Cornish hens, depending on size.
• Fresh green peppercorns are simply unripe berries. They are sold on the stem. Look for them at Thai and Asian supermarkets. If unavailable, substitute bottled green peppercorns, but rinse well and drain them first.

Turkey Stew with Chilli and Sesame

This rich Mexican stew is traditionally served on a festive occasion.

Serves 4
115g/4oz/³⁄₄ cup sesame seeds
50g/2oz/¹⁄₂ cup whole blanched almonds
50g/2oz/¹⁄₂ cup shelled unsalted peanuts, skinned
50g/2oz/¹⁄₄ cup white cooking fat, or 60ml/4 tbsp oil
1 small onion, finely chopped
2 garlic cloves, crushed
50g/2oz/¹⁄₃ cup canned tomatoes
1 ancho chilli and 1 guajillo chilli, seeded, soaked in hot water for 30 minutes and chopped
1 ripe plantain, sliced diagonally
50g/2oz/¹⁄₃ cup raisins
75g/3oz/¹⁄₂ cup ready-to-eat prunes, pitted
5ml/1 tsp dried oregano
2.5ml/¹⁄₂ tsp ground cloves
2.5ml/¹⁄₂ tsp crushed allspice berries
5ml/1 tsp ground cinnamon
25g/1oz/¹⁄₄ cup unsweetened cocoa powder
4 turkey breast steaks
tortillas, to serve

1 Toast the sesame seeds in a frying pan until golden all over. Set aside 45ml/3 tbsp of the toasted seeds for the garnish and tip the rest into a bowl. Toast the almonds and peanuts in the same way and add them to the bowl.

2 Heat half the cooking fat or oil in a frying pan. Cook the onion and garlic for 2–3 minutes. Add the tomatoes and chilli. Cook gently for 10 minutes.

3 Add the plantain, raisins, prunes, dried oregano, spices and cocoa to the pan. Stir in 250ml/8fl oz/1 cup of the chilli water. Add the toasted sesame seeds, almonds and peanuts. Simmer for 10 minutes, stirring frequently, then allow to cool slightly. Blend the sauce in a food processor or blender until smooth.

4 Heat the remaining fat or oil in a flameproof casserole. Add the turkey and brown over a moderate heat. Pour the sauce over the steaks and cover the casserole. Simmer for 25 minutes or until the turkey is cooked, and the sauce has thickened.

5 Sprinkle with sesame seeds and serve with warm tortillas.

Jungle Spiced Curry Energy 368kcal/1540kJ; Protein 56.8g; Carbohydrate 1.4g, of which sugars 0.9g; Fat 14g, of which saturates 3.2g; Cholesterol 0mg; Calcium 82mg; Fibre 1.1g; Sodium 454mg.
Turkey Stew Energy 700kcal/2920kJ; Protein 50.6g; Carbohydrate 27.7g, of which sugars 19.1g; Fat 43.8g, of which saturates 6.9g; Cholesterol 86mg; Calcium 267mg; Fibre 7g; Sodium 178mg.

Italian Lamb Meatballs with Chilli Tomato Sauce

Serve these piquant Italian-style meatballs with pasta and a leafy salad. Sprinkle with a little grated Parmesan cheese for that extra Italian touch.

Serves 4
450g/1lb lean minced (ground) lamb
1 large onion, grated
1 garlic clove, crushed
50g/2oz/1 cup fresh white breadcrumbs
15ml/1 tbsp chopped fresh parsley
1 small egg, lightly beaten
30ml/2 tbsp olive oil

salt and ground black pepper
60ml/4 tbsp finely grated Parmesan cheese, pasta and rocket (arugula) leaves, to serve

For the sauce
1 onion, finely chopped
400g/14oz can chopped tomatoes
200ml/7fl oz/scant 1 cup passata (bottled strained tomatoes)
5ml/1 tsp sugar
2 green chillies, seeded and finely chopped
30ml/2 tbsp chopped fresh oregano
salt and ground black pepper

1 Soak a small clay pot in cold water for 15 minutes, then drain. Place the minced lamb, onion, garlic, breadcrumbs, parsley and seasoning in a bowl and mix well. Add the beaten egg and mix to bind the meatball mixture together.

2 Roll the mixture in your hands and shape into about 20 even balls, about the size of walnuts. Wetting your hands slightly will prevent the mixture sticking to them.

3 Heat the olive oil in a frying pan, add the meatballs and cook over a high heat, stirring occasionally, until browned all over.

4 Meanwhile, to make the sauce, mix together the chopped onion, tomatoes, passata, sugar, seeded and chopped chillies and oregano. Season well and pour the sauce into the clay pot.

5 Place the meatballs in the sauce, then cover and place in an unheated oven. Set the oven to 200°C/400°F/Gas 6 and cook for 1 hour, stirring after 30 minutes. Serve over pasta with Parmesan cheese and rocket.

Lamb Tagine with Lemon and Spices

Meatballs are poached gently with lemon and spices to make a dish that is quite light, and ideal for lunch. Serve it with a salad or plain couscous. A popular dish in Morocco, it has no discernible boundaries. It can be found in the tiniest rural villages, in street stalls in the towns and cities, or in the finest restaurants of Casablanca, Fez and Marrakech.

Serves 4
450g/1lb finely minced (ground) lamb
3 large onions, grated

small bunch of flat leaf parsley, chopped
5–10ml/1–2 tsp ground cinnamon
5ml/1 tsp ground cumin
pinch of cayenne pepper
40g/1½oz/3 tbsp butter
25g/1oz fresh root ginger, peeled and finely chopped
1 hot chilli, seeded and finely chopped
pinch of saffron threads
small bunch of fresh coriander (cilantro), finely chopped
juice of 1 lemon
300ml/½ pint/1¼ cups water
1 lemon, quartered
salt and ground black pepper
crusty bread, to serve

1 To make the meatballs, pound the minced lamb in a bowl by using your hand to lift it up and slap it back down into the bowl. Knead in half the grated onions, the parsley, cinnamon, cumin and cayenne pepper. Season with salt and pepper, and continue pounding the mixture by hand for a few minutes. Break off pieces and shape them into walnut-size balls.

2 In a heavy lidded frying pan, melt the butter and add the remaining onion with the ginger, chilli and saffron. Stirring frequently, cook just until the onion begins to colour, then stir in the coriander and lemon juice.

3 Pour in the water, season with salt and bring to the boil. Drop in the meatballs, reduce the heat and cover the pan. Poach the meatballs gently, turning them occasionally, for about 20 minutes.

4 Remove the lid, tuck the lemon quarters around the meatballs and cook, uncovered, for a further 10 minutes to reduce the liquid slightly. Serve hot, straight from the pan with lots of crusty fresh bread to mop up the delicious juices.

Italian Lamb Meatballs Energy 443kcal/1853kJ; Protein 33.1g; Carbohydrate 22.5g, of which sugars 11.1g; Fat 25.3g, of which saturates 10.3g; Cholesterol 148mg; Calcium 246mg; Fibre 3g; Sodium 389mg.
Lamb Tagine Energy 362kcal/1503kJ; Protein 424.5g; Carbohydrate 12.9g, of which sugars 9.3g; Fat 24g, of which saturates 12.2g; Cholesterol 108mg; Calcium 134mg; Fibre 4g; Sodium 155mg.

Lamb Cutlets with Piquant Tomato Sauce

Lamb cutlets are more readily available in Turkey, but veal can also be used for this recipe. Very fine cutlets are prepared by bashing them flat with a heavy meat cleaver. The cutlets are then quickly cooked on a griddle in their own fat, or a little butter, and served with a sprinkling of dried oregano, as in this recipe, or with wedges of lemon. For a tasty supper, serve this dish with a pilaff, or with sautéed potatoes.

Serves 4

30ml/2 tbsp olive oil
10ml/2 tsp butter
12 lamb cutlets (US rib chops), trimmed and flattened with a cleaver
1 onion, finely chopped
1 fresh green chilli, seeded and finely chopped
2 garlic cloves, finely chopped
5ml/1 tsp sugar
5–10ml/1–2 tsp white wine vinegar
2–3 large tomatoes, skinned and chopped, or 400g/14oz can chopped tomatoes
1 green (bell) pepper, seeded and finely chopped
a sprinkling of dried oregano
salt and ground black pepper

1 Heat the oil and butter in a large, heavy pan and quickly fry the cutlets on both sides until evenly browned.

2 Remove the cutlets from the pan, add the onion, chilli and garlic, and fry until the onion begins to brown.

3 Stir in the sugar and vinegar, then add the tomatoes and green pepper. Lower the heat, cover and simmer for about 30 minutes, until the mixture is thick and saucy. Season with salt and pepper.

4 Return the cutlets to the pan, covering them in the sauce. Cook for about 15 minutes, until the meat is tender.

5 Transfer the cutlets to a serving dish, arranging them around the edge with the bones sticking outwards. Sprinkle with the dried oregano, spoon the sauce into the middle of the cutlets and serve immediately.

Chargrilled Chilli Kebabs

This is the ultimate kebab: spicy chargrilled meat served on day-old pide, a Turkish flat bread, as well as yogurt and tomatoes.

Serves 4

12 plum tomatoes
30ml/2 tbsp butter
1 large pide, or 4 pitta or small naan, cut into bitesize chunks
5ml/1 tsp ground sumac
5ml/1 tsp dried oregano
225g/8oz/1 cup thick and creamy natural (plain) yogurt
salt and ground black pepper
1 bunch fresh flat leaf parsley, chopped, to garnish

For the kebabs

500g/1¼lb minced (ground) lamb
2 onions, finely chopped
1 green chilli, seeded and chopped
4 garlic cloves, crushed
5ml/1 tsp Turkish red pepper or paprika
5ml/1 tsp ground sumac
1 bunch flat leaf parsley, chopped

For the sauce

30ml/2 tbsp olive oil
15ml/1 tbsp butter
1 onion, finely chopped
2 garlic cloves, finely chopped
1 green chilli, seeded and chopped
5–10ml/1–2 tsp sugar
400g/14oz can chopped tomatoes

1 Make the kebabs. Put the lamb in a bowl with all the other ingredients and knead to a paste. Cover and chill for 15 minutes.

2 Make the sauce. Heat the oil and butter in a pan, stir in the onion, garlic and chilli and cook until they colour. Add the sugar and tomatoes and cook for 30 minutes. Season and set aside.

3 Light the barbecue and shape the kebabs. Cook on the barbecue for 6–8 minutes, turning once. Meanwhile, thread the tomatoes on to skewers and cook on the barbecue until charred.

4 While the kebabs are cooking, melt the butter in a heavy pan and fry the pide or other bread until golden. Sprinkle with sumac and oregano, then arrange on a serving dish. Splash a little sauce over the pide and spoon half the yogurt on top.

5 Cut the kebab meat into bitesize pieces. Arrange on the bread with the tomatoes, sprinkle with salt and the rest of the sumac and oregano, and garnish with the chopped parsley. Serve hot, topped with dollops of the remaining sauce and yogurt.

Lamb Cutlets Energy 683kcal/2822kJ; Protein 23.2g; Carbohydrate 7.4g, of which sugars 6.9g; Fat 62.4g, of which saturates 29.2g; Cholesterol 122mg; Calcium 24mg; Fibre 1.7g; Sodium 114mg.
Chargrilled Kebabs Energy 642kcal/2688kJ; Protein 35.2g; Carbohydrate 52.8g, of which sugars 24.1g; Fat 33.9g, of which saturates 15.1g; Cholesterol 121mg; Calcium 253mg; Fibre 6.3g; Sodium 456mg.

Balti Spiced Lamb with Peas and Potatoes

Fresh mint leaves are used in this dish, but if they are not available, use ready-minted frozen peas to bring an added freshness to the spicy sauce.

Serves 4
225g/8oz lean spring lamb
120ml/4 fl oz/½ cup natural
   (plain) low-fat yogurt
1 cinnamon stick
2 green cardamom pods
3 black peppercorns
5ml/1 tsp crushed garlic
5ml/1 tsp crushed ginger
5ml/1 tsp chilli powder
5ml/1 tsp garam masala
5ml/1 tsp salt
30ml/2 tbsp chopped fresh mint
15ml/3 tbsp corn oil
2 medium onions, sliced
300ml/½ pint/1¼ cups water
1 large potato, diced
115g/4oz frozen peas
1 firm tomato, skinned, seeded
   and diced
cooked rice, to serve

1 Using a sharp knife, cut the lamb into even strips, then place the pieces in a bowl.

2 Add the yogurt, cinnamon, cardamoms, peppercorns, garlic, ginger, chilli powder, garam masala, salt and half the mint. Leave to marinate for about 2 hours.

3 Heat the oil in a non-stick wok or frying pan and fry the onions until golden brown. Stir in the lamb and the marinade and stir-fry for about 3 minutes.

4 Pour in the water, lower the heat and simmer gently until the meat is cooked right through, about 15 minutes, depending on the age of the lamb.

5 Meanwhile, cook the potato in boiling water until it is just soft, but not mushy.

6 Add the peas and potato to the lamb and stir to mix gently.

7 Finally, add the remaining mint and the tomato and cook for a further 5 minutes. Serve immediately with cooked rice.

Stir-fried Lamb with Chilli, Ginger and Coriander

This dish benefits from being cooked a day in advance and kept in the refrigerator, which helps the flavours to deepen.

Serves 4
225–275g/8–10oz boned lean
   spring lamb
3 medium onions
15ml/1 tbsp olive oil
15ml/1 tbsp tomato purée (paste)
5ml/1 tsp crushed garlic
7.5ml/1½ tsp crushed ginger
5ml/1 tsp salt
1.5ml/¼ tsp ground turmeric
600ml/1 pint/2½ cups water
15ml/1 tbsp lemon juice
15ml/1 tbsp grated fresh
   root ginger
15ml/1 tbsp chopped fresh
   coriander (cilantro)
15ml/1 tbsp chopped fresh mint
1 red chilli, seeded and chopped
chapatis, to serve

1 Cut the lamb into small cubes. Dice the onions. Heat the oil in a non-stick wok or frying pan and fry the onions until soft.

2 Meanwhile, mix the tomato purée, garlic, ginger, salt and turmeric. Add to the wok and briefly stir-fry until fragrant.

3 Add the lamb and stir-fry for about 2–3 minutes. Add the water, lower the heat, cover and cook for 15–20 minutes, stirring occasionally.

4 When the water has almost evaporated, start bhooning over a medium heat (see the Cook's Tip below), making sure that the sauce does not catch on the bottom of the wok. Continue for 5–7 minutes.

5 Pour in the lemon juice, followed by the ginger, coriander, mint and red chilli, then serve immediately with chapatis.

> **Cook's Tip**
> *Bhooning is a traditional way of stir-frying which involves scraping the bottom of the wok each time in the centre.*

Balti Lamb Energy 317kcal/1322kJ; Protein 18.1g; Carbohydrate 25.6g, of which sugars 10.7g; Fat 16.8g, of which saturates 4.4g; Cholesterol 43mg; Calcium 113mg; Fibre 3.8g; Sodium 89mg.
Stir-fried Lamb Energy 184kcal/767kJ; Protein 13.3g; Carbohydrate 11.7g, of which sugars 7.5g; Fat 9.8g, of which saturates 3.4g; Cholesterol 43mg; Calcium 44mg; Fibre 1.9g; Sodium 554mg.

Balti Lamb with Cauliflower

Cauliflower and lamb go beautifully together. This curry is given a final *tarka* – an Indian garnish – of cumin seeds and curry leaves, which enhances the flavour.

Serves 4
10ml/2 tsp corn oil
2 medium onions, sliced
7.5ml/1½ tsp crushed ginger
5ml/1 tsp chilli powder
5ml/1 tsp crushed garlic
1.5ml/¼ tsp ground turmeric
2.5ml/½ tsp ground coriander

30ml/2 tbsp fresh fenugreek leaves
275g/10oz boned lean spring
    lamb, cut into strips
1 small cauliflower, cut into
    small florets
300ml/½ pint/1¼ cups water
30ml/2 tbsp fresh coriander
    (cilantro) leaves
½ red (bell) pepper, sliced
15ml/1 tbsp lemon juice

For the tarka
10ml/2 tsp corn oil
2.5ml/½ tsp white cumin seeds
4–6 curry leaves

1 Heat the oil in a non-stick wok or frying pan and fry the onions until golden brown. Lower the heat and add the crushed ginger, chilli powder, crushed garlic, turmeric and ground coriander, followed by the fenugreek.

2 Add the lamb strips to the wok and stir-fry until the lamb is completely coated with the spices. Add half the cauliflower florets and stir the mixture well.

3 Pour in the water, cover the wok, and simmer for 5–7 minutes until the cauliflower and lamb are almost cooked through.

4 Add the remaining cauliflower, half the fresh coriander, the red pepper and lemon juice and stir-fry for about 5 minutes, making sure that the sauce does not catch on the bottom of the wok.

5 Check that the lamb is completely cooked, then remove from the heat and set aside.

6 To make the tarka, heat the oil and fry the seeds and curry leaves for about 30 seconds. While it is still hot, pour the seasoned oil over the cauliflower and lamb and serve garnished with the remaining fresh coriander leaves.

Spicy Lamb Korma

This is a delicious creamy and aromatic dish with no 'hot' taste. So it is perfect for guests who like the spiciness of Asian cuisine without the extra fiery kick.

Serves 4 to 6
15ml/1 tbsp white sesame seeds
15ml/1 tbsp white poppy seeds
50g/2oz almonds, blanched
2 green chillies, seeded
5cm/2in piece fresh root
    ginger, sliced

6 garlic cloves, sliced
1 onion, finely chopped
45ml/3 tbsp ghee or vegetable oil
6 green cardamoms
5cm/2in piece cinnamon stick
4 cloves
900g/2lb lean lamb, cubed
5ml/1 tsp ground cumin
5ml/1 tsp ground coriander
salt, to taste
300ml/½ pint/1¼ cups double
    (heavy) cream mixed with
    ½ tsp cornflour (cornstarch)
roasted sesame seeds, to garnish

1 Heat a frying pan without any liquid and dry-roast the sesame and poppy seeds, almonds, chillies, ginger, garlic and onion for about 3–5 minutes until the fragrances of the spices are released.

2 Cool the mixture and grind to a fine paste using a mortar and pestle or a food processor. Heat the ghee or oil in a wok or frying pan.

3 Add the cardamoms, cinnamon and cloves to the pan. Stir-fry the spices until the cloves begin to swell.

4 Add the lamb, ground cumin and coriander, and the prepared paste to the pan. Season with salt, to taste.

5 Cover the pan and cook over a low heat until the lamb is almost done, about 30–40 minutes.

6 Remove the pan from the heat, leave it to cool a little and then gradually fold in the double cream, reserving 15ml/1 tsp to use as a garnish.

7 To serve, gently reheat the lamb uncovered and serve hot, garnished with the sesame seeds and the remaining cream.

Balti Lamb Energy 277kcals/1154kJ; Protein 18.7g; Carbohydrate 14.4g, of which sugars 9g; Fat 16.7g, of which saturates 4.7g; Cholesterol 52mg; Calcium 62mg; Fibre 3.2g; Sodium 73mg
Spicy Lamb Korma Energy 220kcal/916kJ; Protein 14.2g; Carbohydrate 14.5g, of which sugars 11.1g; Fat 12.2g, of which saturates 3.8g; Cholesterol 42mg; Calcium 101mg; Fibre 2.1g; Sodium 90mg.

Sticky Pork Ribs with Ginger and Chilli

Ginger, garlic and chilli are used to flavour the sweet-and-sour sauce that coats these ribs. Cook the pork ribs in a covered clay pot first to tenderize the meat, then uncover the dish so the ribs become deliciously sticky and brown.

Serves 4

16–20 small meaty pork ribs, about 900g/2lb total weight

1 onion, finely chopped
5cm/2in piece fresh root ginger, peeled and grated
2 garlic cloves, crushed
2.5–5ml/½–1 tsp chilli powder
60ml/4 tbsp soy sauce
45ml/3 tbsp tomato purée (paste)
45ml/3 tbsp clear honey
30ml/2 tbsp red wine vinegar
45ml/3 tbsp dry sherry
60ml/4 tbsp water
salt and ground black pepper

1 Soak the clay pot in cold water for 20 minutes, then drain. Place the ribs in the clay pot, arranging them evenly.

2 Mix together the onion, ginger, garlic, chilli powder, soy sauce, tomato purée, honey, wine vinegar, sherry and water.

3 Pour the sauce over the ribs and toss to coat them. Cover the clay pot and place in an unheated oven. Set the oven to 220°C/425°F/Gas 7. Cook for 1 hour.

4 Remove the lid, baste the ribs and season to taste with salt and pepper. Cook uncovered for 15–20 minutes, basting the ribs two to three times during the cooking until they are sticky and dark brown.

Cook's Tips
• *For a stronger flavour, coat the ribs evenly with the sauce and leave to marinate for 2 hours before cooking in the clay pot.*
• *If you cannot find fresh root ginger, crushed ginger, also known as ginger pulp, is available from supermarkets. Use 10ml/2 tsp of the paste instead of 5cm/2in of fresh root ginger.*

Sichuan Pork Ribs with Ginger, Garlic and Chilli Relish

This spicy dish works best when the pork ribs are grilled in whole, large slabs, then sliced to serve.

Serves 4

4 pork rib slabs, each with 6 ribs, total weight about 2kg/4½lb
40g/1½oz/3 tbsp light muscovado sugar
3 garlic cloves, crushed
5cm/2in piece fresh root ginger, finely grated
10ml/2 tsp Sichuan peppercorns, finely crushed
2.5ml/½ tsp ground black pepper
5ml/1 tsp finely ground star anise
5ml/1 tsp Chinese five-spice powder

90ml/6 tbsp dark soy sauce
45ml/3 tbsp sunflower oil
15ml/1 tbsp sesame oil

For the relish
60ml/4 tbsp sunflower oil
300g/11oz banana shallots, finely chopped
9 garlic cloves, crushed
7.5cm/3in piece fresh root ginger, finely grated
60ml/4 tbsp rice wine vinegar
45ml/3 tbsp sweet chilli sauce
105ml/7 tbsp tomato ketchup
90ml/6 tbsp water
60ml/4 tbsp chopped fresh coriander (cilantro) leaves
salt

1 Lay the slabs of pork ribs in a large dish. Mix the remaining ingredients and pour over the ribs. Cover and chill overnight.

2 Make the relish. Heat the oil in a heavy pan, add the shallots and cook for 5 minutes. Add the garlic and ginger and cook for 4 minutes. Add the remaining ingredients except the fresh coriander. Cover and simmer for 10 minutes. Stir in the coriander.

3 Prepare the barbecue. Remove the ribs from the marinade. Pour the marinade into a pan. Boil, then simmer for 3 minutes.

4 When the coals are hot, lay the ribs on a rack and cook for 3 minutes on each side. Move them to a cooler part of the barbecue, cover with a lid or tented foil and cook for 30 minutes, turning and basting occasionally with the marinade, until tender.

5 Stop basting with the marinade 5 minutes before the end of the cooking time. Cut into single ribs to serve, with the relish.

Sticky Pork Ribs Energy 633kcal/2637kJ; Protein 42.9g; Carbohydrate 11.5g, of which sugars 11.2g; Fat 45.2g, of which saturates 14.1g; Cholesterol 149mg; Calcium 43mg; Fibre 0.5g; Sodium 250mg.
Sichuan Pork Ribs Energy 633kcal/2637kJ; Protein 42.9g; Carbohydrate 11.5g, of which sugars 11.2g; Fat 45.2g, of which saturates 14.1g; Cholesterol 149mg; Calcium 43mg; Fibre 0.5g; Sodium 250mg.

Pork Belly with Sesame Dip and Chilli Sauce

Thinly sliced pork belly is griddled until the outside is crisp, leaving a smooth texture at the centre. The meat is then immersed in a salty sesame dip, before being wrapped in lettuce leaves with a spoonful of red chilli paste.

Serves 3
675g/1½lb pork belly
2 round (butterhead) lettuces

For the dip
45ml/3 tbsp sesame oil
10ml/2 tsp salt
ground black pepper

For the sauce
45ml/3 tbsp gochujang (red chilli paste)
75ml/5 tbsp doenjang (soya bean paste)
2 garlic cloves, crushed
1 spring onion (scallion), chopped
5ml/1 tsp sesame oil

1 Freeze the pork belly for 30 minutes and then slice it very thinly, to about 3mm/⅛in thick. (You could ask the butcher to do this, or buy the meat pre-sliced at an Asian store.)

2 To make the dip, combine the sesame oil, salt and pepper in a small serving bowl.

3 To make the sauce, blend the chilli paste, doenjang soya bean paste, garlic, spring onion and sesame oil in a bowl, mixing the oil thoroughly into the paste. Transfer to a serving bowl.

4 Remove the outer leaves from the heads of lettuce, keeping them whole. Rinse well and place in a serving dish.

5 Heat a griddle pan or heavy frying pan over high heat (the griddle can be used over charcoal). Add the pork to the pan and cook until the surface is crisp and golden brown.

6 Serve the pork with the accompanying dishes of lettuce, sesame dip and chilli sauce. To eat, take a strip of pork and dip it into the sesame dip. Then place the meat in the middle of a lettuce leaf and add a small spoonful of the chilli sauce. Fold the sides of the leaf inwards and roll up into a parcel.

Jamaican Jerk Pork with Red Chillies

This is a Jamaican way of spicing meat or poultry before roasting in the oven or over a fire.

Serves 4
15ml/1 tbsp oil
2 onions, finely chopped
2 fresh red chillies, seeded and finely chopped
1 garlic clove, crushed
2.5cm/1in piece fresh root ginger, grated
5ml/1 tsp dried thyme
5ml/1 tsp ground allspice
5ml/1 tsp hot pepper sauce
30ml/2 tbsp rum
grated rind and juice of 1 lime
4 pork chops
salt and ground black pepper
fresh thyme, small red chillies and lime wedges, to garnish

1 Heat the oil in a frying pan. Add the onions and cook for 10 minutes until soft and translucent.

2 Add the chillies, garlic, ginger, thyme and allspice and fry for 2 minutes. Stir in the hot pepper sauce, rum, lime rind and juice.

3 Lower the heat and simmer gently until the mixture has formed a dark paste. Season with salt and pepper to taste, and set aside to cool.

4 Rub the paste all over the chops, ensuring they are well covered. Place them in a shallow dish, cover and marinate overnight in the refrigerator.

5 Preheat the oven to 190°C/375°F/Gas 5. Place the chops on a rack in a roasting pan and roast in the oven for 30 minutes until fully cooked.

6 Serve garnished with thyme, chillies and lime wedges.

> **Variation**
> Chicken joints or even a whole chicken can also be coated with this delicious spicy paste before roasting.

Pork Belly Energy 991kcal/4093kJ; Protein 37g; Carbohydrate 1.1g, of which sugars 0.6g; Fat 93.1g, of which saturates 31.4g; Cholesterol 162mg; Calcium 37mg; Fibre 1.2g; Sodium 1475mg.
Jerk Pork Energy 271kcal/1134kJ; Protein 33.9g; Carbohydrate 9.2g, of which sugars 5.6g; Fat 9.4g, of which saturates 2.5g; Cholesterol 95mg; Calcium 42mg; Fibre 1.4g; Sodium 109mg.

Chipotle Chilli Meatballs

The chipotle chilli gives the sauce a distinctive, slightly smoky flavour.

Serves 4
225g/8oz minced (ground) pork
225g/8oz lean minced
   (ground) beef
1 onion, finely chopped
50g/2oz/1 cup fresh
   white breadcrumbs
5ml/1 tsp dried oregano
2.5ml/½ tsp ground cumin
2.5ml/½ tsp salt
2.5ml/½ tsp ground black pepper

1 egg, beaten
vegetable oil, for frying
fresh oregano sprigs, to garnish
boiled rice, to serve

For the sauce
1 chipotle chilli, seeded
15ml/1 tbsp vegetable oil
1 onion, finely chopped
2 garlic cloves, crushed
175ml/6fl oz/¾ cup beef stock
400g/14oz can chopped tomatoes
105ml/7 tbsp passata (bottled
   strained tomatoes)

1 Mix the minced pork and beef in a bowl. Add the onion, breadcrumbs, oregano, cumin, salt and pepper. Mix with clean hands until all the ingredients are well combined.

2 Stir in the egg, mix well, then roll into 4cm/1½in balls. Put these on a baking sheet and chill while you make the sauce.

3 Soak the dried chilli in hot water for 15 minutes. Heat the oil in a pan and fry the onion and garlic for 3–4 minutes until soft.

4 Drain the chilli, reserving the soaking water, then chop it and add it to the onion mixture. Fry for 1 minute, then stir in the beef stock, tomatoes, passata and soaking water, with salt and pepper to taste. Bring to the boil, lower the heat and simmer, stirring occasionally, while you cook the meatballs.

5 Heat the oil for frying in a frying pan and fry the meatballs in batches for about 5 minutes, turning occasionally, until browned.

6 Drain off the oil and transfer the meatballs to a shallow casserole. Pour over the sauce and simmer for 10 minutes, stirring occasionally so that the meatballs are coated. Garnish with the oregano and serve with boiled rice, if you like.

Chilli Pork in Chinese Leaves

Meltingly tender pork, imbued with the flavours of Korean doenjang soya bean paste and garlic, is combined with a refreshingly zesty mooli stuffing and wrapped in parcels of Chinese leaves.

Serves 3 to 4
1 head Chinese leaves
   (Chinese cabbage)
5 garlic cloves, roughly chopped
½ onion, roughly chopped
1 leek, roughly chopped
15ml/1 tbsp doenjang soya
   bean paste
100ml/3½fl oz/scant ½ cup sake
   or rice wine

675g/1½lb pork neck
salt
sugar

For the stuffing
500g/1¼lb mooli (daikon), peeled
   and thinly sliced
3 chestnuts, sliced
½ Asian pear, sliced
65g/2½oz watercress, or rocket
   (arugula), chopped
45ml/3 tbsp Korean chilli powder
5ml/1 tsp Thai fish sauce
2 garlic cloves, crushed
2.5ml/½ tsp grated fresh
   root ginger
5ml/1 tsp honey
5ml/1 tsp sesame seeds

1 Soak the whole head of Chinese leaves in salty water (using 50g/2oz/¼ cup of salt) for about 1 hour, or until softened.

2 Make the stuffing. Put the mooli into a colander and sprinkle with salt. Leave to stand for 10 minutes, then rinse well and transfer to a large bowl. Add the chestnuts, pear and chopped watercress or rocket to the bowl and mix well. Add all the other stuffing ingredients, with salt to taste, and mix well.

3 Prepare the poaching liquid. Put the garlic, onion and leek in a large pan. Mix in the doenjang paste and sake or rice wine, and add the pork. Add water to cover then bring to the boil. Cook the pork for 30–40 minutes, until tender.

4 Drain the Chinese leaves and tear off whole leaves and place on a serving plate. Transfer the stuffing mixture to a serving dish. Slice the pork into bitesize pieces.

5 Place a slice of pork on a Chinese leaf. Spoon stuffing on to the meat, and wrap it into a parcel before eating it.

Chilli Pork Energy 332kcal/1391kJ; Protein 40.2g; Carbohydrate 18.7g, of which sugars 14.9g; Fat 7.9g, of which saturates 2.6g; Cholesterol 106mg; Calcium 136mg; Fibre 5.9g; Sodium 507mg.
Chilli Meatballs Energy 412kcal/1717kJ; Protein 26.2g; Carbohydrate 16g, of which sugars 5.9g; Fat 27.6g, of which saturates 7.7g; Cholesterol 118mg; Calcium 50mg; Fibre 1.9g; Sodium 265mg.

Stir-fried Chilli Beef with Ginger, Chilli and Oyster Sauce

In Thailand this spicy dish is often made with just straw mushrooms, which are readily available fresh, but oyster mushrooms make a good substitute and if you use a mixture, the dish will be more interesting.

Serves 4 to 6
450g/1lb rump (round) steak
30ml/2 tbsp soy sauce
15ml/1 tbsp cornflour
(cornstarch)

45ml/3 tbsp vegetable oil
15ml/1 tbsp chopped garlic
15ml/1 tbsp chopped fresh
root ginger
225g/8oz/3¼ cups mixed
mushrooms such as shiitake,
oyster and straw
30ml/2 tbsp oyster sauce
5ml/1 tsp sugar
4 spring onions (scallions), cut into
short lengths
ground black pepper
2 fresh red chillies, seeded and
cut into strips, to garnish

1 Place the steak in the freezer for 30 minutes, until firm, then slice diagonally into long thin strips. Mix the soy sauce and cornflour in a bowl. Add the steak, turning to coat well, cover with clear film (plastic wrap) and leave to marinate for 1–2 hours.

2 Heat half the oil in a wok or large, heavy frying pan. Add the garlic and ginger and cook for 1–2 minutes, until fragrant. Drain the steak, add it to the wok or pan and stir well. Cook, stirring frequently, for 1–2 minutes, until the steak is browned all over and tender. Remove from the wok or pan and set aside.

3 Heat the remaining oil in the wok or pan. Add the shiitake, oyster and straw mushrooms. Stir-fry over a medium heat until golden brown.

4 Return the steak to the wok and mix it with the mushrooms. Spoon in the oyster sauce and sugar, stir well, then add ground black pepper to taste. Toss over the heat until all the ingredients are thoroughly combined.

5 Stir in the spring onions. Tip the mixture on to a serving platter, garnish with the strips of red chilli and serve.

Chilli Beef with Sesame Sauce

Variations of this dish can be found all over Vietnam and Cambodia. This version has a deliciously rich, spicy and nutty flavour.

Serves 4
450g/1lb beef sirloin or fillet,
cut into thin strips
15ml/1 tbsp groundnut (peanut)
or sesame oil
2 garlic cloves, finely chopped
2 red Thai chillies, seeded and
finely chopped

7.5ml/1½ tsp sugar
30ml/2 tbsp sesame paste
30–45ml/2–3 tbsp beef stock
or water
coarse sea salt and ground
black pepper
red chilli strips, to garnish
1 lemon, cut into quarters, to serve

For the marinade
15ml/1 tbsp groundnut
(peanut) oil
30ml/2 tbsp tuk trey
30ml/2 tbsp soy sauce

1 In a bowl, mix together the ingredients for the marinade. Toss in the beef, making sure it is well coated. Leave to marinate for about 30 minutes.

2 Heat the groundnut or sesame oil in a wok or heavy pan. Add the garlic and chillies and cook until golden and fragrant. Stir in the sugar. Add the beef, tossing it in the wok to sear it.

3 Stir in the sesame paste and enough stock or water to thin it down. Cook for 1–2 minutes, making sure the beef is coated with the sauce. Season with salt and pepper, garnish with chilli strips and and serve with lemon wedges.

> **Variation**
> Chicken breast fillet or pork fillet (tenderloin) can be used in this recipe instead of beef.

> **Cook's Tip**
> Jars of sesame paste, also known as tahini, are available in South-east Asian and Middle Eastern stores.

Stir-fry Beef Energy 282kcal/1177kJ; Protein 25.4g; Carbohydrate 10.7g, of which sugars 3.4g; Fat 15.5g, of which saturates 4.2g; Cholesterol 69mg; Calcium 16mg; Fibre 0.8g; Sodium 697mg.
Chilli Beef with Sesame Energy 269kcal/1119kJ; Protein 26.2g; Carbohydrate 20g, of which sugars 2.0g; Fat 18g, of which saturates 5g; Cholesterol 65mg; Calcium 31mg; Fibre 0.3g; Sodium 73mg.

Spicy Beef and Mushroom Casserole

In this perfect example of a spicy Korean casserole dish, wild mushrooms are slow-cooked together in a sauce seasoned with garlic and sesame. Ideal as a warming winter dish, its earthy mushroom flavour is enlivened with spring onions and chillies.

Serves 2
150g/5oz beef
2 dried shiitake mushrooms, soaked in warm water for about 30 minutes until softened
25g/1oz enoki mushrooms
1 onion, sliced

400ml/14fl oz/1⅔ cups water or beef stock
25g/1oz oyster mushrooms, thinly sliced
6 pine mushrooms, cut into thin strips
10 spring onions (scallions), sliced
2 chrysanthemum leaves, and ½ red and ½ green chilli, seeded and shredded, to garnish
steamed rice, to serve

For the seasoning
30ml/2 tbsp dark soy sauce
3 spring onions (scallions), sliced
2 garlic cloves, crushed
10ml/2 tsp sesame seeds
10ml/2 tsp sesame oil

1 Slice the beef into thin strips and place in a bowl. Add the seasoning ingredients and mix well, coating the beef evenly. Set aside for 20 minutes so the beef strips can absorb the flavours of the seasonings.

2 When the soaked shiitake mushrooms have reconstituted and become soft, drain and thinly slice them, discarding the stems. Discard the caps from the enoki mushrooms.

3 Place the seasoned beef and the onion in a heavy pan or flameproof casserole and add the water or beef stock. Add all the mushrooms and the spring onions, and bring to the boil.

4 Once the mixture is bubbling in the pan, reduce the heat and simmer gently for 20 minutes.

5 Transfer to a serving dish or serve from the casserole. Garnish with the chrysanthemum leaves and shredded chilli, and then serve with steamed rice.

Chilli Beef and Tomato Curry

When served with boiled yam or rice, this delicious curry makes a hearty dish, certain to be popular with anybody who likes their food spicy.

Serves 4
450g/1lb stewing beef
5ml/1 tsp dried thyme
45ml/3 tbsp palm or vegetable oil
1 large onion, finely chopped
2 garlic cloves, crushed

4 canned plum tomatoes, chopped, plus 60ml/4 tbsp of the juice
15ml/1 tbsp tomato purée (paste)
2.5ml/½ tsp mixed spice
1 fresh red chilli, seeded and chopped
900ml/1½ pints/3¾ cups chicken stock or water
1 large aubergine (eggplant), about 350g/12oz
salt and ground black pepper

1 Cut the beef into cubes and season with 2.5ml/½ tsp of the thyme and salt and pepper.

2 Heat 15ml/1 tbsp of the oil in a large pan and fry the meat, in batches if necessary, for 8–10 minutes, stirring constantly, until evenly browned all over. Transfer to a bowl using a slotted spoon and set aside.

3 Heat the remaining oil in the pan and fry the onion and garlic for a few minutes until the onion begins to soften.

4 Add the tomatoes and tomato juice to the pan and simmer for a further 8–10 minutes, stirring occasionally.

5 Add the tomato purée, mixed spice, chilli and remaining thyme to the pan and stir well.

6 Add the cubed beef and the chicken stock or water to the pan. Bring to the boil, reduce the heat, cover the pan and simmer gently for 30 minutes.

7 Cut the aubergine into 1cm/½in dice. Stir into the beef mixture and cook, covered, for a further 30 minutes until the beef is completely tender. Taste the sauce, adjust the seasoning if necessary and serve immediately.

Spicy Beef Casserole Energy 227kcal/945kJ; Protein 21.1g; Carbohydrate 5.5g, of which sugars 4.4g; Fat 13.6g, of which saturates 3.9g; Cholesterol 44mg; Calcium 72mg; Fibre 2.4g; Sodium 1125mg.
Chilli Beef Curry Energy 251kcal/1050kJ; Protein 27.2g; Carbohydrate 7.2g, of which sugars 6.2g; Fat 12.8g, of which saturates 2.9g; Cholesterol 75mg; Calcium 29mg; Fibre 3g; Sodium 87mg.

Beef and Aubergine Curry with Fresh Red Chillies

Aubergines are popular in Vietnam and are often paired with beef.

Serves 6

120ml/4fl oz/½ cup sunflower oil
2 onions, thinly sliced
2.5cm/1in fresh root ginger, sliced
　　and cut in matchsticks
1 garlic clove, crushed
2 fresh red chillies, seeded and
　　very finely sliced
5ml/1 tsp ground turmeric
1 lemon grass stem, lower part
　　sliced finely, top bruised
675g/1½ lb braising steak, cut in
　　even-size strips
400ml/14fl oz can coconut milk
300ml/½ pint/1¼ cups water
1 aubergine (eggplant), sliced and
　　patted dry
5ml/1 tsp tamarind pulp, soaked
　　in 60ml/4 tbsp warm water
salt and ground black pepper
finely sliced chilli, (optional) and
　　fried onions, to garnish
boiled rice, to serve

1 Heat half the oil and fry the onions, ginger and garlic until they give off a rich aroma. Add the chillies, turmeric and the lower part of the lemon grass. Push to one side and then turn up the heat and add the steak, stirring until the meat changes colour. Add the coconut milk, water, lemon grass top and seasoning to taste. Cover and simmer gently for 1½ hours, or until the meat is tender.

2 Towards the end of the cooking time heat the remaining oil in a frying pan. Fry the aubergine slices until brown on both sides.

3 Add the browned aubergine slices to the beef curry and cook for a further 15 minutes. Stir gently from time to time. Strain the tamarind and stir the juice into the curry. Taste and adjust the seasoning. Put into a warm serving dish. Garnish with the sliced chilli, if using, and fried onions, and serve with boiled rice.

Cook's Tip
If you want to make this curry ahead, follow the above method to the end of step 2 and finish later.

Beef Stew with Star Anise and Chilli Spices

The Vietnamese eat this dish for breakfast, and on chilly mornings people queue up for a steaming bowl of this spicy stew on their way to work. In southern Vietnam, it is often served with chunks of baguette, but in the other regions it is served with noodles. For the midday or evening meal, it is served with steamed or sticky rice. Traditionally, it has an orange hue from the oil in which annatto seeds have been fried, but in this recipe the colour comes from the turmeric.

Serves 4 to 6

500g/1¼lb lean beef, cut into
　　bitesize cubes
10–15ml/2–3 tsp ground turmeric
30ml/2 tbsp sesame or
　　vegetable oil
3 shallots, chopped
3 garlic cloves, chopped
2 red chillies, seeded
　　and chopped
2 lemon grass stalks, cut into
　　several pieces and bruised
15ml/1 tbsp curry powder
4 star anise, roasted and ground
　　to a powder
700ml/scant 1¼ pints hot beef
　　or chicken stock, or
　　boiling water
45ml/3 tbsp Thai fish sauce
30ml/2 tbsp soy sauce
15ml/1 tbsp raw cane sugar
1 bunch of fresh basil,
　　stalks removed
salt and ground black pepper
1 onion, halved and finely sliced,
　　and chopped fresh coriander
　　(cilantro) or leaves, to garnish

1 Toss the beef in the ground turmeric and set aside. Heat a wok or heavy pan and add the oil. Stir in the shallots, garlic, chillies and lemon grass, and cook until they become fragrant.

2 Add the curry powder and all but 10ml/2 tsp of the roasted star anise, followed by the beef. Brown the beef a little, then pour in the stock or water, the fish sauce, soy sauce and sugar. Stir well and bring to the boil. Reduce the heat and simmer for 40 minutes, or until the meat is tender and the liquid has reduced.

3 Season to taste with salt and pepper, stir in the reserved roasted star anise, and add the basil. Transfer the stew to a serving dish and garnish with the onion and coriander leaves.

Beef and Aubergine Curry Energy 394kcal/1638kJ; Protein 26g; Carbohydrate 12g, of which sugars 10g; Fat 27g, of which saturates 5g; Cholesterol 71mg; Calcium 54mg; Fibre 203g; Sodium 700mg.
Beef Stew Energy 314kcal/1312kJ; Protein 33g; Carbohydrate 17g, of which sugars 11g; Fat 14g, of which saturates 4g; Cholesterol 64mg; Calcium 64mg; Fibre 1.7g; Sodium 1500mg

Hot Pineapple and Coconut Curry

This sweet and spicy curry from the Maluku spice islands in Indonesia benefits from being made the day before eating, enabling the flavours to mingle longer. It is often eaten at room temperature, but it is also delicious hot.

Serves 4

1 small, firm pineapple
15–30ml/1–2 tbsp palm or
    coconut oil
4–6 shallots, finely chopped
2 garlic cloves, finely chopped
1 red chilli, seeded and
    finely chopped
15ml/1 tbsp palm sugar (jaggery)
400ml/14fl oz/1²⁄₃ cups
    coconut milk
salt and ground black pepper
1 small bunch fresh coriander
    (cilantro) leaves, finely chopped,
    to garnish

For the spice paste

4 cloves
4 cardamom pods
1 small cinnamon stick
5ml/1 tsp coriander seeds
2.5ml/½ tsp cumin seeds
5–10ml/1–2 tsp water

1 First make the spice paste. Using a mortar and pestle or electric spice grinder, grind all the spices together to a powder. In a small bowl, mix the spice powder with the water to make a paste. Put aside.

2 Remove the skin from the pineapple, then cut the flesh lengthways into quarters and remove the core. Cut each quarter widthways into chunky slices and put aside.

3 Heat the oil in a wok or large, heavy frying pan, stir in the shallots, garlic and chilli and stir-fry until fragrant and beginning to colour. Stir in the spice paste and fry for 1 minute. Toss in the pineapple, making sure the slices are coated in the spicy mixture.

4 Stir the sugar into the coconut milk and pour into the wok. Stir and bring to the boil. Reduce the heat and simmer for 3–4 minutes to thicken the sauce, but do not allow the pineapple to become too soft. Season with salt and pepper to taste.

5 Transfer the curry to a serving dish and sprinkle with the coriander to garnish. Serve hot or at room temperature.

Spicy Black-eyed Bean and Potato Curry

This spicy curry can be served for a light lunch or supper, or use as a side dish as part of a larger meal.

Serves 4 to 6

225g/8oz/2¼ cups black-eyed
    beans (peas), soaked overnight
    and drained
1.5ml/¼ tsp bicarbonate of soda
    (baking soda)
5ml/1 tsp five-spice powder
1.5ml/¼ tsp asafoetida
2 onions, finely chopped
2.5cm/1in piece fresh root
    ginger, crushed
a few mint leaves
450ml/³⁄₄ pint/scant 2 cups water
60ml/4 tbsp vegetable oil
2.5ml/½ tsp each ground
    turmeric, coriander, cumin
    and chilli powder
4 fresh green chillies, chopped
75ml/2½fl oz/⅓ cup
    tamarind juice
2 potatoes, peeled, cubed
    and boiled
115g/4oz coriander (cilantro)
    leaves, chopped
2 firm tomatoes, chopped
salt

1 Place the black-eyed beans with the bicarbonate of soda, five-spice powder, asafoetida, onion, ginger and mint in a large, heavy pan. Pour in the measured water.

2 Bring the mixture to the boil, reduce the heat and simmer gently until the beans are soft, about 1–2 hours depending on the age of the dried beans. Remove any excess water from the pan and reserve.

3 Heat the vegetable oil in a large pan. Add the ground spices, chillies and tamarind juice, and fry gently for 3–4 minutes until the spices release their fragrances.

4 Pour the black-eyed bean mixture into the pan with the spice paste and stir until thoroughly combined.

5 Add the potatoes, coriander leaves, tomatoes and salt to the pan. Mix well, and if the curry is a little dry, add a little of the reserved water. Reheat the curry for a few minutes until just bubbling. Serve immediately.

Hot Pineapple Curry Energy 135kcal/573kJ; Protein 1.6g; Carbohydrate 25.4g, of which sugars 23.6g; Fat 3.8g, of which saturates 0.5g; Cholesterol 0mg; Calcium 87mg; Fibre 2.9g; Sodium 131mg.
Spicy Beans Energy 266kcal/1118kJ; Protein 11.8g; Carbohydrate 36.8g, of which sugars 8.5g; Fat 9g, of which saturates 1.1g; Cholesterol 0mg; Calcium 110mg; Fibre 8.8g; Sodium 28mg.

Chilli Dhal Curry

This is an Anglo-Indian version of dhal, a spicy dish made from lentils or other beans and peas. It is characteristically hot and spicy and can be served as a meal in itself with some Indian breads or plain rice or as part of a main course with a dry meat curry.

Serves 4 to 6
175g/6oz Bengal gram, washed
450ml/3/4 pint/scant 2 cups water
60ml/4 tbsp vegetable oil
2 fresh green chillies, chopped
1 onion, chopped
2 garlic cloves, crushed
5cm/2in piece fresh root
  ginger, crushed
6–8 curry leaves
5ml/1 tsp chilli powder
5ml/1 tsp ground turmeric
450g/1lb bottle gourd or
  marrow (large zucchini),
  courgettes (zucchini), squash
  or pumpkin, peeled, pithed
  and sliced
60ml/4 tbsp tamarind juice
2 tomatoes, chopped
a handful fresh coriander
  (cilantro) leaves, chopped
salt

1 In a large pan, cook the Bengal gram in the measured water until the grains are tender but not mushy. Set aside without draining away any excess water.

2 Heat the vegetable oil in a large pan. Add the chillies, onion, garlic, ginger, curry leaves, chilli powder, turmeric and salt to the pan. Fry the mixture for 4–5 minutes, stirring constantly, until the onions begin to soften and turn translucent.

3 Add the gourd pieces, or other vegetables if using, to the spice mixture and stir until well combined. Cover the pan and cook gently, stirring frequently, until the vegetables are just beginning to soften.

4 Add the Bengal gram and the cooking water to the vegetable pan. Stir well and bring the mixture to the boil.

5 Stir in the tamarind juice, tomatoes and coriander to the pan. Reduce the heat and simmer until the vegeatables are tender.

6 Serve immediately with rice or Indian breads.

Tofu and Green Bean Red Chilli Curry

This is one of those versatile recipes that should be in every chilli-loving cook's repertoire. This version uses green beans, but other types of vegetable work equally well. The tofu takes on the flavour of the spice paste and also boosts the nutritional value.

Serves 4 to 6
600ml/1 pint/2 1/2 cups canned
  coconut milk
15ml/1 tbsp Thai red curry paste
45ml/3 tbsp Thai fish sauce
10ml/2 tsp palm sugar (jaggery)
  or light muscovado
  (brown) sugar
225g/8oz/3 1/4 cups button
  (white) mushrooms
115g/4oz/scant 1 cup green
  beans, trimmed
175g/6oz firm tofu, rinsed,
  drained and cut into
  2cm/3/4in cubes
4 kaffir lime leaves, torn
2 fresh red chillies, seeded
  and sliced
fresh coriander (cilantro) leaves,
  to garnish

1 Pour about one-third of the coconut milk into a wok or pan. Cook until it starts to separate and an oily sheen appears on the surface.

2 Add the red curry paste, fish sauce and sugar to the coconut milk. Mix thoroughly. Add the button mushrooms. Stir the mixture and cook for 1–2 minutes.

3 Stir in the remaining coconut milk. Bring the mixture slowly back to the boil. Add the green beans and tofu cubes. Reduce the heat and simmer gently for 4–5 minutes more.

4 Stir in the kaffir lime leaves and sliced red chillies. Heat the curry for a couple of minutes until bubbling. Spoon the curry into warmed individual bowls. Sprinkle the coriander leaves over the top of each serving as a garnish and serve at once.

Cook's Tip
Tofu or bean curd is quite bland in flavour but it readily picks up strong tastes, such as chillies and spices.

Chilli Dhal Curry Energy 196kcal/828kJ; Protein 10.7g; Carbohydrate 29.2g, of which sugars 5.7g; Fat 5g, of which saturates 0.7g; Cholesterol 0mg; Calcium 47mg; Fibre 3.1g; Sodium 20mg.
Tofu and Bean Curry Energy 110kcal/460kj; Protein 5.7g; Carbohydrate 10.2g, of which sugars 9.6g; Fat 5.5g, of which saturates 0.9g; Cholesterol 0mg; Calcium 282mg; Fibre 1.3g; Sodium 437mg.

Chilli-stuffed Pan-fried Tofu

An easy accompaniment for a main course, or a great lunch. Squares of fried tofu stuffed with a blend of chilli and chestnut give a piquant jolt to the delicate flavour.

Serves 2
2 blocks firm tofu
30ml/2 tbsp Thai fish sauce
5ml/1 tsp sesame oil
2 eggs
7.5ml/1½ tsp cornflour (cornstarch)
vegetable oil, for shallow-frying

For the filling
2 green chillies, finely chopped
2 chestnuts, finely chopped
6 garlic cloves, crushed
10ml/2 tsp sesame seeds

1 Cut the block of tofu into 2cm/¾in slices, and then cut each slice in half. Place the tofu slices on a piece of kitchen paper to absorb any excess water.

2 Mix together the Thai fish sauce and sesame oil. Transfer the tofu slices to a plate and coat them evenly with the fish sauce mixture. Leave to marinate for 20 minutes. Meanwhile, put all the filling ingredients into a bowl and combine them thoroughly. Set aside until needed.

3 Beat the egg in a shallow dish. Add the cornflour and whisk until the mixture is well combined. Take the slices of tofu and dip them into the beaten egg mixture, ensuring an even coating on all sides.

4 Place a frying pan over medium heat and add the vegetable oil. Add the tofu slices to the pan and fry, turning over once, until golden brown.

5 Once cooked, make a slit down the middle of each slice with a sharp knife, without cutting all the way through. Gently push a large pinch of the filling into each slice, and serve.

> **Variation**
> Alternatively, you could serve the tofu with a light soy dip instead of the spicy filling.

Green Beans with Tofu and Chilli Flakes

Yard-long beans are so-called because they grow to 35cm/14in in length, and more. Look for them in Asian stores and markets, but if you have trouble finding them, you can substitute other green beans instead.

Serves 4
500g/1¼lb yard-long beans, thinly sliced
200g/7oz silken tofu, cut into cubes
2 shallots, thinly sliced
200ml/7fl oz/scant 1 cup coconut milk
115g/4oz/1 cup roasted peanuts, chopped
juice of 1 lime
10ml/2 tsp palm sugar (jaggery) or light muscovado (brown) sugar
60ml/4 tbsp soy sauce
5ml/1 tsp dried chilli flakes

1 Bring a pan of lightly salted water to the boil. Add the beans and blanch them for 30 seconds.

2 Drain the beans immediately, then refresh under cold running water and drain again, shaking them well to remove as much water as possible. Place in a serving bowl and set aside until needed.

3 Put the tofu and shallots in a pan, then add the coconut milk. Heat gently, stirring constantly, until the tofu begins to crumble.

4 Add the peanuts, lime juice, sugar, soy sauce and chilli flakes to the pan. Heat, stirring frequently, until the sugar has dissolved. Pour the sauce over the prepared beans, toss to combine and serve immediately.

> **Variation**
> The sauce also works very well with other vegetables, for example, mangetouts (snow peas). Alternatively, stir in sliced yellow or red (bell) pepper.

Chilli-stuffed Tofu Energy 291kcal/1213kJ; Protein 23g; Carbohydrate 7.8g, of which sugars 1.3g; Fat 19.1g, of which saturates 3.4g; Cholesterol 209mg; Calcium 1014mg; Fibre 0.8g; Sodium 88mg.
Beans with Tofu Energy 263kcal/1091kJ; Protein 14.5g; Carbohydrate 13.3g, of which sugars 10g; Fat 17.2g, of which saturates 3g; Cholesterol 0mg; Calcium 335mg; Fibre 4.7g; Sodium 1353mg.

Tofu and Vegetable Thai Chilli Curry

Traditional Thai ingredients – chillies, galangal, lemon grass and kaffir lime leaves – give this curry a wonderfully fragrant aroma.

Serves 4

175g/6oz firm tofu
45ml/3 tbsp dark soy sauce
15ml/1 tbsp sesame oil
5ml/1 tsp chilli sauce
2.5cm/1in piece fresh root ginger, peeled and finely grated
1 head broccoli, about 225g/8oz
1/2 head cauliflower, about 225g/8oz
30ml/2 tbsp vegetable oil
1 onion, sliced
400ml/14fl oz/1 2/3 cups coconut milk
150ml/1/4 pint/2/3 cup water

1 red (bell) pepper, seeded and chopped
175g/6oz/generous 1 cup green beans, halved
115g/4oz shiitake or button (white) mushrooms, halved
shredded spring onions (scallions), to garnish
jasmine rice or noodles, to serve

For the curry paste

2 fresh red or green chillies, seeded and chopped
1 lemon grass stalk, chopped
2.5cm/1in piece fresh galangal, chopped
2 kaffir lime leaves
10ml/2 tsp ground coriander
a few fresh coriander (cilantro) sprigs, including the stalks
45ml/3 tbsp water

1 Rinse and drain the tofu. Using a sharp knife, cut it into 2.5cm/1in cubes. Place the cubes in an ovenproof dish that is large enough to hold them all in a single layer.

2 Mix together the soy sauce, sesame oil, chilli sauce and grated ginger in a jug (pitcher) and pour over the tofu. Toss gently to coat all the cubes evenly, cover with clear film (plastic wrap) and leave to marinate for at least 2 hours or overnight if possible, turning and basting the tofu occasionally.

3 Make the curry paste. Place the chillies, lemon grass, galangal, lime leaves, ground coriander and fresh coriander in a food processor or blender and whizz until well blended. Add the water and process to a thick paste.

4 Preheat the oven to 190°C/375°F/Gas 5. Cut the broccoli and cauliflower into small florets. Cut any stalks into thin slices.

5 Heat the vegetable oil in a frying pan and add the sliced onion. Cook over a low heat for about 8 minutes, until soft and lightly browned. Stir in the curry paste and the coconut milk. Add the water and bring to the boil.

6 Stir in the red pepper, green beans, broccoli and cauliflower. Transfer to a terracotta pot or earthenware casserole. Cover and place towards the bottom of the oven.

7 Stir the tofu and marinade, then place the dish on a shelf near the top of the oven. Cook for 30 minutes. Remove both the dish and the terracotta pot or casserole from the oven. Add the tofu, with any remaining marinade, to the curry, with the mushrooms, and stir well.

8 Return the pot or casserole to the oven, reduce the temperature to 180°C/350°F/Gas 4 and cook for 15 minutes. Garnish with spring onions and serve with the rice or noodles.

Blanched Tofu with Chilli and Soy Dressing

The silky consistency of the tofu absorbs the dark smoky taste of the soy dressing in this rich and flavourful dish. Tofu has a nutty quality that blends agreeably with the salty sweetness of the soy sauce and the hints of garlic, chilli and spring onion. Several flavoured tofus are available, such as smoked tofu, which could also be used in this recipe.

Serves 2

2 blocks firm tofu
salt

For the dressing

10ml/2 tsp finely sliced spring onion (scallion)
5ml/1 tsp finely chopped garlic
60ml/4 tbsp dark soy sauce
10ml/2 tsp chilli powder
5ml/1 tsp sugar
10ml/2 tsp sesame seeds

1 To make the dressing, mix the spring onion and garlic in a bowl with the soy sauce, chilli powder, sugar and sesame seeds. Leave the dressing to stand for a few minutes, allowing the flavours to mingle.

2 Meanwhile, bring a large pan of water to the boil and season with a pinch of salt. Place the whole blocks of tofu in the water, being careful not to let them break apart.

3 Blanch the tofu for 3 minutes. Remove and place on kitchen paper to remove any excess water.

4 Transfer the tofu to a warmed serving plate. Pour the dressing evenly over the plate of tofu. Serve immediately, slicing the tofu as desired.

Cook's Tip
Koreans traditionally eat this dish without slicing the tofu, preferring instead to either eat it directly with a spoon or pick it apart with chopsticks. It may be easier, however, to slice it in advance if you are serving it as an accompanying dish.

Tofu and Vegetable Curry Energy 210kcal/873kJ; Protein 11g; Carbohydrate 13.1g, of which sugars 13.1g; Fat 12g, of which saturates 1.8g; Cholesterol 0mg; Calcium 328mg; Fibre 5g; Sodium 927g.
Blanched Tofu with Dressing Energy 160kcal/669kJ; Protein 16.1g; Carbohydrate 6.7g, of which sugars 5.6g; Fat 7.8g, of which saturates 0.9g; Cholesterol 0mg; Calcium 954mg; Fibre 0.1g; Sodium 2144mg.

Vegetable Curry with Ginger and Chilli

This is a delicious vegetable curry, in which fresh mixed vegetables are cooked in a spicy, aromatic yogurt sauce.

Serves 4

10ml/2 tsp cumin seeds
8 black peppercorns
2 green cardamom pods, seeds only
5cm/2in cinnamon stick
2.5ml/½ tsp grated nutmeg
45ml/3 tbsp vegetable oil
1 green chilli, chopped
2.5cm/1in piece fresh root
   ginger, grated

5ml/1 tsp chilli powder
2.5ml/½ tsp salt
2 large potatoes, cut into
   2.5cm/1in chunks
225g/8oz cauliflower, broken
   into florets
225g/8oz okra, thickly sliced
150ml/¼ pint/⅔ cup natural
   (plain) yogurt
150ml/¼ pint/⅔ cup
   vegetable stock
toasted flaked (sliced) almonds
   and fresh coriander (cilantro)
   sprigs, to garnish

1 Grind the cumin seeds, peppercorns, cardamom seeds, cinnamon stick and nutmeg to a fine powder using a blender or a mortar and pestle.

2 Heat the oil in a large pan and fry the chilli and ginger for about 2 minutes, stirring all the time.

3 Add the chilli powder, salt and ground spice mixture and fry for about 2–3 minutes, stirring all the time to prevent the spices from sticking.

4 Stir in the potatoes, cover, and cook for 10 minutes over a low heat, stirring occasionally.

5 Add the cauliflower and okra to the pan and mix well. Cook for about 5 minutes.

6 Add the yogurt and stock. Bring to the boil, then reduce the heat. Cover and simmer for 20 minutes, or until all the vegetables are tender. Garnish with toasted almonds and coriander sprigs, and serve immediately.

Spicy Spinach Dhal

There are many different types of dhals eaten in India, with each region having its own speciality. This is a delicious, lightly spiced dish with a mild nutty flavour from the lentils, which combine beautifully with the spinach. Serve as a main meal with rice and breads or with a meat dish.

Serves 4

175g/6oz/1 cup chana dhal or
   yellow split peas

175ml/6fl oz/¾ cup water
30ml/2 tbsp vegetable oil
1.5ml/¼ tsp black mustard seeds
1 onion, thinly sliced
2 garlic cloves, crushed
2.5cm/1in piece fresh root
   ginger, grated
1 red chilli, seeded and
   finely chopped
275g/10oz frozen
   spinach, thawed
1.5ml/¼ tsp chilli powder
2.5ml/½ tsp ground coriander
2.5ml/½ tsp garam masala
2.5ml/½ tsp salt

1 Wash the chana dhal or split peas in several changes of cold water, carefully picking through it to remove any stones. Place in a bowl and cover with plenty of cold water. Leave to soak for 30 minutes.

2 Drain the chana dhal or split peas and place in a large pan with the measured water. Bring to the boil, cover the pan, and simmer for about 20–25 minutes, or until the dhal or peas are soft and tender.

3 Meanwhile, heat the oil in a wok or large frying pan and fry the mustard seeds for 2 minutes until they begin to splutter.

4 Add the onion, garlic, ginger and chilli to the pan and fry for 5–6 minutes, stirring constantly. Add the spinach and cook for about 10 minutes, or until the spinach is dry and the liquid has been absorbed.

5 Stir in the chilli powder, coriander, garam masala and salt and cook for a further 2–3 minutes.

6 Drain the chana dhal or split peas, add to the spinach mixture and cook for about 5 minutes. Serve immediately.

Vegetable Curry Energy 238kcal/996kJ; Protein 9.1g; Carbohydrate 26.7g, of which sugars 6.9g; Fat 11.6g, of which saturates 1.8g; Cholesterol 1mg; Calcium 202mg; Fibre 4.3g; Sodium 56mg.
Spicy Spinach Dhal Energy 226kcal/949kJ; Protein 13.3g; Carbohydrate 28.7g, of which sugars 2.9g; Fat 7.3g, of which saturates 0.9g; Cholesterol 0mg; Calcium 152mg; Fibre 3.8g; Sodium 114mg.

Curried Kidney Beans with Chilli

This is a very popular Punjabi-style dish using red kidney beans, but you can substitute the same quantity of other beans of your choice, such as butter beans or black-eyed beans.

Serves 4
225g/8oz dried red kidney beans
30ml/2 tbsp vegetable oil
2.5ml/½ tsp cumin seeds
I onion, thinly sliced
I green chilli, finely chopped
2 garlic cloves, crushed
2.5cm/Iin piece fresh root
   ginger, grated
30ml/2 tbsp curry paste
5ml/I tsp ground cumin
5ml/I tsp ground coriander
2.5ml/½ tsp chilli powder
2.5ml/½ tsp salt
400g/14oz can
   chopped tomatoes
30ml/2 tbsp chopped fresh
   coriander (cilantro)

1 Place the kidney beans in a large bowl of cold water, then leave them to soak overnight.

2 Drain the beans and place in a large pan with double the volume of water. Boil vigorously for 10 minutes. Skim off any scum from the surface of the water. Cover the pan and cook for about 1–1½ hours, or until the beans are soft.

3 Meanwhile, heat the oil in a large frying pan and fry the cumin seeds for 2 minutes until they begin to splutter. Add the onion, chilli, garlic and ginger and fry for 5 minutes. Stir in the curry paste, cumin, coriander, chilli powder and salt and cook for 5 minutes.

4 Add the tomatoes and simmer for about 5 minutes. Add the beans and fresh coriander to the pan, reserving a little coriander for the garnish. Cover and cook for 15 minutes, adding a little water if necessary. Serve immediately, garnished with the reserved coriander.

Cook's Tip
If you want to reduce the cooking time, cook the beans in a pressure cooker for 20–25 minutes.

Yellow Lentils with Courgettes and Green Chillies

Spicy dhal dishes are often runny but this one provides texture owing to the addition of courgettes.

Serves 4 to 6
175g/6oz moong dhal
2.5ml/½ tsp ground turmeric
300ml/½ pint/1¼ cups water
60ml/4 tbsp vegetable oil
I large onion, finely sliced
2 garlic cloves, crushed
2 green chillies, chopped
2.5ml/½ tsp mustard seeds
2.5ml/½ tsp cumin seeds
1.5ml/¼ tsp asafoetida
a few coriander (cilantro) and
   mint leaves, chopped
6–8 curry leaves
2.5ml/½ tsp sugar
200g/7oz can chopped tomatoes
225g/8oz courgettes (zucchini),
   cut into small pieces
60ml/4 tbsp lemon juice
salt, to taste

1 In a pan, boil the moong dhal and turmeric in the water then simmer until the dhal is cooked but not mushy. Drain and reserve both the liquid and the dhal.

2 Heat the oil in a wok or frying pan and fry the onion for about 3–4 minutes, until it has softened. Add the garlic, chillies, spice seeds and asafoetida, and fry for a few minutes.

3 Add the coriander, mint and curry leaves, sugar, tomatoes and courgettes. Cover and cook until the courgettes are tender but still crunchy.

4 Stir in the dhal and the lemon juice. If the dish is dry, add a little of the reserved water. Reheat and serve immediately.

Cook's Tip
Asafoetida is a pungent spice obtained from the resin of a fennel-like plant. It has a very strong odour of garlic and onion and should only be used sparingly. Its pungency may seem too much at first, but it will reduce somewhat while cooking, and does add a deep onion flavour to the dish.

Curried Beans Energy 274kcal/1155kJ; Protein 15.9g; Carbohydrate 34.5g, of which sugars 4.7g; Fat 9.2g, of which saturates 1.1g; Cholesterol 0mg; Calcium 168mg; Fibre 12.8g; Sodium 76mg.
Yellow Lentils with Courgettes Energy 210kcal/878kJ; Protein 9.4g; Carbohydrate 25.1g, of which sugars 6.1g; Fat 8.7g, of which saturates 1.1g; Cholesterol 0mg; Calcium 52mg; Fibre 3g; Sodium 18mg.

Spiced Potatoes and Tomatoes

Diced potatoes are cooked gently in a fresh and spicy tomato sauce, which is flavoured with curry leaves and green chillies.

Serves 4

2 medium potatoes
15ml/1 tbsp olive oil
2 medium onions, finely chopped
4 curry leaves
1.5ml/¼ tsp onion seeds

1 green chilli, seeded
   and chopped
4 tomatoes, sliced
5ml/1 tsp crushed ginger
5ml/1 tsp crushed garlic
5ml/1 tsp chilli powder
5ml/1 tsp ground coriander
5ml/1 tsp lemon juice
15ml/1 tbsp chopped fresh
   coriander (cilantro)
salt
3 hard-boiled eggs, to garnish

1 Peel the potatoes and cut into bitesize cubes. Try to keep them to a uniform size so they cook at the same time.

2 Heat the oil in a non-stick wok or frying pan over a medium heat. Fry the onions, curry leaves, onion seeds and green chilli for about 2–3 minutes, until the seeds start to splutter and the onions are softened slightly.

3 Add the tomato slices to the pan and continue to cook for about 3 minutes over a low heat, stirring occasionally, until the tomatoes are just heated through.

4 Add the ginger, garlic, chilli powder and ground coriander to the pan, mixing well. Add salt to the mixture and taste the sauce, adding more salt if necessary. Continue to cook, stirring constantly, for about 1–2 minutes.

5 Add the potatoes to the pan. Cover the pan and continue to cook over a low heat, stirring occasionally, for 8–10 minutes until the potatoes are tender.

6 Add the lemon juice and the fresh coriander and stir well to mix together.

7 Shell the hard-boiled eggs, cut into quarters and add as a garnish to the finished dish. Serve immediately.

Red Bean Chilli

This vegetarian chilli can be adapted to accommodate meat eaters by adding either minced beef or lamb in place of the lentils. Add the meat once the onions are soft and fry until nicely browned before adding the tomatoes.

Serves 4

30ml/2 tbsp vegetable oil
1 onion, chopped
400g/14oz can chopped tomatoes
2 garlic cloves, crushed
300ml/½ pint/1¼ cups white wine

about 300ml/½ pint/1¼ cups
   vegetable stock
115g/4oz red lentils
2 thyme sprigs or 5ml/1 tsp
   dried thyme
10ml/2 tsp ground cumin
45ml/3 tbsp dark soy sauce
½ hot chilli pepper, finely chopped
5ml/1 tsp mixed spice
15ml/1 tbsp oyster sauce (optional)
225g/8oz can red kidney
   beans, drained
10ml/2 tsp sugar
salt
boiled rice and corn, to serve

1 Heat the oil in a large pan and fry the onion over a moderate heat for a few minutes until slightly softened.

2 Add the tomatoes and garlic, cook for 10 minutes, then stir in the wine and stock.

3 Add the lentils, thyme, cumin, soy sauce, hot pepper, mixed spice and oyster sauce, if using.

4 Cover and simmer for 40 minutes, or until the lentils are soft, stirring occasionally and adding water if the lentils dry out.

5 Stir in the kidney beans and sugar and continue cooking for 10 minutes, adding a little extra stock or water if necessary. Season to taste with salt and serve hot with boiled rice and corn.

> **Cook's Tip**
> *Fiery chillies can irritate the skin, so always wash your hands well after handling them and take care not to touch your eyes. If you like really hot, spicy food, then include the seeds from the chilli in this dish.*

Spiced Potatoes and Tomatoes Energy 188kcals/790kJ; Protein 8.54g; Fat 7.62g; Saturated Fat 1.66g; Carbohydrate 23.40g; Fibre 3.10g; Added Sugar 0.01g; Salt 570mg.
Red Bean Chilli Energy 240kcal/1011kJ Protein 13g; Carbohydrate 35g; of which sugars 10g; Fat 7g; of which saturates 1g; Cholesterol 0mg; Calcium 79mg; Fibre 5.4g; Sodium 1200mg.

Chilli Bean Loaf

This recipe is a vegetarian dish using delicious flavours, such as pickled ginger, which is available at Asian stores.

Serves 4

225g/8oz/1¼ cups red kidney beans, soaked overnight
15g/½oz/1 tbsp butter or margarine
1 onion, finely chopped
2 garlic cloves, crushed
½ red (bell) pepper, seeded and chopped
½ green (bell) pepper, seeded and chopped
1 green chilli, seeded and finely chopped
5ml/1 tsp mixed herbs
2 eggs
15ml/1 tbsp lemon juice
75ml/5 tbsp gari (pickled ginger)
salt and ground black pepper

1 Drain the kidney beans, then place in a pan, cover with water and boil rapidly for 15 minutes. Reduce the heat and continue boiling for about 1 hour, until the beans are tender, adding more water if needed. Drain, reserving the cooking liquid. Preheat the oven to 190°C/375°F/Gas 5 and grease a 900g/2lb loaf tin (pan).

2 Melt the butter or margarine in a large frying pan and fry the onion, garlic and peppers for 5 minutes, then add the chilli, mixed herbs and a little salt and pepper.

3 Place the cooked kidney beans in a large bowl or in a food processor and mash or process to a pulp. Add the onion and pepper mixture and stir well. Cool slightly, then stir in the eggs and lemon juice.

4 Place the gari in a separate bowl and sprinkle generously with warm water. The gari should become soft and fluffy after about 5 minutes.

5 Pour the gari into the bean and onion mixture and stir together thoroughly. If the consistency is too stiff, add a little of the bean liquid. Spoon the mixture into the prepared loaf tin and bake in the oven for 35–45 minutes, until firm to the touch.

6 Cool the loaf in the tin and then turn out on to a plate. Cut into thick slices and serve immediately.

Vegetables in Spicy Peanut Sauce

This nutritious and aromatic dish is quick and easy to prepare, ideal for when you want a little spice for a mid-week dinner.

Serves 4

15ml/1 tbsp palm or vegetable oil
1 onion, chopped
2 garlic cloves, crushed
400g/14oz can chopped tomatoes, puréed
45ml/3 tbsp smooth peanut butter, preferably unsalted
750ml/1¼ pint/3 cups water
5ml/1 tsp dried thyme
1 green chilli, seeded and finely chopped
1 vegetable stock (bouillon) cube
2.5ml/½ tsp ground allspice
2 carrots
115g/4oz white cabbage
175g/6oz okra
½ red (bell) pepper
150ml/¼ pint/⅔ cup good quality vegetable stock
salt

1 Heat the oil in a wok or large frying pan. Cook the onion and garlic over a moderate heat for 5 minutes, stirring frequently until the onion has softened. Be careful not to burn the garlic or it will taste bitter.

2 Add the puréed tomatoes and the peanut butter to the pan and stir well until combined. Cook for a further 1–2 minutes until the tomatoes begin to bubble.

3 Stir in the measured water, thyme, chopped chilli, stock cube, allspice and a little salt, to taste. Bring the mixture to the boil, reduce the heat and then simmer gently, uncovered, for about 35 minutes.

4 Prepare the vegetables. Cut the carrots into even sticks, finely shred the white cabbage, top and tail the okra, and seed and slice the red pepper.

5 Place the vegetables in a separate pan with the vegetable stock. Bring to the boil, then simmer until tender but still with a little crunch, about 7–10 minutes.

6 Drain the vegetables and place in a warmed serving dish. Pour the sauce over the top and serve immediately.

Chilli Bean Loaf Energy 304kcal/1280kJ; Protein 17.7g; Carbohydrate 44.2g, of which sugars 5.3g; Fat 7g, of which saturates 2.9g; Cholesterol 103mg; Calcium 83mg; Fibre 9.9g; Sodium 70mg.
Vegetables in Peanut Sauce Energy 172kcal/719kJ; Protein 7g; Carbohydrate 15g, of which sugars 12g; Fat 10g, of which saturates 2g; Cholesterol 0mg; Calcium 130mg; Fibre 3.5g; Sodium 600mg.

Noodles with Spicy Beansprout Broth

The components for this dish are served separately so diners can help themselves.

Serves 4 to 6
250g/9oz tofu block
corn or vegetable oil, for deep-frying
200g/7oz/1 cup long grain
    jasmine rice
4–6 spring onions (scallions), sliced
chilli sambal

For the broth
15ml/1 tbsp palm or corn oil
2 garlic cloves, finely chopped
1–2 red or green chillies, seeded
    and finely chopped
1 lemon grass stalk, finely chopped
45ml/3 tbsp soy sauce
2 litres/3½ pints chicken stock
450g/1lb fresh mung beansprouts

For the noodles
500g/1¼lb fresh egg noodles or
    225g/8oz dried egg noodles,
    softened in warm water
30ml/2 tbsp palm or corn oil
4 shallots, finely sliced
2 garlic cloves, finely chopped
450g/1lb fresh shelled
    prawns (shrimp)
30ml/2 tbsp kecap manis
    (Indonesian sweet soy sauce)
ground black pepper

1 Prepare the tofu. Cut it into four rectangles. Heat enough oil in a wok or heavy pan for deep-frying. Add the tofu and fry for 2–3 minutes, until golden brown. Drain on kitchen paper. Cut the tofu into thin slices and pile on a serving plate. Set aside.

2 Rinse the rice under cold water, then drain. Place in a pan with 600ml/1 pint/2½ cups water. Bring to the boil, then simmer for 15 minutes. Turn off the heat, cover and steam for 10–15 minutes.

3 Make the broth. Heat the oil in a heavy pan, fry the garlic, chillies and lemon grass until fragrant. Add 15ml/1 tbsp soy sauce and the stock. Bring to the boil, then simmer for 10–15 minutes. Season with soy sauce and pepper and stir in the beansprouts.

4 Prepare the noodles. Heat the oil in a wok, fry the shallots and garlic for 2 minutes. Cook the prawns for 2 minutes. Stir in the kecap manis with 30ml/2 tbsp water. Add the noodles and season.

5 Transfer the rice and noodles on to warmed serving dishes. Serve with the tofu, a bowl of spring onions, chilli sambal and a bowl of the broth, so that everyone can help themselves.

Thai Noodles with Chinese Chives and Chilli

This is a filling and tasty vegetarian dish, ideal for a weekend lunch.

Serves 4
350g/12oz dried rice noodles
1cm/½in piece fresh root ginger,
    peeled and grated
30ml/2 tbsp light soy sauce
45ml/3 tbsp vegetable oil
225g/8oz Quorn (mycoprotein),
    cut into small cubes
2 garlic cloves, crushed
1 large onion, cut into thin wedges
115g/4oz fried tofu, thinly sliced
1 fresh green chilli, seeded and
    thinly sliced
175g/6oz/2 cups beansprouts
2 large bunches garlic chives, total
    weight about 115g/4oz, cut
    into 5cm/2in lengths
50g/2oz/½ cup roasted
    peanuts, ground
30ml/2 tbsp dark soy sauce
30ml/2 tbsp chopped fresh
    coriander (cilantro), and
    1 lemon, cut into wedges,
    to garnish

1 Place the noodles in a bowl, cover with warm water and leave to soak for 30 minutes. Drain and set aside.

2 Mix the ginger, light soy sauce and 15ml/1 tbsp of the oil in a bowl. Add the Quorn, then set aside for 10 minutes. Drain, reserving the marinade.

3 Heat 15ml/1 tbsp of the remaining oil in a frying pan and cook the garlic for a few seconds. Add the Quorn and stir-fry for 3–4 minutes. Transfer to a plate and set aside.

4 Heat the remaining oil in the pan and stir-fry the onion for 3–4 minutes, until softened and tinged brown. Add the tofu and chilli, stir-fry briefly and then add the noodles. Stir-fry over a medium heat for 4–5 minutes.

5 Stir in the beansprouts, garlic chives and most of the peanuts, reserving a little for the garnish. Stir well, then add the Quorn, the dark soy sauce and the reserved marinade.

6 When hot, spoon on to serving plates and garnish with the remaining ground peanuts, the coriander and lemon.

Noodles with Broth Energy 690kcal/2900kJ; Protein 32.6g; Carbohydrate 97g, of which sugars 5.9g; Fat 20.7g, of which saturates 3.6g; Cholesterol 171mg; Calcium 328mg; Fibre 4.2g; Sodium 833mg.
Thai Noodles Energy 444kcal/1857kJ; Protein 16g; Carbohydrate 77.6g, of which sugars 4.3g; Fat 6.5g, of which saturates 0.9g; Cholesterol 0mg; Calcium 230mg; Fibre 5g; Sodium 1227mg.

Cellophane Noodles with Spicy Pork

The magic paste in this dish is a mix of garlic, coriander root and white pepper.

Serves 2
200g/7oz cellophane noodles
30ml/2 tbsp vegetable oil
15ml/1 tbsp magic paste
200g/7oz minced (ground) pork
1 fresh green or red chilli, seeded and finely chopped

300g/11oz/3½ cups beansprouts
5 spring onions (scallions), sliced
30ml/2 tbsp soy sauce
30ml/2 tbsp Thai fish sauce
30ml/2 tbsp sweet chilli sauce
15ml/1 tbsp palm sugar (jaggery) or light muscovado (brown) sugar
30ml/2 tbsp rice vinegar
30ml/2 tbsp roasted peanuts, chopped, and chopped fresh coriander (cilantro), to garnish

1 Place the noodles in a large bowl, cover with boiling water and soak for 10 minutes. Drain the noodles and set aside.

2 Heat the oil in a wok or large, heavy frying pan. Add the magic paste and stir-fry for 2–3 seconds, then add the pork. Stir-fry the meat for 2–3 minutes, until browned all over.

3 Add the chilli to the meat and stir-fry for 3–4 seconds. Add the beansprouts and spring onions, stir-frying for a few seconds after each addition.

4 Cut the noodles into 5cm/2in lengths and add to the wok, with the soy sauce, fish sauce, chilli sauce, sugar and rice vinegar.

5 Toss the ingredients together until well combined and the noodles have warmed through. Pile into a large bowl. Sprinkle over the peanuts and coriander and serve immediately.

Chilli Ribs in Noodle Soup

This slow-cooked dish of ribs in a rich soup includes a piquant chilli seasoning.

Serves 4
900g/2lb beef short ribs, cut into 5cm/2in squares
350g/12oz mooli (daikon), peeled
5ml/1 tsp salt
90g/3½oz dangmyun noodles

For the seasoning
45ml/3 tbsp soy sauce
15ml/1 tbsp chilli powder
50g/2oz spring onions (scallions), roughly chopped
5ml/1 tsp sesame oil
1 chilli, finely sliced
ground black pepper

1 Soak the ribs in cold water for 10 hours, changing the water halfway through. Drain and place in a large pan, cover with fresh water. Bring to the boil, then rinse in cold water and set aside.

2 Cut the mooli into 2cm/¾in cubes. Place the seasoning ingredients in a bowl and mix thoroughly.

3 Place the ribs in a pan and cover with 1 litre/1¾ pints/4 cups water. Simmer for 20 minutes. Add the mooli and salt and cook for 7 minutes. Add the noodles and cook for 3 minutes more.

4 Ladle the soup into bowls and add a generous spoonful of the seasoning just before serving.

Special Chow Mein with Chinese Sausage and Chilli

Lap cheong is a spicy Chinese sausage, available from most Chinese markets.

Serves 4 to 6
450g/1lb egg noodles
45ml/3 tbsp vegetable oil
2 garlic cloves, sliced
5ml/1 tsp chopped fresh root ginger
2 fresh red chillies, seeded and chopped
2 lap cheong, about 75g/3oz in total, rinsed and sliced (optional)
1 skinless chicken breast fillet, thinly sliced

16 uncooked tiger prawns (jumbo shrimp), peeled, tails left intact, and deveined
115g/4oz/2 cups green beans
225g/8oz/2½ cups beansprouts
small bunch garlic chives, about 50g/2oz
30ml/2 tbsp soy sauce
15ml/1 tbsp oyster sauce
15ml/1 tbsp sesame oil
salt and ground black pepper
2 shredded spring onions (scallions) and fresh coriander (cilantro) leaves, to garnish

1 Cook the noodles in a large pan of boiling water, according to the instructions on the packet. Drain well.

2 Heat 15ml/1 tbsp of the oil in a wok or large frying pan. Add the garlic, ginger and chillies and stir-fry for about 2 minutes. Add the lap cheong, if using, chicken, prawns and beans. Stir-fry over a high heat for a further 2 minutes, or until the chicken and prawns are cooked through. Transfer the mixture to a bowl then set aside.

3 Heat the rest of the oil in the wok. Toss in the beansprouts and garlic chives and stir-fry for 1–2 minutes. Add the drained noodles and toss over the heat to mix. Season with the soy sauce, oyster sauce and salt and pepper to taste.

4 Return the prawn mixture to the wok. Mix well with the noodles and toss until heated through.

5 Stir the sesame oil into the noodles. Spoon into a warmed bowl and serve immediately, garnished with the spring onions and coriander leaves.

Noodles with Pork Energy 720kcal/3009kJ; Protein 29.4g; Carbohydrate 99.9g, of which sugars 15.4g; Fat 21.6g, of which saturates 5.1g; Cholesterol 66mg; Calcium 58mg; Fibre 2.4g; Sodium 1933mg.
Chilli Ribs Energy 437kcal/1830kJ; Protein 52.1g; Carbohydrate 19.8g, of which sugars 3.1g; Fat 17g, of which saturates 6.7g; Cholesterol 126mg; Calcium 40mg; Fibre 1.6g; Sodium 1174mg.
Chow Mein Energy 624kcal/2631kJ; Protein 29.3g; Carbohydrate 84.5g, of which sugars 4.6g; Fat 21.2g, of which saturates 4.2g; Cholesterol 107mg; Calcium 76mg; Fibre 4.8g; Sodium 808mg.

Chilli Meatballs, Chinese Leaves and Noodles

This fragrant combination of spiced meatballs, noodles and vegetables cooked slowly in a richly flavoured broth makes for a very hearty, warming soup.

Serves 4

10 dried shiitake mushrooms, soaked in hot water for 30 minutes, soaking liquid reserved
90g/3¹⁄₂oz bean thread noodles
675g/1¹⁄₂lb minced (ground) beef
10ml/2 tsp finely grated garlic
10ml/2 tsp finely grated fresh root ginger
1 red chilli, seeded and chopped
6 spring onions (scallions), sliced
1 egg white
15ml/1 tbsp cornflour (cornstarch)
15ml/1 tbsp Chinese rice wine
30ml/2 tbsp sunflower oil
1.5 litres/2¹⁄₂ pints/6¹⁄₄ cups chicken or beef stock
50ml/2fl oz/¹⁄₄ cup light soy sauce
5ml/1 tsp sugar
150g/5oz enoki mushrooms, trimmed
200g/7oz Chinese leaves (Chinese cabbage), very thinly sliced
salt and ground black pepper
sesame oil and chilli oil (optional)

1 Discard the stems from the reconstituted mushrooms and then thickly slice the caps and set aside. Put the noodles in a large bowl and pour over boiling water to cover. Leave to soak for 3–4 minutes, then drain, rinse and set aside.

2 Place the beef, garlic, ginger, chilli, spring onions, egg white, cornflour, rice wine and seasoning in a food processor. Process to combine well. Divide into 30 portions, then shape into balls.

3 Heat the oil in a wok. Fry the meatballs for 2–3 minutes on each side until browned. Remove and drain on kitchen paper. Wipe out the wok and add the stock, soy sauce, sugar and shiitake mushrooms with the soaking liquid and bring to the boil.

4 Add the meatballs to the boiling stock, reduce the heat and cook gently for 20–25 minutes. Add the noodles, enoki mushrooms and cabbage to the wok and cook gently for 4–5 minutes. Serve ladled into wide shallow bowls. Drizzle with sesame oil and chilli oil, if you like.

Thai Crispy Noodles with Chilli Beef

Rice vermicelli is deep-fried before being added to this dish, and in the process the vermicelli expands to at least four times its original size.

Serves 4

450g/1lb rump (round) steak
teriyaki sauce, for brushing
175g/6oz rice vermicelli
groundnut (peanut) oil, for deep-frying and stir-frying
8 spring onions (scallions), diagonally sliced
2 garlic cloves, crushed
4–5 carrots, cut into julienne strips
1–2 fresh red chillies, seeded and finely sliced
2 small courgettes (zucchini), diagonally sliced
5ml/1 tsp grated fresh root ginger
60ml/4 tbsp rice vinegar
90ml/6 tbsp light soy sauce
475ml/16fl oz/2 cups spicy stock

1 Beat the steak to about 2.5cm/1in thick. Place in a shallow dish, brush with the teriyaki sauce and set aside for 2–4 hours. Separate the rice vermicelli into manageable loops. Pour oil into a large wok to a depth of about 5cm/2in, and heat until a strand of vermicelli cooks as soon as it is lowered into the oil.

2 Add a loop of vermicelli to the oil. Almost immediately, turn to cook on the other side, then remove and drain on kitchen paper. Repeat with the remaining loops. Transfer the cooked noodles to a separate wok or serving bowl and keep warm.

3 Strain the oil from the wok into a heatproof bowl and set it aside. Heat 15ml/1 tbsp groundnut oil in the clean wok. When it sizzles, fry the steak for about 30 seconds on each side, until browned. Transfer to a board and cut into thick slices. The meat should be well browned on the outside but pink inside. Set aside.

4 Add a little extra oil to the wok, add the spring onions, garlic and carrots and fry for 5–6 minutes, until the carrots are just soft. Add the chillies, courgettes and ginger and fry for 1–2 minutes. Stir in the rice vinegar, soy sauce and stock. Cook for about 4 minutes, or until the sauce has thickened slightly. Return the slices of steak to the wok and cook for a further 1–2 minutes.

5 Spoon the steak, vegetables and sauce over the noodles and toss lightly and carefully to mix. Serve immediately.

Meatballs and Noodles Energy 548kcal/2279kJ; Protein 36.8g; Carbohydrate 24.9g, of which sugars 3g; Fat 33.3g, of which saturates 12.4g; Cholesterol 101mg; Calcium 52mg; Fibre 1.7g; Sodium 161mg.
Thai Crispy Noodles Energy 493kcal/2052kJ; Protein 29.5g; Carbohydrate 43.4g, of which sugars 7.2g; Fat 21.9g, of which saturates 5.7g; Cholesterol 65mg; Calcium 43mg; Fibre 2g; Sodium 1697mg.

Fried Rice with Okra and Chillies

Okra features in many tasty Indian and Asian dishes. In this dish, it is cooked with rice.

Serves 3 to 4
30ml/2 tbsp vegetable oil
15ml/1 tbsp butter or margarine
1 garlic clove, crushed
½ red onion, finely chopped
115g/4oz okra, topped and tailed
30ml/2 tbsp diced green and red
  (bell) peppers
2.5ml/½ tsp dried thyme
2 green chillies, finely chopped
2.5ml/½ tsp five-spice powder
1 vegetable stock (bouillon) cube
30ml/2 tbsp soy sauce
15ml/1 tbsp chopped fresh
  coriander (cilantro)
225g/8oz/2½ cups cooked rice
salt and ground black pepper
coriander (cilantro) sprigs,
  to garnish

1 Heat the oil and butter or margarine in a frying pan or wok, add the garlic and onion and cook over a moderate heat for 5 minutes until soft.

2 Thinly slice the okra, add to the pan or wok and fry gently for a further 6–7 minutes.

3 Add the green and red peppers, the dried thyme, the green chillies and five-spice powder and cook, stirring constantly, for 3 minutes, then crumble in the stock cube. Stir well to dissolve the stock cube.

4 Add the soy sauce, the chopped fresh coriander and the cooked rice to the pan and heat through, stirring well.

5 Season with salt and ground black pepper to taste. Serve the dish immediately, garnished with the sprigs of fresh coriander.

> **Cook's Tip**
> *Okra, also known as lady's fingers, has a ridged skin and a tapered, oblong shape. Buy okra that is firm and brightly coloured. When cooked, okra gives off a viscous substance that helps to thicken any liquid in which it is cooked.*

Chilli Coconut Rice

This is a delicious, mildly spiced and creamy rice dish. Use thin coconut milk, which is rich, yet won't dominate the other ingredients in the dish.

Serves 4
30ml/2 tbsp vegetable oil
1 onion, chopped
30ml/2 tbsp tomato
  purée (paste)
600ml/1 pint/2½ cups
  coconut milk
2 carrots
1 yellow (bell) pepper
5ml/1 tsp dried thyme
2.5ml/½ tsp mixed spice
1 fresh green chilli, seeded
  and chopped
350g/12oz/1½ cups long
  grain rice
salt

1 Heat the oil in a large pan and fry the onion for about 2–3 minutes, until it is beginning to soften and turn translucent.

2 Add the tomato purée to the pan and cook over a moderate heat for 5–6 minutes, stirring all the time.

3 Pour the coconut milk into the pan and stir until well combined. Bring the mixture to the boil.

4 Roughly chop the carrots. Remove the seeds from the yellow pepper and roughly chop the flesh.

5 Stir the carrots, pepper, thyme, mixed spice, chilli and rice into the onion mixture, season with salt and bring to the boil.

6 Cover the pan and simmer over a low heat until the rice has absorbed most of the liquid.

7 Cover the rice with foil, secure with the lid and steam very gently until the rice is fully cooked. Serve immediately.

> **Cook's Tip**
> *If you prefer a little more heat, then use the seeds from the chilli pepper or increase the amount of chillies you use.*

Fried Rice with Okra Energy 247kcal/1034kJ; Protein 5g; Carbohydrate 29g, of which sugars 3g; Fat 13g, of which saturates 4g; Cholesterol 11mg; Calcium 99mg; Fibre 2.2g; Sodium 1100mg.
Coconut Rice Energy 448kcal/1876kJ; Protein 8.6g; Carbohydrate 87.8g, of which sugars 17g; Fat 6.9g, of which saturates 1.1g; Cholesterol 0mg; Calcium 82mg; Fibre 2.6g; Sodium 194mg.

Spicy Bulgur and Pine Nut Pilaff

Although not rice, bulgur makes a delicious pilaff, and is a popular staple throughout the Middle East and Africa. This version comes from North Africa.

Serves 4
30ml/2 tbsp olive oil
1 onion, chopped
1 garlic clove, crushed
5ml/1 tsp ground saffron
   or turmeric
2.5ml/½ tsp ground cinnamon
1 fresh green chilli, seeded
   and chopped
600ml/1 pint/2½ cups chicken or
   vegetable stock
150ml/¼ pint/⅔ cups white wine
225g/8oz/1⅓ cups bulgur wheat
15g/½oz/1 tbsp butter
   or margarine
30–45ml/2–3 tbsp pine nuts
30ml/2 tbsp chopped fresh
   parsley

1 Heat the oil in a large pan and fry the onion until soft. Add the garlic, saffron or turmeric, ground cinnamon and chopped chilli, and fry for a few seconds more.

2 Add the stock and wine to the pan and mix well. Bring to the boil, then reduce the heat and simmer for 8 minutes.

3 Rinse the bulgur wheat under cold water, drain and add to the pan. Cover and simmer gently for about 15 minutes until the stock has been absorbed.

4 Melt the butter in a small pan, add the pine nuts and fry for a few minutes until golden. Add to the pan containing the other ingredients. Add the chopped parsley to the pan and stir with a fork to mix.

5 Spoon into a warmed serving dish and serve immediately. This pilaff would make a tasty accompaniment to grilled and roasted meats or a vegetable stew.

Cook's Tip
You can leave out the wine, if you prefer, and replace with water or stock. It is not essential, but it adds extra flavour.

Rice with Chilli Chicken and Potatoes

This tasty Indian dish is generally only made on special occasions.

Serves 4 to 6
1.3kg/3lb skinless chicken breast
   fillet, cut into large pieces
60ml/4 tbsp biryani masala paste
2 green chillies, chopped
15ml/1 tbsp crushed fresh
   root ginger
15ml/1 tbsp crushed garlic
50g/2oz coriander (cilantro)
   leaves, chopped
6–8 mint leaves, chopped
150ml/½ pint/⅔ cup natural
   (plain) yogurt, beaten
30ml/2 tbsp tomato purée (paste)
4 onions, finely sliced, deep-fried
   and crushed
450g/1lb basmati rice, washed
   and drained
5ml/1 tsp black cumin seeds
5cm/2in cinnamon stick
4 green cardamoms
2 black cardamoms
vegetable oil, for shallow-frying
4 large potatoes, peeled
   and quartered
175ml/6fl oz/¾ cup milk, mixed
   with 75ml/2½fl oz/⅓ cup water
1 sachet saffron powder, mixed
   with 90ml/6 tbsp milk
30ml/2 tbsp ghee or unsalted
   butter
salt, to taste

For the garnish
ghee or unsalted (sweet) butter,
   for shallow-frying
50g/2oz cashew nuts
50g/2oz sultanas (golden raisins)
deep-fried onion slices

1 Mix the chicken with the next ten ingredients and marinate for 2 hours. Place in a pan and cook for 10 minutes. Set aside. Boil a pan of salted water and soak the rice with the cumin seeds, cinnamon and cardamoms for 5 minutes. Drain well. Heat the oil for frying. Cook the potatoes until browned. Set aside.

2 Place half the rice on top of the chicken, then an even layer of potatoes. Add the remaining rice on the potatoes. Sprinkle the milky water all over the rice. Make a few holes through the rice and pour in a little saffron milk. Dot the surface with ghee or butter, cover and cook over a low heat for 35–45 minutes.

3 Make the garnish. Heat the ghee or butter and fry the nuts and sultanas until they swell. Set aside. When the rice is ready, gently toss the layers together. Garnish with the nut mixture and onion slices and serve immediately.

Spicy Bulgur Pilaff Energy 295kcal/1225kJ; Protein 4.8g; Carbohydrate 32.4g, of which sugars 2.7g; Fat 14.4g, of which saturates 3.1g; Cholesterol 8mg; Calcium 25mg; Fibre 0.7g; Sodium 26mg.
Rice with Chicken Energy 940kcal/3944kJ; Protein 66g; Carbohydrate 107.1g, of which sugars 15.5g; Fat 28.4g, of which saturates 5.9g; Cholesterol 153mg; Calcium 166mg; Fibre 4.9g; Sodium 195mg.

Fiery Lamb Pilau

In this Indian rice dish, lamb is first marinated in spices then pan-fried and cooked with the rice to create a tasty dish that can be served on its own or accompanied with Indian breads or a moist dhal.

Serves 4
450g/1lb stewing lamb
15ml/1 tbsp curry powder
1 onion, chopped
2 garlic cloves, crushed
2.5ml/½ tsp dried thyme
2.5ml/½ tsp dried oregano
1 fresh or dried chilli
25g/1oz/2 tbsp butter or
    margarine, plus more for serving
600ml/1 pint/2½ cups beef
    stock or chicken stock or
    coconut milk
5ml/1 tsp ground black pepper
2 tomatoes, chopped
10ml/2 tsp sugar
30ml/2 tbsp chopped spring
    onions (scallions)
450g/1lb basmati rice
spring onion (scallion) strips,
    to garnish

1 Cut the lamb into bitesize cubes and place in a shallow glass or china dish. Sprinkle with the curry powder, onion, garlic, herbs and chilli and stir until the spices are well combined and the lamb pieces are thoroughly coated. Cover the dish loosely with clear film (plastic wrap) and leave to marinate in a cool place for 1 hour.

2 Melt the butter or margarine in a large, heavy pan and fry the lamb for 5–10 minutes, until evenly browned on all sides.

3 Add the stock or coconut milk to the pan and stir well. Bring the mixture to the boil, then lower the heat and simmer for about 35 minutes or until the meat is tender.

4 Add the black pepper, tomatoes, sugar, spring onions and rice, stir well and reduce the heat. Make sure that the rice is covered by about 2.5cm/1in of liquid and add a little more water if necessary.

5 Simmer the pilau gently for about 25 minutes, or until the rice is tender and the liquid has been absorbed. Stir a little extra butter or margarine into the rice before serving. Garnish with the spring onion strips.

Spiced Chicken Biryani

Biryanis originated in Persia and are traditionally made with meat and rice.

Serves 4
275g/10oz/1½ cups basmati rice
30ml/2 tbsp vegetable oil
1 onion, thinly sliced
2 garlic cloves, crushed
1 green chilli, finely chopped
2.5cm/1in fresh root ginger,
    finely chopped
675g/1½lb skinless chicken breast
    fillets, cut into 2.5cm/1in cubes
45ml/3 tbsp curry paste
1.5ml/¼ tsp salt
1.5ml/¼ tsp garam masala
3 tomatoes, cut into thin wedges
1.5ml/¼ tsp ground turmeric
2 bay leaves
4 green cardamom pods
4 cloves
1.5ml/¼ tsp saffron strands
fresh coriander (cilantro), to garnish

1 Wash the rice in several changes of cold water. Put into a large bowl, cover with plenty of water and leave to soak for 30 minutes.

2 Meanwhile, heat the oil in a large frying pan and fry the onion for about 5–7 minutes until lightly browned, then add the garlic, chilli and ginger and fry for about 2 minutes.

3 Add the chicken to the pan and fry for about 5 minutes, stirring occasionally.

4 Add the curry paste, salt and garam masala and cook for 5 minutes. Add the tomatoes and continue to cook for a further 3–4 minutes. Remove from the heat and set aside.

5 Preheat the oven to 190°C/375°F/Gas 5. Bring a large pan of water to the boil. Drain the rice and add it to the pan with the turmeric. Cook for about 10 minutes, or until the rice is almost tender. Drain the rice and toss together with the bay leaves, cardamoms, cloves and saffron.

6 Layer the rice and chicken in a shallow, ovenproof dish until all the mixture has been used, finishing off with a layer of rice. Cover and bake in the oven for 15–20 minutes, or until the chicken is tender. Serve immediately, garnished with a fresh coriander sprig.

Chicken Biryani Energy 377kcal/1579kJ; Protein 30.3g; Carbohydrate 47.2g, of which sugars 8.3g; Fat 7.5g, of which saturates 1.2g; Cholesterol 71mg; Calcium 86mg; Fibre 1.8g; Sodium 255mg.
Fiery Lamb Pilau Energy 652kcal/2726kJ; Protein 32.1g; Carbohydrate 96.3g, of which sugars 5.7g; Fat 15g, of which saturates 7.3g; Cholesterol 97mg; Calcium 51mg; Fibre 1g; Sodium 231mg.

Squid Risotto with Coriander

Squid is marinated in lime and kiwi fruit before being cooked in this spicy risotto.

Serves 3 to 4

450g/1lb squid, cleaned and gutted
about 45ml/3 tbsp olive oil
15g/½oz/1 tbsp butter
1 onion, finely chopped
2 garlic cloves, crushed
1 fresh red chilli, seeded and
   finely sliced
275g/10oz/1½ cups risotto rice
175ml/6fl oz/¾ cup white wine
1 litre/1¾ pints/4 cups fish stock
30ml/2 tbsp chopped fresh
   coriander (cilantro)
salt and ground black pepper

For the marinade
2 kiwi fruit, chopped
1 fresh red chilli, seeded and
   finely sliced
30ml/2 tbsp fresh lime juice

1 Cut the squid body into thin strips and the tentacles into short pieces. Mash the kiwi fruit for the marinade in a bowl, then stir in the chilli and lime juice. Add the squid, stirring to coat. Season with salt and ground black pepper, cover with clear film (plastic wrap) and chill for 4 hours or overnight.

2 Drain the squid. Heat 15ml/1 tbsp of the olive oil in a frying pan and cook, in batches if necessary, for 30–60 seconds over a high heat. It is important that the squid cooks very quickly. Transfer to a plate and set aside. If too much juice accumulates in the pan, pour this into a jug (pitcher) and add more olive oil when cooking the next batch. Reserve the accumulated juices.

3 Heat the remaining oil with the butter in a large pan and gently fry the onion and garlic for 5–6 minutes until soft. Add the sliced chilli to the pan and fry for 1 minute more. Add the rice. Cook for a few minutes, stirring, until the rice is coated with oil, then stir in the wine until it has been absorbed.

4 Heat the stock, and gradually add it and the reserved liquid from the squid, a ladleful at a time, to the pan. Stir constantly and wait until each addition is absorbed before adding the next.

5 When the rice is about three-quarters cooked, add the squid and cook until the stock has gone and the rice is tender. Stir in the coriander, cover, and leave for a few minutes before serving.

Chilli Rice with Chinese Sausage

Traditional Vietnamese stir-fried rice includes cured Chinese pork sausage, or thin strips of pork combined with prawns or crab meat. Prepared this way, the dish can be eaten as a snack, or as part of the meal with grilled and roasted meats accompanied by a vegetable dish or salad.

Serves 4

25g/1oz dried cloud ear (wood
   ear) mushrooms, soaked for
   20 minutes
15ml/1 tbsp vegetable or
   sesame oil
1 onion, sliced
2 green or red Thai
   chillies, seeded and
   finely chopped
2 Chinese sausages (15cm/6in
   long), each sliced into
   10 pieces
175g/6oz prawns (shrimp),
   shelled and deveined
30ml/2 tbsp Thai fish sauce, plus
   extra for drizzling
10ml/2 tsp five-spice
   powder
1 bunch of fresh coriander
   (cilantro), stalks removed, leaves
   finely chopped
450g/1lb/4 cups cold
   steamed rice
ground black pepper

1 Drain the soaked cloud ear mushrooms then cut into thin strips. Heat a wok or large, heavy pan and add the oil. Add the onion and chillies and fry until they begin to colour, then stir in the cloud ear mushrooms.

2 Add the Chinese sausage slices, moving them around the wok or pan until they begin to brown.

3 Add the prawns and move them around until they turn opaque. Stir in the fish sauce, the five-spice powder and 30ml/ 2 tbsp of the coriander.

4 Season well with ground black pepper. Add the rice, and cook, stirring constantly to make sure it doesn't stick to the pan.

5 As soon as the rice is heated through, sprinkle with the remainder of the chopped fresh coriander and serve with Thai fish sauce to drizzle over it.

Squid Risotto Energy 645kcal/2722kJ; Protein 31g; Carbohydrate 86g, of which sugars 5g; Fat 22g, of which saturates 6g; Cholesterol 348mg; Calcium 84mg; Fibre 1.2g; Sodium 1000mg.
Chilli Rice Energy 398kcal/1673kJ; Protein 19g; Carbohydrate 44g, of which sugars 4g; Fat 18g, of which saturates 5g; Cholesterol 116mg; Calcium 158mg; Fibre 2g; Sodium 800mg.

Spicy Beef and Vegetable Rice

This dish looks a little daunting but is well worth the effort. It is the perfect dish to serve on a special occasion for guests who like spicy food.

Serves 4
400g/14oz/2 cups short grain
 rice or pudding rice, rinsed
a drop of sunflower oil
1 sheet dried seaweed
4 quail's eggs
vegetable oil, for shallow-frying
sesame seeds, to garnish

For the marinated beef
30ml/2 tbsp dark soy sauce
15ml/1 tbsp garlic, crushed
15ml/1 tbsp sliced spring
 onions (scallions)
5ml/1 tsp sesame oil
5ml/1 tsp rice wine
200g/7oz beef, shredded
10ml/2 tsp vegetable oil
salt and ground black pepper

For the namul vegetables
150g/5oz mooli (daikon), peeled
1 courgette (zucchini)
150g/5oz/generous ½ cup soya
 beansprouts, trimmed
150g/5oz fern fronds (optional)
6 dried shiitake mushrooms,
 soaked in warm water for about
 30 minutes until softened
½ cucumber

For the namul seasoning
5ml/1 tsp sugar
12.5ml/2½ tsp salt
30ml/2 tbsp sesame oil
5ml/1 tsp crushed garlic
a splash of dark soy sauce
1.5ml/¼ tsp chilli powder
5ml/1 tsp sesame seeds
vegetable oil, for stir-frying

For the gochujang sauce
15ml/3 tbsp gochujang
7.5ml/1½ tsp sugar or honey
10ml/2 tsp sesame oil

1 Place the rice in a pan and add water to 5mm/¼in above the rice. Add the sunflower oil, cover and bring to the boil. Simmer for 12–15 minutes. Remove from the heat and leave for 5 minutes.

2 For the marinade, blend the soy sauce, garlic, spring onions, sesame oil, rice wine, and salt and pepper. Add the beef, mix well and marinate for 1 hour. Roll up the seaweed and slice into strips. Mix the gochujang sauce ingredients and place in a serving bowl.

3 Cut the mooli and courgette into strips. Blend 5ml/ 1 tsp sugar, 5ml/1 tsp salt and 5ml/1 tsp sesame oil, with 2.5ml/ ½ tsp garlic, and fry. Use to coat the mooli. Transfer to a plate.

4 Blend 5ml/1 tsp salt and 5ml/1 tsp sesame oil with 2.5ml/½ tsp garlic and a little water. Use to coat the courgette. Heat 5ml/1 tsp vegetable oil and fry the courgette until soft. Transfer to the plate.

5 Briefly boil the beansprouts. Mix 15ml/1 tbsp sesame oil with 2.5ml/½ tsp salt, 1.5ml/¼ tsp chilli powder and 2.5ml/½ tsp sesame seeds and sugar. Use to coat the beansprouts. Transfer to the plate.

6 Parboil the fern fronds, if using, and drain. Stir-fry in 5ml/1 tsp sesame oil, with a little soy sauce and 2.5ml/½ tsp sesame seeds. Drain and slice the mushrooms, discarding the stems. Quickly fry in 5ml/1 tsp vegetable oil and season. Transfer to the plate. Seed the cucumber, cut into thin strips and add to the mushrooms.

7 Heat 10ml/2 tsp vegetable oil and fry the beef until tender. Serve the rice in four bowls and top with the vegetables and beef. Fry the eggs, and place one in each bowl. Garnish with sesame seeds and dried seaweed. Serve with gochujang sauce.

Fried Rice with Pork and Chillies

This classic rice dish looks particularly pretty garnished with strips of omelette.

Serves 4 to 6
45ml/3 tbsp vegetable oil
1 onion, chopped
15ml/1 tbsp chopped garlic
115g/4oz pork, cut into
 small cubes
2 eggs, beaten
1kg/2¼lb/4 cups cooked rice

30ml/2 tbsp Thai fish sauce
15ml/1 tbsp dark soy sauce
2.5ml/½ tsp caster
 (superfine) sugar

For the garnish
4 spring onions (scallions),
 finely sliced
2 fresh red chillies, seeded and
 finely sliced
1 lime, cut into wedges

1 Heat the oil in a wok or large frying pan. Add the onion and garlic and cook for about 2–3 minutes until the onion is beginning to turn soft and translucent.

2 Add the pork to the softened onion and garlic. Fry, stirring constantly, until the pork changes colour and is cooked through.

3 Add the beaten eggs to the pan and cook, stirring, until they are scrambled into small lumps.

4 Add the cooked rice to the pan and continue to stir and toss, to coat it with the oil and prevent it from sticking to the base of the pan.

5 Add the fish sauce, soy sauce and sugar and mix well. Continue to fry until the rice is thoroughly heated.

6 Spoon the rice into warmed individual bowls and serve immediately, garnished with sliced spring onions, sliced chillies and lime wedges.

Cook's Tip
To make 1kg/2¼lb/4 cups cooked rice, you will need approximately 400g/14oz/2 cups uncooked rice.

Spicy Beef Energy 645kcal/2688kJ; Protein 23.7g; Carbohydrate 88.5g, of which sugars 7.7g; Fat 21.4g, of which saturates 4.4g; Cholesterol 86mg; Calcium 73mg; Fibre 2.3g; Sodium 1781mg.
Rice with Pork Energy 513kcal/2165kJ; Protein 17.1g; Carbohydrate 80g, of which sugars 2.1g; Fat 16.1g, of which saturates 2.3g; Cholesterol 132mg; Calcium 75mg; Fibre 0.7g; Sodium 511mg.

Thai Asparagus with Ginger and Chilli

This is an excitingly different way of cooking asparagus. The crunchy texture is retained and the flavour is complemented by the addition of galangal and chilli.

Serves 4
350g/12oz asparagus stalks
30ml/2 tbsp vegetable oil
1 garlic clove, crushed
15ml/1 tbsp sesame
   seeds, toasted
2.5cm/1in piece fresh galangal,
   finely shredded
1 fresh red chilli, seeded and
   finely chopped
15ml/1 tbsp Thai fish sauce
15ml/1 tbsp light soy sauce
45ml/3 tbsp water
5ml/1 tsp palm sugar (jaggery) or
   light muscovado (brown) sugar

1 Snap the asparagus stalks. They will break naturally at the junction between the woody base and the more tender upper portion of the stalk. Discard the woody parts of the stems.

2 Heat the oil in a wok and stir-fry the garlic, sesame seeds and galangal for 3–4 seconds. Do not allow to brown but cook until the garlic is just beginning to turn golden.

3 Add the asparagus stalks and chilli to the pan. Cook for 1 minute, stirring constantly, then add the fish sauce, soy sauce, water and sugar.

4 Using two spoons, toss over the heat for a further 2 minutes, or until the asparagus just begins to soften and the liquid is reduced by about half.

5 Carefully transfer the asparagus to a warmed serving dish and serve immediately.

> **Variation**
> This is a very versatile recipe. Try using broccoli or pak choi (bok choy) in place of the asparagus. The sauce will also work very well with green beans.

Stir-fried Asparagus with Chilli, Galangal and Lemon Grass

One of the culinary legacies of French colonization in Vietnam and Cambodia is asparagus. Today it is grown in Vietnam and finds its way into stir-fries in both countries. Cambodian in style, this is a lovely spicy way to eat asparagus.

Serves 2 to 4
30ml/2 tbsp groundnut
   (peanut) oil
2 garlic cloves, finely chopped
2 Thai chillies, seeded and
   finely chopped
25g/1oz galangal, finely shredded
1 lemon grass stalk, trimmed and
   finely sliced
350g/12oz fresh asparagus
   stalks, trimmed
30ml/2 tbsp tuk trey
30ml/2 tbsp soy sauce
5ml/1 tsp sugar
30ml/2 tbsp unsalted roasted
   peanuts, finely chopped
1 small bunch fresh coriander
   (cilantro), finely chopped

1 Heat a large wok and add the oil. Stir in the garlic, chillies, galangal and lemon grass and stir-fry until they become fragrant and begin to turn golden.

2 Add the asparagus and stir-fry for a further 1–2 minutes, until it is just tender but not too soft.

3 Stir in the tuk trey, soy sauce and sugar. Stir in the peanuts and coriander and serve immediately.

> **Cook's Tip**
> Tuk trey is a popular condiment in Cambodian cuisine. It is a nutty and pungent fish sauce made from fermented fish with the addition of ground, roasted peanuts.

> **Variation**
> This recipe also works well with broccoli, green beans and courgettes (zucchini), cut into strips.

Thai Asparagus Energy 120kcal/492kJ; Protein 4.1g; Carbohydrate 2.4g, of which sugars 2.3g; Fat 10.4g, of which saturates 1.4g; Cholesterol 0mg; Calcium 75mg; Fibre 2.1g; Sodium 537mg.
Stir-fried Asparagus Energy 117kcal/482kJ; Protein 5g; Carbohydrate 3.3g, of which sugars 2.7g; Fat 9g, of which saturates 1g; Cholesterol 0mg; Calcium 30mg; Fibre 2g; Sodium 535mg.

Refried Chilli Beans

If the only refried beans you've tried have been the canned ones, you may have found them rather bland. These, however, are superb.

Serves 4
25g/1oz/2 tbsp lard or white cooking fat
2 onions, finely chopped
5ml/1 tsp ground cumin
5ml/1 tsp ground coriander
250g/9oz/1¼ cups dried pinto beans, soaked overnight and cooked
3 garlic cloves, crushed
small bunch of fresh coriander (cilantro) or 4–5 dried avocado leaves
50g/2oz feta cheese
salt

1 Melt the lard in a large frying pan. Add the onions, cumin and ground coriander. Cook gently over a low heat for about 30 minutes, or until the onions caramelize and become soft.

2 Add a ladleful of the soft, cooked beans. Fry them for only a few minutes simply to heat. Mash the beans into the onions as they cook, using a fork or a potato masher. Continue until all the beans have been added, a little at a time, then stir in the crushed garlic.

3 Lower the heat and cook the beans to form a thick paste. Season with salt and spoon into a warmed serving dish. Chop the coriander or crumble the avocado leaves, and sprinkle most of them over the beans. Crumble the feta cheese over the top, then garnish with the reserved sprigs or leaves.

Mung Bean Stew with Chillies

This is a simple and tasty stew from Kenya.

Serves 4
225g/8oz/1¼ cups mung beans, soaked overnight in water
25g/1oz/2 tbsp ghee or butter
2 garlic cloves, crushed
1 red onion, chopped
30ml/2 tbsp tomato purée (paste)
½ green (bell) pepper, seeded and cut into small cubes
½ red (bell) pepper, seeded and cut into small cubes
1 green chilli, seeded and finely chopped
300ml/½ pint/1¼ cups water

1 Drain the mung beans, put them in a large pan, cover with fresh water and boil until the beans are soft and the water has evaporated. Remove from the heat and mash roughly with a fork or potato masher until smooth.

2 Heat the ghee or butter in a separate pan, add the garlic and onion and fry for 4–5 minutes until golden brown, then add the tomato purée and cook for a further 2–3 minutes, stirring all the time.

3 Stir in the mashed beans, then the green and red peppers and the chopped chilli. Add the water, stirring well to mix all the ingredients together.

4 Pour the mixture back into a clean pan and simmer for about 10 minutes, then spoon into a serving dish and serve immediately.

Spiced Mexican Beans

Traditionally, clay pots are used in Mexico for this spicy dish, which give the beans a wonderful, slightly earthy flavour.

Serves 4
250g/9oz/1¼ cups dried pinto beans, soaked overnight in water to cover
1.75 litres/3 pints/7½ cups water
2 onions
10 whole garlic cloves, peeled
small bunch of fresh coriander (cilantro)
salt

For the toppings
2 fresh red fresno chillies
1 tomato, peeled and chopped
2 spring onions (scallions), finely chopped
60ml/4 tbsp sour cream
50g/2oz feta cheese

1 Drain the beans, rinse them under cold water and drain again. Put the water in a large pan, bring to the boil and add the beans. Cut the onions in half and add them to the pan, with the whole garlic cloves. Boil again, then simmer for 1½ hours, until the beans are tender and there is only a little liquid remaining.

2 While the beans are cooking, prepare the toppings. Spear the chillies on a long-handled metal skewer and roast them over the flame of a gas burner until the skins blister and darken. Alternatively, dry fry them in a griddle pan until the skins are scorched. Put the roasted chillies in a plastic bag and tie the top immediately to keep the steam in. Set aside for 20 minutes.

3 Remove the chillies from the bag and peel. Discard the stalks, then slit the chillies and discard the seeds. Slice into thin strips and put in a bowl. Put the other toppings into separate bowls.

4 Ladle about 250ml/8fl oz/1 cup of the beans and liquid into a food processor or blender. Process to a smooth purée. Return the purée to the pan, and stir it in. Chop the coriander and stir it in, reserving some for the garnish. Season with salt.

5 Serve the beans in individual bowls along with the toppings and add coriander to garnish. Each guest spoons a little of the chillies, tomatoes and spring onions over the beans, then adds a spoonful of sour cream, and finally a crumbling of feta cheese.

Refried Beans Energy 279kcal/1174kJ; Protein 16.9g; Carbohydrate 32.8g, of which sugars 5.4g; Fat 9.9g, of which saturates 4.4g; Cholesterol 15mg; Calcium 148mg; Fibre 11.3g; Sodium 197mg.
Mung Bean Stew Energy 229kcal/965kJ; Protein 14.5g; Carbohydrate 31.1g, of which sugars 5.5g; Fat 6g, of which saturates 3.5g; Cholesterol 13mg; Calcium 61mg; Fibre 6.8g; Sodium 65mg.
Spiced Beans Energy 259kcal/1094kJ; Protein 17.6g; Carbohydrate 34.1g, of which sugars 6.9g; Fat 6.8g, of which saturates 3.8g; Cholesterol 18mg; Calcium 166mg; Fibre 11.7g; Sodium 2,700mg.

Cauliflower and Potatoes Chilli-style

Cauliflower and potatoes are encrusted with Indian spices in this delicious recipe. It is a popular side dish or can be served as a main course with other dishes such as a salad, dhal or simply with Indian breads.

Serves 4

450g/1lb potatoes, cut into
  2.5 cm/1in chunks
30ml/2 tbsp vegetable oil
5ml/1 tsp cumin seeds
1 green chilli, finely chopped
450g/1lb cauliflower, broken
  into florets
5ml/1 tsp ground coriander
5ml/1 tsp ground cumin
1.5ml/¼ tsp chilli powder
2.5ml/½ tsp ground turmeric
2.5ml/½ tsp salt
chopped fresh coriander (cilantro),
  to garnish
tomato and onion salad and
  pickle, to serve

1 Par-boil the potatoes in a large pan of boiling water for 10 minutes. Drain well and set aside.

2 Heat the oil in a wok or large frying pan and fry the cumin seeds for about 2 minutes, until they begin to splutter and release their fragrance. Add the chilli to the pan and fry, stirring constantly, for a further 1 minute.

3 Add the cauliflower florets to the pan and fry, stirring constantly, for 5 minutes.

4 Add the potatoes, the ground spices and salt and cook for 7–10 minutes, or until both the vegetables are tender.

5 Garnish with fresh coriander and serve with a tomato and onion salad and pickle.

Variation

Try using sweet potatoes instead of ordinary potatoes for an alternative curry with a sweeter flavour. The cauliflower could also be replaced with the same amount of broccoli.

Spiced Eggs and Spinach

This is a superbly balanced dish for those who don't eat meat. Egusi, or ground melon seed, is widely used in West African cooking, adding a creamy texture and a nutty flavour to many recipes. It is especially good with fresh spinach.

Serves 4

900g/2lb fresh spinach
115g/4oz ground egusi
90ml/6 tbsp groundnut (peanut)
  or vegetable oil
4 tomatoes, peeled and chopped
1 onion, chopped
2 garlic cloves, crushed
1 slice fresh root ginger,
  finely chopped
150ml/¼ pint/⅔ cup
  vegetable stock
1 fresh red chilli, seeded and
  finely chopped
6 eggs
salt

1 Roll up the spinach into bundles and slice into strips. Place the strips in a bowl. Cover with boiling water, then drain through a sieve (strainer). Press with your fingers to remove excess water.

2 Place the egusi in a bowl and gradually add enough water to form a paste, stirring all the time.

3 Heat the oil in a pan, add the tomatoes, onion, garlic and ginger and fry for about 10 minutes, stirring frequently.

4 Add the egusi paste, stock, chilli and salt, and cook for about 10 minutes, then add the spinach and stir into the sauce. Cook for 15 minutes, uncovered, stirring frequently.

5 Meanwhile hard-boil the eggs, stand them in cold water for a few minutes to cool and then shell and cut in half. Arrange in a serving dish and pour the egusi spinach over the top. Serve hot.

Cook's Tip

Instead of using boiled eggs, you could make an omelette flavoured with herbs and garlic. Serve it either whole, or sliced, with the egusi sauce. If you can't find egusi, use ground almonds as a substitute.

Cauliflower Chilli-style Energy 181kcal/759kJ; Protein 6.7g; Carbohydrate 23.2g, of which sugars 4.3g; Fat 7.5g, of which saturates 1.1g; Cholesterol 0mg; Calcium 40mg; Fibre 3.2g; Sodium 24mg.
Spiced Eggs Energy 436kcal/1803kJ; Protein 21.5g; Carbohydrate 12.6g, of which sugars 7.5g; Fat 33.3g, of which saturates 5.1g; Cholesterol 285mg; Calcium 464mg; Fibre 7.3g; Sodium 428mg.

Korean Spicy Cabbage

There are many varieties of kimchi, which is fermented vegetables. This version takes two days to prepare.

Serves 10
1 head Chinese leaves (Chinese cabbage), about 2kg/4½lb
30ml/2 tbsp table salt
50g/2oz/½ cup coarse sea salt

For the seasoning
2 oysters (optional)
½ mooli (daikon), about 500g/1¼lb, peeled and sliced
25g/1oz Korean chives
25g/1oz minari or watercress
5 garlic cloves
15g/½oz fresh root ginger, peeled
½ onion
½ Asian pear, or ½ kiwi fruit
1 chestnut, sliced
3 spring onions (scallions), sliced
50g/2oz Korean chilli powder
120ml/4fl oz/½ cup Thai fish sauce
5ml/1 tsp sugar
1 red chilli, sliced
salt

1 Make a deep cut across the base of the head of Chinese leaves and split it into two. Split the two halves into quarters. Place the quartered head in a bowl and cover with water, adding the table salt. Leave to soak for 2 hours.

2 Drain the cabbage and sprinkle with the sea salt, making sure to coat between the leaves. Leave for 4 hours.

3 Hold an oyster with the rounded shell up. Push the tip of a short-bladed knife into the hinge of the oyster and twist to prise open. Cut the two muscles. Run the blade between the shells to open. Remove the oyster from the shell. Season with salt.

4 Cut the mooli slices into fine strips. Cut the chives and minari or watercress into 5cm/2in lengths. Finely chop or blend the garlic, ginger, onion and Asian pear or kiwi fruit. Mix all the seasoning ingredients together with 120ml/4fl oz/½ cup water.

5 Rinse the quarters of Chinese leaves in cold running water. Place in a bowl and coat with the seasoning mixture. Place the Chinese leaves in an airtight container. Leave at room temperature for 5 hours, then chill for 24 hours.

Stir-fried Pineapple with Ginger and Chilli

Throughout South-east Asia, fruit is often treated like a vegetable and tossed in a salad, or stir-fried, to accompany spicy dishes. In this Cambodian dish, the pineapple is combined with the tangy flavours of ginger and chilli and served as a side dish.

Serves 4
30ml/2 tbsp groundnut (peanut) oil
2 garlic cloves, finely shredded
40g/1½oz fresh root ginger, peeled and finely shredded
2 red Thai chillies, seeded and finely shredded
1 pineapple, trimmed, peeled, cored and cut into bitesize chunks
15ml/1 tbsp fish sauce
30ml/2 tbsp soy sauce
15ml–30ml/1–2 tbsp sugar
30ml/2 tbsp roasted unsalted peanuts, finely chopped
1 lime, cut into quarters, to serve

1 Heat a large wok or large, heavy frying pan and add the groundnut oil. Stir in the garlic, ginger and chillies. Stir-fry for 2 minutes until the ingredients begin to colour. Ensure that the garlic does not burn, otherwise it will impart a bitter taste to the rest of the dish.

2 Add the pineapple to the pan and stir-fry for a further 1–2 minutes, until the edges turn golden.

3 Add the fish sauce and soy sauce to the pan and mix well. Add sugar to taste and continue to stir-fry until the pineapple begins to caramelize.

4 Transfer to a serving dish, sprinkle with the roasted peanuts and serve with lime wedges.

> **Cook's Tip**
> *This dish is an excellent accompaniment to grilled (broiled) meats, and will be perfect on a summer's day to be eaten alongside spicy chicken or satays cooked on the barbecue.*

Korean Spicy Cabbage Energy 73kcal/303kJ; Protein 3.6g; Carbohydrate 13.5g, of which sugars 12.9g; Fat 0.6g, of which saturates 0.1g; Cholesterol 0mg; Calcium 121mg; Fibre 5.1g; Sodium 383mg.
Stir-fried Pineapple Energy 185kcal/780kJ; Protein 3g; Carbohydrate 24.1g, of which sugars 23.6g; Fat 9g, of which saturates 1g; Cholesterol 0mg; Calcium 43mg; Fibre 2.9g; Sodium 271mg.

Banana Curry with Chilli Spices

An unusual partnership, but the sweetness of bananas combines well with the spices used, producing a mild, sweet curry. Choose bananas that are slightly under-ripe so that they retain their shape and do not become mushy.

Serves 4

4 under-ripe bananas
30ml/2 tbsp ground coriander
15ml/1 tbsp ground cumin
5ml/1 tsp chilli powder
2.5ml/½ tsp salt
1.5ml/¼ tsp ground turmeric
5ml/1 tsp sugar
15ml/1 tbsp gram flour
45ml/3 tbsp chopped
   fresh coriander (cilantro)
90ml/6 tbsp vegetable oil
1.5ml/¼ tsp cumin seeds
1.5ml/¼ tsp black mustard seeds
fresh coriander (cilantro) sprigs,
   to garnish
chapatis, to serve

1 Trim the bananas and cut each into three equal pieces leaving the skin on. Make a lengthways slit in each piece of banana, without cutting through.

2 Mix together on a plate, the coriander, cumin, chilli powder, salt, turmeric, sugar, gram flour, fresh coriander and 15ml/1 tbsp of the oil.

3 Carefully stuff each piece of banana with the spice mixture, taking care not to break them in half.

4 Heat the remaining oil in a large heavy pan and fry the cumin and mustard seeds for 2 minutes, or until they begin to splutter and release their fragrances.

5 Add the stuffed banana pieces to the pan and toss very gently in the oil until coated in the seeds. Cover the pan and simmer over a low heat for 15 minutes, stirring from time to time until the bananas are soft, but be careful to avoid letting them go too mushy.

6 When the bananas are ready, transfer them to a warmed serving dish. Garnish with the fresh coriander and serve with warm chapatis.

Curried Spiced Cauliflower

In this tasty and popular Indian side dish, the creamy, aromatic and spicy coconut sauce complements the texture and mild flavour of the cauliflower. Serve with a fiery meat curry, together with Indian breads.

Serves 4 to 6

15ml/1 tbsp gram flour
100ml/3½fl oz/scant ½ cup water
5ml/1 tsp chilli powder
15ml/1 tbsp ground coriander
5ml/1 tsp ground cumin
5ml/1 tsp mustard powder
5ml/1 tsp ground turmeric
60ml/4 tbsp vegetable oil
6–8 curry leaves
5ml/1 tsp cumin seeds
1 cauliflower, broken into florets
175ml/6fl oz/¾ cup thick
   coconut milk
juice of 2 lemons
salt, to taste

1 In a bowl, mix together the gram flour with a little of the water to make a smooth paste.

2 Add the chilli, coriander, cumin, mustard and turmeric, and season with a little salt. Slowly add the remaining water to the bowl and keep mixing to ensure all the ingredients are thoroughly blended together.

3 Heat the oil in a frying pan and fry the curry leaves and cumin seeds for 1–2 minutes, until the seeds begin to splutter and release their fragrance.

4 Add the spice paste to the pan and cook, stirring constantly, for about 5 minutes. If the sauce has become too thick, add a little hot water to thin it down.

5 Add the cauliflower florets to the pan and pour in the coconut milk, stirring until it is well combined with the other ingredients in the pan.

6 Bring the mixture to the boil, reduce the heat, cover the pan and cook until the cauliflower is tender but still slightly crunchy. Cook longer, if you prefer.

7 Add the lemon juice, and mix well. Serve immediately.

Banana Curry Energy 321kcal/1340kJ; Protein 4g; Carbohydrate 36.7g, of which sugars 26.4g; Fat 18.7g, of which saturates 2.3g; Cholesterol 0mg; Calcium 56mg; Fibre 2.1g; Sodium 10mg.
Spiced Cauliflower Energy 122kcal/504kJ; Protein 3.7g; Carbohydrate 7.4g, of which sugars 3.3g; Fat 8.8g, of which saturates 1.2g; Cholesterol 0mg; Calcium 34mg; Fibre 1.4g; Sodium 41mg.

Fragrant Chilli Mushrooms in Lettuce Leaves

This quick and easy vegetable dish is served on lettuce leaf 'saucers' so can be eaten with the fingers – a great treat for children.

Serves 2
30ml/2 tbsp vegetable oil
2 garlic cloves, finely chopped
2 baby cos or romaine lettuces, or 2 Little Gem (Bibb) lettuces
1 lemon grass stalk, finely chopped
2 kaffir lime leaves, rolled in cylinders and thinly sliced
200g/7oz/3 cups oyster or chestnut mushrooms, sliced
1 small fresh red chilli, seeded and finely chopped
juice of ½ lemon
30ml/2 tbsp light soy sauce
5ml/1 tsp palm sugar (jaggery) or light muscovado (brown) sugar
small bunch fresh mint, leaves removed from the stalks

1 Heat the oil in a wok or frying pan. Add the garlic and cook over a medium heat, stirring occasionally, until golden. Do not let it burn or it will taste bitter.

2 Meanwhile, separate the individual lettuce leaves into a stack and set aside until needed.

3 Increase the heat under the wok or pan and add the lemon grass, lime leaves and sliced mushrooms. Stir-fry for about 2 minutes.

4 Add the chilli, lemon juice, soy sauce and sugar to the wok or pan. Toss the mixture over the heat to combine the ingredients together, then stir-fry for a further 2 minutes.

5 Arrange the lettuce leaves on a large plate. Spoon a small amount of the mushroom mixture on to each leaf, top with a mint leaf and serve.

> **Cook's Tip**
> If serving this dish to children, ensure that the amount of chilli used won't make it too spicy for them to enjoy.

Mushrooms with Chipotle Chillies

Chipotle chillies are jalapeños that have been smoke-dried and are extremely popular in Mexican and Tex-Mex cuisine. Their smoky flavour and significant spicy kick is the perfect foil for the earthy taste of the mushrooms in this simple and delicious salad.

Serves 6
2 chipotle chillies
450g/1lb/6 cups button (white) mushrooms
60ml/4 tbsp vegetable oil
1 onion, finely chopped
2 garlic cloves, crushed or chopped
salt
small bunch of fresh coriander (cilantro), to garnish

1 Soak the dried chillies in a bowl of hot water for about 10 minutes until they are softened. Drain them, cut off the stalks, then slit the chillies and scrape out the seeds. Chop the flesh finely.

2 Trim the mushrooms, then clean them with a damp cloth or kitchen paper. If they are large, cut them in half.

3 Heat the oil in a large, heavy frying pan. Add the onion and cook, stirring, for 2–3 minutes until just beginning to soften and turn translucent.

4 Add the garlic, chillies and mushrooms to the pan and stir until evenly coated in the oil. Fry for 6–8 minutes, stirring occasionally, until the onion and mushrooms are cooked.

5 Season to taste and spoon into a serving dish. Chop some of the coriander, leaving some whole leaves, and use to garnish. Serve immediately.

> **Variation**
> Baby button mushrooms are perfect for this dish, if you can get them. You can, of course, use other varieties of mushrooms, such as brown cap (cremini) or chestnut, but larger ones will work better if halved or quartered.

Fragrant Mushrooms Energy 136kcal/561kJ; Protein 3.1g; Carbohydrate 4.7g, of which sugars 4.4g; Fat 11.7g, of which saturates 1.4g; Cholesterol 0mg; Calcium 22mg; Fibre 1.3g; Sodium 1076mg.
Mushrooms with Chillies Energy 84kcal/346kJ; Protein 1.7g; Carbohydrate 1.9g, of which sugars 1.4g; Fat 7.8g, of which saturates 1.2g; Cholesterol 0mg; Calcium 9mg; Fibre 1.4g; Sodium 5mg..

Hot Mushroom Curry

This is a deliciously spicy way of cooking mushrooms, and they will go perfectly well with any meat dish.

Serves 4
30ml/2 tbsp vegetable oil
2.5ml/½ tsp cumin seeds
1.5ml/¼ tsp black peppercorns
4 green cardamom pods
1.5ml/¼ tsp ground turmeric
1 onion, finely chopped
5ml/1 tsp ground cumin
5ml/1 tsp ground coriander

2.5ml/½ tsp garam masala
1 fresh green chilli, seeded and finely chopped
2 garlic cloves, crushed
2.5cm/1in piece fresh root ginger, grated
400g/14oz can chopped tomatoes
1.5ml/¼ tsp salt
450g/1lb button (white) mushrooms, halved
chopped fresh coriander (cilantro), to garnish

1 Heat the oil in a large pan and fry the cumin seeds, peppercorns, cardamom pods and turmeric for about 2–3 minutes, until the seeds start to splutter and the spices release their fragrances.

2 Add the onion to the pan and fry, stirring occasionally, for about 5–7 minutes, until soft and beginning to turn golden.

3 Stir in the cumin, coriander and garam masala and fry for a further 2 minutes, stirring constantly.

4 Add the chilli, garlic and ginger and fry for 2–3 minutes, stirring all the time to prevent the spices from sticking to the bottom of the pan.

5 Add the tomatoes and salt. Bring to the boil and simmer for 5 minutes.

6 Add the mushrooms to the pan and mix well to coat with the spices and sauce. Cover the pan and simmer over a low heat for 10 minutes until the mushrooms are tender.

7 Transfer to a warmed serving dish. Garnish with chopped fresh coriander and serve immediately.

Chilli Mushrooms in a Creamy Garlic Sauce

This is a simple and delicious dish which makes a great accompaniment to a spicy rice dish, or a fiery curry.

Serves 4
350g/12oz/4½ cups button (white) mushrooms
45ml/3 tbsp olive oil
1 bay leaf
3 garlic cloves, roughly chopped

2 fresh green chillies, seeded and chopped
225g/8oz/1 cup fromage frais or low-fat cream cheese
15ml/1 tbsp chopped fresh mint
15ml/1 tbsp chopped fresh coriander (cilantro)
5ml/1 tsp salt
fresh mint and coriander (cilantro) leaves, to garnish

1 Trim the mushrooms, then clean them with a damp cloth or kitchen paper. Cut them in half, or quarters if particularly large, and set them aside.

2 Heat the oil in a non-stick wok or large frying pan, then add the bay leaf, garlic and chillies and cook for about 1–2 minutes, until just beginng to soften and colour. Ensure that the garlic does not burn, otherwise it will taste bitter.

3 Add the mushrooms. Continue to stir-fry for about 2 minutes, until the juices are released from the mushrooms.

4 Remove the pan from the heat and stir in the fromage frais or low-fat cream cheese, followed by the mint, coriander and salt. Cook for about 2 minutes, until the sauce is bubbling and all the ingredients are heated through and combined.

5 Transfer to a warmed serving dish and garnish with mint and coriander leaves. Serve immediately.

Cook's Tip
Cook the mushrooms for longer if you prefer them well cooked and browned.

Hot Mushroom Curry Energy 110kcal/459kJ; Protein 4.2g; Carbohydrate 7.1g, of which sugars 3.3g; Fat 7.7g, of which saturates 1.1g; Cholesterol 0mg; Calcium 32mg; Fibre 2.2g; Sodium 18mg.
Chilli Mushrooms Energy 75kcal/314kJ; Protein 6.5g; Carbohydrate 4.9g, of which sugars 2.8g; Fat 3.4g, of which saturates 0.5g; Cholesterol 5mg; Calcium 90mg; Fibre 1.1g; Sodium 520mg.

Green Butter Beans in a Chilli Sauce

Make the most of butter beans or broad beans by teaming them with tomatoes and fresh chillies in this simple accompaniment.

Serves 4

450g/1lb fresh butter (wax) beans or broad (fava) beans
30ml/2 tbsp olive oil
1 onion, finely chopped
2 garlic cloves, crushed
400g/14oz can plum tomatoes, drained and chopped
25g/1oz/about 3 tbsp drained pickled jalapeño chilli slices, chopped
salt
fresh coriander (cilantro) and lemon slices, to garnish

1 Bring a pan of lightly salted water to the boil. Add the butter beans or broad beans and cook for 15 minutes, or until the beans are just tender.

2 Meanwhile, heat the olive oil in a frying pan, add the onion and garlic and fry, stirring occasionally, for 5–6 minutes until the onion is soft and translucent.

3 Add in the tomatoes and continue to cook, stirring, until the mixture thickens. Add the chilli slices and cook for 1–2 minutes. Season with salt to taste.

4 Drain the beans and return them to the pan. Pour over the tomato mixture and stir over the heat for a few minutes until the beans are heated through. If the sauce thickens too quickly add a little water.

5 Spoon the spicy beans into a warmed serving dish, garnish with the coriander and lemon slices and serve immediately.

> **Cook's Tip**
> Pickled chillies can often be hotter than roasted chillies – taste one before adding to the dish and adjust the quantity to suit your personal taste.

Pumpkin with Spices

Roasted pumpkin has a wonderful, rich flavour. Eat it straight from the skin, eat the skin too, or scoop out the cooked flesh, add a spoonful of salsa and wrap it in a warm tortilla. Pumpkin is also a wonderful vegetable in flavoursome soups, stews and sauces.

Serves 6

1kg/2¼lb pumpkin
50g/2oz/¼ cup butter
10ml/2 tsp hot chilli sauce
2.5ml/½ tsp salt
2.5ml/½ tsp ground allspice
5ml/1 tsp ground cinnamon
chopped fresh herbs, to garnish
tomato salsa and crème fraîche, to serve

1 Preheat the oven to 220°C/425°F/Gas 7. Cut the pumpkin into large pieces. Scoop out and discard the fibre and seeds, then put the pumpkin pieces in a roasting pan.

2 Melt the butter in a pan over a low heat, or in a heatproof bowl in the microwave. Mix together the melted butter and chilli sauce and drizzle the mixture evenly over the pumpkin pieces in the roasting pan.

3 Put the salt in a small bowl and add the ground allspice and cinnamon. Mix together well and sprinkle the mixture over the pumpkin pieces.

4 Place the roasting pan in the oven and roast for 25 minutes, turning halfway through the cooking. The pumpkin flesh should yield when pressed gently when it is ready.

5 Transfer the spiced pumpkin pieces to a warmed serving dish and serve. Offer the salsa and crème fraîche separately.

> **Cook's Tip**
> Green, grey or orange-skinned pumpkins all roast well and would work in this recipe. The orange-fleshed varieties are, however, the most vibrantly coloured and will look wonderful when used in this dish.

Green Butter Beans Energy 170kcal/714kJ; Protein 10.1g; Carbohydrate 18.7g, of which sugars 6.3g; Fat 6.6g, of which saturates 1g; Cholesterol 0mg; Calcium 80mg; Fibre 8.7g; Sodium 19mg.
Pumpkin with Spices Energy 84kcal/347kJ; Protein 1.2g; Carbohydrate 3.7g, of which sugars 2.9g; Fat 7.2g, of which saturates 4.5g; Cholesterol 18mg; Calcium 50mg; Fibre 1.7g; Sodium 214mg.

Spicy Mooli Salad

The sweet, slightly vinegary taste of mooli provides a refreshing foundation to this healthy dish. The red chilli and sesame oil dressing adds an understated spiciness and nutty aftertaste. The mooli, also known as Chinese white radish or daikon, is a commonly used ingredient in Asian cooking and is highly valued for its medicinal properties.

Serves 2

225g/8oz mooli (daikon), peeled
¼ red chilli, shredded, and
  1.5ml/¼ tsp sesame seeds,
  to garnish

For the marinade

5ml/1 tsp cider vinegar
2.5ml/½ tsp sugar
1.5ml/¼ tsp salt
7.5ml/1½ tsp lemon juice
2.5ml/½ tsp Korean chilli powder

1 Using a sharp knife, slice the mooli into thin strips approximately 5cm/2in long.

2 To make the marinade, mix the cider vinegar, sugar, salt, lemon juice and chilli powder together in a small bowl, ensuring the ingredients are thoroughly blended.

3 Place the mooli strips in a bowl, and pour over the marinade, mixing well to ensure all the ingredients are well combined. Leave in a cool place to marinate for 20 minutes, then place the bowl in the refrigerator until the salad has chilled thoroughly.

4 Garnish the salad with the shredded chilli and sesame seeds before serving.

Variation

The mooli in this salad will take on some of the red colouring of the chilli powder. For an interesting alternative you could try replacing the chilli powder with about 2.5ml/½ tsp of wasabi, the Japanese pungent paste made from a root with a similar taste to horseradish. Wasabi will give the salad an unusual green colour from the as well as giving it a sharper taste.

Korean Green Chilli and Chive Salad

This dish is the perfect accompaniment for any grilled meat, and is a tasty alternative to the classic shredded spring onion salad.

Serves 2

180g/7oz fresh Korean or
  Chinese chives
1 fresh green chilli, seeded and
  finely sliced
10ml/2 tsp sesame seeds,
  to garnish

For the seasoning

30ml/2 tbsp dark soy sauce
2 garlic cloves, crushed
10ml/2 tsp Korean chilli powder
10ml/2 tsp sesame oil
10ml/2 tsp sugar

1 Clean the chives, then trim off the bulbs and discard. Slice the chives roughly into 4cm/1½in lengths. Combine with the chilli in a bowl.

2 To make the seasoning, mix the soy sauce, garlic, chilli powder, sesame oil and sugar together, and then add it to the bowl with the chives and chilli. Mix until well coated, then chill.

3 Garnish with sesame seeds and serve.

Cook's Tip

The Korean chive has a garlic nuance in both taste and aroma, and the leaves have a soft, grasslike texture. Look for it in Asian supermarkets and food stores. If unavailable you can substitute Chinese chives.

Variation

For a traditional alternative to this chive salad, use about 150g/5oz shredded spring onion (scallion) in place of the Korean chives, and add 15ml/1 tbsp cider vinegar and 15ml/1 tbsp soy sauce to the seasoning.

Spicy Mooli Salad Energy 22kcal/91kJ; Protein 1g; Carbohydrate 3.2g, of which sugars 3.2g; Fat 0.7g, of which saturates 0.2g; Cholesterol 0mg; Calcium 27mg; Fibre 1.1g; Sodium 209mg.
Korean Green Chilli Salad Energy 105kcal/434kJ; Protein 4.3g; Carbohydrate 7g, of which sugars 6.7g; Fat 6.7g, of which saturates 0.9g; Cholesterol 0mg; Calcium 196mg; Fibre 2.3g; Sodium 1196mg.

Hot Pepper, Mango and Tomato Salad

This salad makes an excellent appetizer. The under-ripe mango has a subtle sweetness and the flavour blends well with the tomato. There is a pleasant kick from the hot pepper sauce.

Serves 4

1 firm under-ripe mango
2 large tomatoes or 1 beefsteak
  tomato, sliced
½ red onion, sliced into rings
½ cucumber, peeled and
  thinly sliced
30ml/2 tbsp sunflower or
  vegetable oil
15ml/1 tbsp lemon juice
1 garlic clove, crushed
2.5ml/½ tsp hot pepper sauce
salt and ground black pepper
sugar, to taste
chopped chives, to garnish

1 Prepare the mango. Cut away two thick slices from either side of the mango stone (pit) and cut them into slices. Peel the skin from the slices.

2 Arrange the mango, tomato, onion and cucumber slices on a large serving plate.

3 Blend the oil, lemon juice, garlic, hot pepper sauce, salt and black pepper in a blender or food processor, or place in a small jar and shake vigorously. Add a pinch of sugar and mix again.

4 Pour the dressing over the salad and garnish with chopped chives before serving.

> **Cook's Tip**
> There are many varieties of hot pepper sauces from around the world available to buy and there will be a version to suit all palates. They range from the surprisingly mild sauces to extremely hot varieties that should be approached with a high degree of caution. As a rule, unless you are familiar with the sauce, start by using a small amount – you can always add more afterwards.

Hot Cajun Potato Salad

In Cajun country in Louisiana, where Tabasco sauce originates, hot means really hot, so you can go to town with this salad if you think you can take it.

Serves 6 to 8

8 waxy potatoes
1 green (bell) pepper, diced
1 large gherkin, chopped
4 spring onions
  (scallions), shredded
3 hard-boiled eggs, shelled
  and chopped
250ml/8fl oz/1 cup mayonnaise
15ml/1 tbsp Dijon mustard
salt and ground black pepper
Tabasco sauce, to taste
pinch or two of cayenne
sliced gherkin, to garnish
mayonnaise, to serve

1 Cook the potatoes in their skins in boiling salted water until tender. Drain and leave to cool.

2 When the potatoes are cool enough to handle, but while they are still warm, peel them and cut into coarse chunks. Place them in a large bowl.

3 Add the green pepper, gherkin, spring onions and hard-boiled eggs to the potatoes and toss gently to combine.

4 In a separate bowl, mix the mayonnaise with the mustard and season with salt, black pepper and Tabasco sauce to taste.

5 Pour the dressing over the potato mixture and toss gently so that the potatoes are well coated. Sprinkle with a pinch or two of cayenne and garnish with a few slices of gherkin. Serve with extra mayonnaise.

> **Cook's Tips**
> • The salad is good to eat immediately, when the potatoes are just cool. If you make it in advance and chill it, let it come back to room temperature before serving.
> • Tabasco is one of thousands of commercial hot pepper sauces on the market, of varying intensity: use your favourite brand to make this salad.

Hot Pepper Salad Energy 93kcal/390kj; Protein 1g; Carbohydrate 10.1g; of which sugars 9.5g; Fat 5.8g; of which saturates 0.7g; Cholesterol 0mg; Calcium 17mg; Fibre 2.1g; Sodium 600mg.
Cajun Salad Energy 289kcal/1197kJ; Protein 4g; Carbohydrate 10.3g, of which sugars 2.7g; Fat 26.1g, of which saturates 4.2g; Cholesterol 95mg; Calcium 21mg; Fibre 0.9g; Sodium 229mg.

Red Hot Seaweed Salad with Green Mango

In the Philippines various types of seaweed are enjoyed in salads and the occasional stir-fry. Serve this spicy salad as an appetizer or as an accompaniment to grilled meats and fish.

Serves 4
50g/2oz fine thread seaweed, reconstituted in water, or 225g/8oz fresh seaweed, cut into strips

1 green mango, grated
2–3 ripe tomatoes, skinned, seeded and chopped
4–6 spring onions (scallions), white parts only, sliced
25g/1oz fresh root ginger, grated
45ml/3 tbsp coconut or cane vinegar
10ml/2 tsp chilli oil
15ml/1 tbsp sugar
salt and ground black pepper

1 Bring a large pan of water to the boil, drop in the seaweed, remove from the heat and leave to soak for 15 minutes. Drain and refresh under cold running water. Using your hands, squeeze the seaweed dry.

2 Put the seaweed, mango, tomatoes, spring onions and ginger into a large bowl and mix to combine.

3 In a separate bowl, mix together the coconut vinegar, chilli oil and sugar until the sugar has dissolved.

4 Pour the dressing over the salad, toss well together and season with salt and pepper to taste. Serve as an appetizer or with grilled (broiled) meat or fish.

Cook's Tip
Fresh and dried seaweeds are widely available from Chinese and South-east Asian supermarkets and food stores. Some dried varieties are also available from health food stores. For this recipe, you need the fine thread seaweed available in Chinese stores.

Thai Seafood Salad with Pomelo and Peanuts

A Thai meal will include a selection of dishes, one of which is often a refreshing and palate-cleansing salad that features tropical fruit, as with the pomelo here.

Serves 4 to 6
30ml/2 tbsp vegetable oil
4 shallots, finely sliced
2 garlic cloves, finely sliced
1 large pomelo, peeled
15ml/1 tbsp roasted peanuts
115g/4oz cooked peeled prawns (shrimp)
115g/4oz cooked crab meat
10–12 small fresh mint leaves

For the dressing
30ml/2 tbsp Thai fish sauce
15ml/1 tbsp palm sugar (jaggery) or light muscovado (brown) sugar
30ml/2 tbsp fresh lime juice

For the garnish
2 spring onions (scallions), thinly sliced
2 fresh red chillies, seeded and thinly sliced
fresh coriander (cilantro) leaves
grated fresh coconut (optional)

1 Make the dressing. Mix the fish sauce, sugar and lime juice in a bowl. Whisk well, then cover and set aside.

2 Heat the oil in a frying pan, add the shallots and garlic and cook until they are golden. Remove from the pan and set aside.

3 Break the pomelo flesh into small pieces, taking care to remove any membranes. Grind the peanuts and mix with the pomelo, prawns, crab, mint and shallots. Toss in the dressing and sprinkle with spring onions, chillies and coriander. Add the coconut, if using. Serve immediately.

Cook's Tip
The pomelo is a large citrus fruit that looks like a grapefruit, although it is not, as is often thought, a hybrid. It is slightly pear-shaped with thick, yellow, dimpled skin and pinkish-yellow flesh that is drier than a grapefruit's. It also has a sharper taste.

Red Hot Seaweed Salad Energy 75kcal/315kJ; Protein 2.4g; Carbohydrate 12g, of which sugars 11.8g; Fat 2.2g, of which saturates 0.3g; Cholesterol 0mg; Calcium 110mg; Fibre 2.8g; Sodium 85mg.
Thai Seafood Salad Energy 159kcal/665kJ; Protein 13.4g; Carbohydrate 8.4g; of which sugars 8.1g; Fat 4.9g; of which saturates 0.9g; Cholesterol 44mg; Calcium 107mg; Fibre 1.1g; Sodium 612mg.

Fruit and Vegetable Salad with a Hint of Chilli

This fruit salad is often presented in traditional style, with the main course, and serves as a cooler to counteract the heat of the chillies that will inevitably be present in the other dishes. It is a typically harmonious balance of flavours.

Serves 4 to 6
1 small pineapple
1 small mango, peeled and sliced
1 green apple, cored and sliced
6 rambutans or lychees, peeled and stoned (pitted)
115g/4oz/1 cup green beans, trimmed and halved
1 red onion, sliced
1 small cucumber, cut into short sticks
115g/4oz/½ cup beansprouts
2 spring onions (scallions), sliced
1 ripe tomato, quartered
225g/8oz cos, romaine or iceberg lettuce leaves
salt

For the coconut dipping sauce
30ml/2 tbsp coconut cream
30ml/2 tbsp sugar
75ml/5 tbsp boiling water
1.5ml/¼ tsp chilli sauce
15ml/1 tbsp Thai fish sauce
juice of 1 lime

1 Make the coconut dipping sauce. Spoon the coconut cream, sugar and boiling water into a screw-top jar. Add the chilli and fish sauces and lime juice, close tightly and shake to mix.

2 Trim both ends of the pineapple with a serrated knife, then cut away the outer skin. Remove the central core with an apple corer. Alternatively, quarter the pineapple lengthways and remove the portion of core from each wedge with a knife. Chop the pineapple and set aside with the other fruits.

3 Bring a small pan of lightly salted water to the boil over a medium heat. Add the green beans and cook for 3–4 minutes, until just tender but still retaining some 'bite'. Drain, refresh under cold running water, drain well again and set aside.

4 To serve, arrange all the fruits and vegetables in small heaps on a platter or in a shallow bowl. Pour the coconut sauce into a small serving bowl and serve separately as a dip.

Thai Spiced Cabbage Salad

This is a simple and delicious way of serving a somewhat mundane vegetable, with classic Thai flavours.

Serves 4 to 6
30ml/2 tbsp vegetable oil
2 large fresh red chillies, seeded and cut into thin strips
6 garlic cloves, thinly sliced
6 shallots, thinly sliced
1 small cabbage, shredded
salt
30ml/2 tbsp coarsely chopped roasted peanuts, to garnish

For the dressing
30ml/2 tbsp Thai fish sauce
grated rind of 1 lime
30ml/2 tbsp fresh lime juice
120ml/4fl oz/½ cup coconut milk

1 Make the dressing by mixing the fish sauce, lime rind and juice and coconut milk together in a bowl. Whisk until thoroughly combined, then set aside.

2 Heat the oil in a wok or large frying pan. Fry the chillies, garlic and shallots over a medium heat, stirring constantly, for 3–4 minutes, until the shallots have turned brown and crisp. Remove the ingredients from the pan with a slotted spoon and set aside until needed.

3 Bring a large pan of lightly salted water to the boil. Add the cabbage and blanch for 2–3 minutes. Transfer it into a colander, drain well and put into a bowl.

4 Whisk the dressing again. Pour it over the warm cabbage and toss to mix until the cabbage is evenly coated in the dressing.

5 Transfer the salad to a serving dish. Sprinkle the fried shallot mixture and the chopped peanuts over the salad. Serve the salad immediately.

> **Variation**
> Other vegetables will also work in this versatile dish. Cauliflower, broccoli and Chinese leaves (Chinese cabbage) can be cooked in this way.

Fruit and Vegetable Salad Energy 159kcal/673kJ; Protein 3.5g; Carbohydrate 32.2g, of which sugars 31g; Fat 2.7g, of which saturates 1.7g; Cholesterol 0mg; Calcium 69mg; Fibre 4.7g; Sodium 188mg.
Thai Spiced Cabbage Salad Energy 124kcal/513kJ; Protein 3.4g; Carbohydrate 7.1g, of which sugars 6.5g; Fat 9.2g, of which saturates 1.4g; Cholesterol 0mg; Calcium 57mg; Fibre 2.3g; Sodium 306mg.

Persimmon and Bamboo Shoot Salad with Chilli

This is a refreshing salad, lightly seasoned with a sweet and sour soy dressing.

Serves 1 to 2
200g/7oz can bamboo shoots, drained and rinsed in water
2 dried shiitake mushrooms, soaked in warm water for about 30 minutes until softened
50g/2oz beef flank, thinly sliced
25ml/1½ tbsp vegetable oil
115g/4oz/½ cup beansprouts
1 egg
90g/3½oz watercress or rocket (arugula)
salt
½ red chilli, seeded and thinly sliced, to garnish

For the seasoning
7.5ml/1½ tsp dark soy sauce
10g/¼oz red persimmon, finely chopped
½ spring onion (scallion), finely chopped
1 garlic clove, crushed
5ml/1 tsp sesame seeds
2.5ml/½ tsp sesame oil
ground white pepper

For the dressing
60ml/4 tbsp dark soy sauce
60ml/4 tbsp water
30ml/2 tbsp rice vinegar
40g/1½oz red persimmon, finely chopped
5ml/1 tsp sesame seeds

1 Thinly slice the bamboo shoots and cut into bitesize pieces. Drain the mushrooms and thinly slice them, discarding the stems. Put the beef slices in a bowl. Add the seasoning ingredients and the shiitake mushrooms, and mix together well.

2 Heat 15ml/1 tbsp of the oil in a frying pan. Stir-fry the beef and mushrooms until cooked. Cool, then put in the refrigerator. Trim the beansprouts and blanch for 3 minutes. Drain.

3 In a bowl, combine all the dressing ingredients and mix well. Set aside. Beat the egg and season with a pinch of salt. Heat the remaining oil, add the egg and make an omelette, browning gently on each side. Remove from the pan and cut into strips.

4 Arrange the beef on a serving plate with the bamboo shoots, watercress or rocket, and beansprouts. Garnish with the sliced chilli and egg strips before serving.

Spicy Bamboo Shoot Salad

This hot, sharp-flavoured salad originated in north-eastern Thailand. Use canned whole bamboo shoots, if you can find them – they have more flavour than the sliced ones.

Serves 4
400g/14oz canned bamboo shoots, in large pieces

25g/1oz glutinous rice
30ml/2 tbsp chopped shallots
15ml/1 tbsp chopped garlic
45ml/3 tbsp chopped spring onions (scallions)
30ml/2 tbsp Thai fish sauce
30ml/2 tbsp fresh lime juice
5ml/1 tsp sugar
2.5ml/½ tsp dried chilli flakes
20–25 small fresh mint leaves
15ml/1 tbsp toasted sesame seeds

1 Rinse the bamboo shoots under cold running water, then drain them, pat thoroughly dry with kitchen paper and set aside.

2 Dry-roast the glutinous rice in a wok or frying pan until it is golden brown. Leave it to cool slightly, then transfer into a mortar and grind to fine crumbs with a pestle, or use a food processor or blender.

3 Transfer the rice to a bowl and add the shallots, garlic, spring onions, fish sauce, lime juice, sugar, chilli flakes and half the mint leaves. Mix well, ensuring that the rice is evenly coated in the other ingredients.

4 Add the bamboo shoots to the bowl and toss to mix. Serve sprinkled with the toasted sesame seeds and the remaining mint leaves.

> **Cook's Tip**
> Glutinous rice does not, in fact, contain any gluten – it is just particularly sticky when boiled due to a higher starch content. This type of rice is generally preferred in much Asian cuisine precisely because it is sticky and therefore easier to handle with chopsticks. It is used in many Chinese and Japanese dishes, especially when it is boiled.

Persimmon Salad Energy 268kcal/1115kJ; Protein 17g; Carbohydrate 9.1g, of which sugars 6.1g; Fat 18.6g, of which saturates 3.6g; Cholesterol 119mg; Calcium 164mg; Fibre 3.5g; Sodium 2489mg.
Spicy Bamboo Shoot Salad Energy 80kcal/336kJ; Protein 4.5g; Carbohydrate 9.4g, of which sugars 2.9g; Fat 2.8g, of which saturates 0.4g; Cholesterol 0mg; Calcium 51mg; Fibre 2g; Sodium 185mg.

Rice Salad with a Touch of Chilli

The sky's the limit with this recipe. Use whatever fruit, vegetables and even leftover meat that you might have, mix with cooked rice, pour over the fragrant dressing and mix together.

Serves 4 to 6

350g/12oz/3 cups cooked rice
1 Asian pear, cored and diced
50g/2oz dried shrimp, chopped
1 avocado, peeled, stoned (pitted) and diced
½ medium cucumber, finely diced
2 lemon grass stalks, finely chopped
30ml/2 tbsp sweet chilli sauce

1 fresh green or red chilli, seeded and finely sliced
115g/4oz/1 cup flaked (sliced) almonds, toasted
small bunch fresh coriander (cilantro), chopped
fresh Thai sweet basil leaves, to garnish

For the dressing

300ml/½ pint/1¼ cups water
10ml/2 tsp shrimp paste
15ml/1 tbsp palm sugar (jaggery) or light muscovado (brown) sugar
2 kaffir lime leaves, torn into small pieces
½ lemon grass stalk, sliced

1 Make the dressing. Put the measured water in a small pan with the shrimp paste, sugar, kaffir lime leaves and lemon grass. Heat gently, stirring, until the sugar dissolves, then bring to boiling point and simmer for 5 minutes. Strain into a bowl and set aside until cold.

2 Put the cooked rice in a large salad bowl and fluff up the grains with a fork.

3 Add the Asian pear, dried shrimp, avocado, cucumber, lemon grass and sweet chilli sauce to the rice. Mix well, ensuring that the rice is evenly coated.

4 Add the sliced chilli, flaked almonds and chopped coriander to the bowl and toss well.

5 Garnish the salad with the Thai basil leaves and serve immediately. Pass around the bowl of dressing so diners can help themselves and spoon it over the top of their individual portions of salad.

Hot and Sour Noodle Salad with Baby Corn

Noodles make the perfect basis for a salad, absorbing the spicy flavours and giving a contrast in texture to the crisp vegetables.

Serves 2

200g/7oz thin rice noodles
small bunch fresh coriander (cilantro)
2 tomatoes, seeded and sliced
130g/4½oz baby corn cobs, sliced

4 spring onions (scallions), thinly sliced
1 red (bell) pepper, seeded and finely chopped
juice of 2 limes
2 small fresh green chillies, seeded and finely chopped
10ml/2 tsp sugar
115g/4oz/1 cup peanuts, toasted and chopped
30ml/2 tbsp soy sauce
salt

1 Bring a large pan of salted water to the boil. Snap the noodles into short lengths, add to the pan and cook for about 4 minutes. Drain, rinse under cold water and drain again.

2 Set aside a few coriander leaves for the garnish. Chop the remaining leaves and place them in a large serving bowl.

3 Add the noodles to the bowl, with the tomato slices, corn cobs, spring onions, red pepper, lime juice, chillies, sugar and toasted peanuts.

4 Season the noodles with the soy sauce, then taste and add a little salt if you think the mixture needs it.

5 Toss the salad if you added salt, to mix it in thoroughly. Garnish the salad with the reserved coriander leaves and serve immediately.

> **Cook's Tip**
> Rice noodles come in a wide range of thicknesses, from the very thin variety often called vermicelli, to the wider ones, which are also known as rice sticks. Use whichever you have available.

Rice Salad Energy 404kcal/1689kj; Protein 16.1g; Carbohydrate 36.7g; of which sugars 8.5g; Fat 22.4g; of which saturates 2.6g; Cholesterol 63mg; Calcium 247mg; Fibre 4g; Sodium 550mg.
Noodle Salad Energy 761kcal/3173kj; Protein 24.1g; Carbohydrate 101.6g; of which sugars 15.6g; Fat 27.7g; of which saturates 5.2g; Cholesterol 0mg; Calcium 117mg; Fibre 7.9g; Sodium 1840mg.

Gypsy Salad with Feta, Chillies and Parsley

There are two common salads eaten as meze in Turkey, or served as accompaniments to meat and fish dishes. One, known as *çoban salatası* or 'shepherd's salad', is made of chopped cucumber, tomatoes, peppers, onion and flat leaf parsley; the other is this gypsy salad, *çingene pilavı*, meaning 'gypsy rice'. The mix is similar to shepherd's salad, only a chilli is included to give the desired kick, and crumbled feta is added to represent the rice.

Serves 3 to 4

2 red onions, cut in half
    lengthways and finely sliced
    along the grain

1 green (bell) pepper, seeded
    and finely sliced
1 fresh green chilli, seeded
    and chopped
2–3 garlic cloves, chopped
1 bunch of fresh flat leaf parsley,
    roughly chopped
225g/8oz firm feta cheese, rinsed
    and grated
2 large tomatoes, skinned, seeded
    and finely chopped
30–45ml/2–3 tbsp olive oil
salt and ground black pepper

To serve

scant 5ml/1 tsp Turkish red
    pepper flakes or paprika
scant 5ml/1 tsp ground sumac

1 Sprinkle the onions with a little salt to draw out the moisture. Leave for about 10 minutes, then rinse and pat dry with kitchen paper.

2 Put the red onions and green pepper in a large bowl. Add the chopped chilli, garlic, flat leaf parsley, feta cheese and tomatoes. Gently mix together.

3 Add the oil and seasoning and toss gently, ensuring that all the ingredients are mixed together and coated in oil.

4 Transfer the salad into a large serving dish and sprinkle with the red pepper or paprika and sumac.

Peppery Egg, Watercress and Chilli Salad

Chillies and eggs may seem unlikely partners, but they actually work very well together. The peppery flavour of the watercress makes it the perfect foundation for this tasty salad.

Serves 2

15ml/1 tbsp groundnut
    (peanut) oil
1 garlic clove, thinly sliced

4 eggs
2 shallots, thinly sliced
2 small fresh red chillies, seeded
    and thinly sliced
½ small cucumber, finely diced
1cm/½in piece fresh root ginger,
    peeled and grated
juice of 2 limes
30ml/2 tbsp soy sauce
5ml/1 tsp caster (superfine) sugar
small bunch coriander (cilantro)
bunch watercress or rocket
    (arugula), coarsely chopped

1 Heat the oil in a frying pan. Add the garlic and cook over a low heat until it starts to turn golden.

2 Crack the eggs into the pan. Break the yolks with a wooden spatula, then fry until the eggs are almost firm. Remove from the pan and set aside.

3 In a bowl, mix together the shallots, chillies, cucumber and ginger until well blended.

4 In a separate bowl, whisk the lime juice with the soy sauce and sugar. Pour this dressing over the vegetables and toss lightly.

5 Set aside a few coriander sprigs for the garnish. Chop the rest and add it to the salad. Toss it again.

6 Reserve a few watercress or rocket sprigs and arrange the remainder on two serving plates. Cut the fried eggs into slices and divide them between the watercress or rocket mounds.

7 Spoon the shallot mixture over the eggs and serve immediately, garnished with the reserved coriander and watercress or rocket.

Gypsy Salad Energy 253kcal/1049kJ; Protein 11.1g; Carbohydrate 13.4g, of which sugars 11g; Fat 17.6g, of which saturates 8.6g; Cholesterol 39mg; Calcium 260mg; Fibre 3.2g; Sodium 824mg.
Egg and Chilli Salad Energy 215kcal/894kJ; Protein 14.2g; Carbohydrate 2.4g, of which sugars 2.2g; Fat 16.9g, of which saturates 4.2g; Cholesterol 381mg; Calcium 112mg; Fibre 0.8g; Sodium 1223mg.

Seafood Salad in Chilli Oil and Mustard Dressing

Though not a traditional ingredient in this Korean dish, English mustard adds a pleasant heat, and perfectly complements the seafood with a unique and slightly mysterious taste. Or, for a more authentic flavour, use Korean mustard. Simple to prepare, this dish is a perfect quick snack or appetizer.

Serves 2

50g/2oz squid, cleaned, gutted
   and prepared
50g/2oz king prawns (jumbo
   shrimp), shelled and deveined
50g/2oz jellyfish (optional)
50g/2oz cooked whelks

90g/3½oz Asian pear
⅓ carrot
½ medium cucumber
25g/1oz Chinese leaves (Chinese
   cabbage), shredded
25g/1oz canned chestnuts,
   drained and sliced
25g/1oz crab meat or
   seafood stick

For the dressing
15ml/1 tbsp ready-made English
   (hot) mustard
30ml/2 tbsp sugar
15ml/1 tbsp milk
45ml/3 tbsp cider vinegar
5ml/1 tsp chilli oil
2.5ml/½ tsp dark soy sauce
5ml/1 tsp salt

1 Score the squid with a criss-cross pattern, and slice into strips about 2cm/¾in wide. Slice the prawns and jellyfish, if using, into similar-sized pieces.

2 Bring a pan of lightly salted water to the boil and blanch the squid, prawns and jellyfish for about 3 minutes, then drain. Thinly slice the whelks.

3 Peel the Asian pear. Cut the pear and carrot into thin julienne strips. Seed the cucumber and cut into thin julienne strips.

4 Mix all the dressing ingredients in a bowl. Take a large serving platter and arrange the julienne vegetables, Chinese leaves and chestnuts in rows, or fan them around the centre of the plate. Add the seafood, including the crab meat or seafood stick. Pour over the dressing and chill in the refrigerator before serving.

Scented Fish Salad with Chilli and Mango

For a tropical taste of the Far East, try this delicious fish salad scented with coconut, fruit and warm Thai spices.

Serves 4

350g/12oz fillet of red mullet, sea
   bream or snapper
1 cos or romaine lettuce
1 papaya or mango, peeled
   and sliced
1 pitaya, peeled and sliced
1 large ripe tomato, cut into
   wedges
½ cucumber, peeled and cut
   into batons
3 spring onions (scallions), sliced
salt

For the marinade
5ml/1 tsp coriander seeds
5ml/1 tsp fennel seeds
2.5ml/½ tsp cumin seeds
5ml/1 tsp caster (superfine) sugar
2.5ml/½ tsp hot chilli sauce
30ml/2 tbsp garlic oil

For the dressing
15ml/1 tbsp coconut cream
45ml/3 tbsp boiling water
60ml/4 tbsp groundnut (peanut) oil
grated rind and juice of 1 lime
1 fresh red chilli, seeded and
   finely chopped
5ml/1 tsp sugar
45ml/3 tbsp chopped fresh
   coriander (cilantro)

1 Cut the fish into even strips, removing any stray bones. Place it on a plate and set aside. Meanwhile, make the marinade. Put the coriander, fennel and cumin seeds in a mortar. Add the sugar and crush with a pestle. Stir in the chilli sauce, garlic oil, and salt to taste and mix to a paste.

2 Spread the paste over the fish, cover and leave to marinate in a cool place for at least 20 minutes. Make the salad dressing. Place the coconut cream and salt in a screw-top jar. Stir in the boiling water. Add the oil, lime rind and juice, chilli, sugar and coriander. Shake well.

3 Wash and dry the lettuce leaves. Place in a bowl and add the papaya or mango, pitaya, tomato, cucumber and spring onions. Pour in the dressing and toss well to coat.

4 Heat a large non-stick frying-pan, add the fish and cook for 5 minutes, turning once. Add to the salad, toss lightly and serve.

Seafood Salad Energy 206kcal/872kJ; Protein 18g; Carbohydrate 29.8g, of which sugars 23.9g; Fat 2.4g, of which saturates 0.6g; Cholesterol 230mg; Calcium 62mg; Fibre 2.4g; Sodium 1282mg.
Fish Salad Energy 304kcal/1269kJ; Protein 17.6g; Carbohydrate 11.7g, of which sugars 11.6g; Fat 21.1g, of which saturates 3.6g; Cholesterol 0mg; Calcium 89mg; Fibre 2.6g; Sodium 88mg.

Chilli Beef and Mushroom Salad

All the ingredients for this traditional, tasty Thai salad, known as *yam nua yang*, are widely available in most large supermarkets as well as in Asian food stores.

Serves 4

675g/1½lb beef fillet or rump
   (round) steak
30ml/2 tbsp olive oil
2 small mild red chillies, seeded
   and sliced
225g/8oz/3¼ cups fresh shiitake
   mushrooms, stems removed
   and caps sliced

For the dressing

3 spring onions (scallions),
   finely chopped
2 garlic cloves, finely chopped
juice of 1 lime
15–30ml/1–2 tbsp Thai fish sauce
5ml/1 tsp soft light brown sugar
30ml/2 tbsp chopped fresh
   coriander (cilantro)

To serve

1 cos or romaine lettuce, in strips
175g/6oz cherry tomatoes,
   halved
5cm/2in piece cucumber, peeled,
   halved and thinly sliced
45ml/3 tbsp toasted sesame seeds

1 Preheat the grill (broiler) to medium, then cook the steak for 2–4 minutes on each side, depending on how well done you like it. (In Thailand, the beef is traditionally served quite rare.) Leave the steak to cool for at least 15 minutes.

2 Slice the beef fillet or rump steak as thinly as possible (freezing it for 30 minutes before slicing will help make this easier). Place the slices in a bowl.

3 Heat the olive oil in a small, heavy frying pan. Add the seeded and sliced red chillies and the sliced shiitake mushroom caps. Cook for 5 minutes, stirring occasionally. Remove from the heat and add the steak slices to the pan. Stir well to coat the beef slices in the chilli and mushroom mixture.

4 Make the dressing by mixing all the ingredients in a bowl, then pour it over the meat mixture and toss gently.

5 Arrange the lettuce, tomatoes and cucumber on a serving plate. Spoon the steak mixture in the centre and sprinkle the sesame seeds over. Serve immediately.

Lime-marinated Beef Salad

This is a great Chinese favourite and versions of it are enjoyed in Vietnam, Thailand, Cambodia and Laos. It is also one of the traditional dishes that appear in the *bo bay mon* – beef seven ways feast – in which there are seven different beef dishes. For the most delicious result, it is worth buying an excellent-quality piece of tender fillet steak because the meat is only just seared before being dressed in the spicy, fragrant lime dressing and tossed in a crunchy salad of beansprouts and fresh, aromatic herbs.

Serves 4

about 7.5ml/1½ tsp vegetable oil
450g/1lb beef fillet, cut into
   steaks 2.5cm/1in thick
115g/4oz/½ cup beansprouts
1 bunch each fresh basil and
   mint, stalks removed,
   leaves shredded
1 lime, cut into quarters,
   to serve

For the dressing

juice (about 80ml/3fl oz/⅓ cup)
   and rind of 2 limes
30ml/2 tbsp Thai fish sauce
30ml/2 tbsp raw cane sugar
2 garlic cloves, crushed
2 lemon grass stalks, very
   finely sliced
2 green serrano chillies, seeded
   and finely sliced

1 To make the marinade, beat the lime juice, rind and Thai fish sauce in a bowl with the sugar, until the sugar dissolves. Stir in the garlic, lemon grass and chillies and set aside.

2 Pour the oil into a heavy pan and rub it over the base with a piece of kitchen paper. Heat the pan and sear the steaks for 1–2 minutes each side. Transfer them to a board and leave to cool a little.

3 Using a sharp knife, cut the meat into thin slices. Toss the slices in the marinade, cover the bowl and leave to marinate for about 1–2 hours.

4 Drain the meat of any excess juice from the marinade and transfer it to a wide serving bowl. Add the beansprouts and herbs and toss it all together. Serve immediately with lime quarters to squeeze over.

Beef and Mushroom Salad Energy 381kcal/1588kJ; Protein 39.7g; Carbohydrate 4g, of which sugars 3.8g; Fat 23g, of which saturates 6.6g; Cholesterol 103mg; Calcium 105mg; Fibre 2.4g; Sodium 352mg.
Lime Beef Salad Energy 233kcal/979kJ; Protein 26g; Carbohydrate 12g, of which sugars 9g; Fat 9g, of which saturates 3g; Cholesterol 69mg; Calcium 74mg; Fibre 0.5g; Sodium 400mg.

Spicy Warm Pork Salad

Tender pork fillet is cut into strips before being grilled. Shredded and then tossed with a delicious sweet and sour sauce, it makes a marvellous warm salad, especially with the extra heat from the chilli.

Serves 4

30ml/2 tbsp dark soy sauce
15ml/1 tbsp clear honey
400g/14oz pork fillet (tenderloin)
6 shallots, very thinly
  sliced lengthways
1 lemon grass stalk, thinly sliced
5 kaffir lime leaves, thinly sliced
5cm/2in piece fresh root ginger,
  peeled and sliced into fine shreds
1/2 fresh long red chilli, seeded
  and sliced into fine shreds
small bunch fresh coriander
  (cilantro), chopped

For the dressing

30ml/2 tbsp palm sugar (jaggery)
  or light muscovado
  (brown) sugar
30ml/2 tbsp Thai fish sauce
juice of 2 limes
20ml/4 tsp thick tamarind juice,
  made by mixing tamarind paste
  with warm water

1 Preheat the grill (broiler) to medium. Mix the soy sauce with the honey in a small bowl or jug (pitcher) and stir until they are well blended.

2 Using a sharp knife, cut the pork fillet lengthways into quarters to make four long, thick strips. Place the pork strips in a grill pan. Brush generously with the soy sauce and honey mixture, then grill (broil) for about 10–15 minutes, until cooked through and tender. Turn the strips over frequently and baste with the soy sauce and honey mixture.

3 Transfer the cooked pork strips to a board. Slice the meat across the grain, then shred it with a fork. Place in a large bowl and add the shallot slices, lemon grass, kaffir lime leaves, ginger, chilli and chopped coriander.

4 Make the dressing. Place the sugar, fish sauce, lime juice and tamarind juice in a bowl. Mix until the sugar has dissolved.

5 Pour the dressing over the pork mixture and toss well to mix, then serve immediately.

Chilli Beef Salad

This hearty main meal salad from Thailand combines tender strips of sirloin steak with thinly shredded cucumber and a piquant chilli and lime dressing.

Serves 4

2 sirloin steaks, each weighing
  about 225g/8oz
1 lemon grass stalk, root trimmed
1 red onion or 4 Thai shallots,
  thinly sliced
1/2 cucumber, cut into strips
30ml/2 tbsp chopped spring
  onion (scallion)
juice of 2 limes
15–30ml/1–2 tbsp Thai
  fish sauce
2–4 fresh red chillies, seeded and
  finely chopped
Chinese mustard cress, salad cress
  or fresh coriander (cilantro),
  to garnish

1 Pan-fry the steaks in a large, heavy frying pan over a medium heat. Cook them for 4–6 minutes for rare, 6–8 minutes for medium and about 10 minutes for well done, depending on their thickness. (In Thailand the beef is traditionally served quite rare.) Alternatively, cook them under a preheated grill (broiler). Remove the steaks from the pan and leave to rest for 10–15 minutes. Meanwhile, cut off the lower 5cm/2in from the lemon grass stalk and chop it finely. Discard the remainder.

2 When the meat is cool, slice it thinly and put the slices in a large bowl. Add the sliced onion or shallots, cucumber, lemon grass and chopped spring onion to the meat slices.

3 Toss the salad and add lime juice and fish sauce to taste. Add the red chillies and toss again. Transfer to a serving bowl or plate. Serve the salad at room temperature or chilled, garnished with the Chinese mustard cress, salad cress or coriander leaves.

> **Cook's Tip**
> Look for gui chai leaves in Thai and Chinese groceries. These look like very thin spring onions (scallions) and are often used as a substitute for the more familiar vegetable.

Spicy Warm Pork Salad Energy 170kcal/718kJ; Protein 22g; Carbohydrate 12.2g, of which sugars 12.1g; Fat 4g, of which saturates 1.4g; Cholesterol 63mg; Calcium 16mg; Fibre 0.2g; Sodium 352mg.
Chilli Beef Salad Energy 161kcal/674kJ; Protein 26.9g; Carbohydrate 1.8g, of which sugars 1.4g; Fat 5.1g, of which saturates 2.3g; Cholesterol 57mg; Calcium 14mg; Fibre 0.3g; Sodium 873mg.

Classic Spiced Tomato Salsa

This is the traditional tomato-based salsa that most people associate with Mexican food. There are innumerable recipes for it, but the basics of onion, tomato, chilli and coriander are common to all. Serve as a condiment with a wide variety of dishes.

Serves 6 as an accompaniment
3–6 fresh serrano chillies
1 large white onion
grated rind and juice of 2 limes,
    plus strips of rind, to garnish
8 ripe, firm tomatoes
bunch of fresh coriander (cilantro)
1.5ml/¼ tsp sugar
salt

1 Use three chillies for a salsa of medium heat; up to six if you like it hot. Spear the chillies on a metal skewer and roast them over a gas flame until the skins blister. Do not let the flesh burn. Alternatively, dry-fry them in a griddle. Place them in a strong plastic bag and tie the top. Set aside for 20 minutes.

2 Meanwhile, chop the onion finely and put it in a bowl with the lime rind and juice. The lime juice will soften the onion.

3 Remove the chillies from the bag and peel off the skins. Cut off the stalks, then slit the chillies and scrape out the seeds with a sharp knife. Chop the flesh roughly and set aside.

4 Cut a small cross in the base of each tomato. Place them in a heatproof bowl and pour over boiling water to cover.

5 Leave the tomatoes in the water for 3 minutes, then lift out and plunge into a bowl of cold water. Drain. The skins will be peeling back from the crosses. Remove the skins completely.

6 Dice the peeled tomatoes and put them in a bowl. Add the chopped onion and lime mixture; the onion should have softened. Chop the fresh coriander finely.

7 Add the coriander, with the chillies and the sugar. Mix gently until the sugar has dissolved and all the ingredients are coated in lime juice. Cover and chill for 2–3 hours. The salsa will keep for 3–4 days in the refrigerator. Garnish with lime rind before serving.

Roasted Tomato and Chilli Salsa

Slow roasting these tomatoes to a semi-dried state results in a very rich, full-flavoured sweet sauce. The costeno amarillo chilli is mild and has a fresh light flavour, making it the perfect partner for the rich tomato taste. This salsa is great to go with tuna or sea bass and makes a marvellous sandwich filling when teamed with creamy cheese.

Serves 6 as an accompaniment
500g/1¼ lb tomatoes
8 small shallots
5 garlic cloves
1 fresh rosemary sprig
2 costeno amarillo chillies
grated rind and juice of
    ½ small lemon
30ml/2 tbsp extra virgin olive oil
1.5ml/¼ tsp soft dark
    brown sugar
sea salt

1 Preheat the oven to 160°C/325°F/Gas 3. Cut the tomatoes into quarters and place them in a roasting pan.

2 Peel the shallots and garlic and add them to the roasting pan. Sprinkle with sea salt. Roast in the oven for 1¼ hours, or until the tomatoes are beginning to dry.

3 Leave the tomatoes to cool, then peel off the skins and chop the flesh finely. Place in a bowl. Remove the outer layer of skin from any shallots that have toughened.

4 Using a large, sharp knife, chop the shallots and garlic roughly, place them with the tomatoes in a bowl and mix.

5 Strip the rosemary leaves from the woody stem and chop finely. Add half to the tomato and shallot mixture and mix lightly.

6 Soak the chillies in hot water for 10 minutes until soft. Drain, remove the stalks, slit them and scrape out the seeds with a sharp knife. Chop the flesh finely and add to the tomato mixture.

7 Stir in the lemon rind and juice, the olive oil and the sugar. Mix well. Cover and chill for at least an hour before serving, sprinkled with the remaining rosemary. The salsa will keep for up to a week in the refrigerator.

Classic Spiced Tomato Salsa Energy 42kcal/176kJ; Protein 2g; Carbohydrate 8g, of which sugars 7g; Fat 1g, of which saturates 0g; Cholesterol 0mg; Calcium 31mg; Fibre 1.7g; Sodium 100mg.
Roasted Tomato Salsa Energy 54kcal/226kJ; Protein 0.8g; Carbohydrate 4.2g, of which sugars 3.7g; Fat 4g, of which saturates 0.6g; Cholesterol 0mg; Calcium 11mg; Fibre 1.1g; Sodium 8mg.

Sweet Potato and Jalapeño Salsa

Very colourful and
delightfully sweet, with
a satisfying heat from
the jalapeño chillies, this
salsa makes the perfect
accompaniment to hot,
spicy Mexican dishes. Add
more dried chilli if you like
your food a little more fiery.

**Serves 4 as an
accompaniment**
675g/1½lb sweet potatoes
juice of 1 small orange
5ml/1 tsp crushed dried
    jalapeño chillies
4 small spring onions (scallions)
juice of 1 small lime (optional)
salt

1 Peel the sweet potatoes and dice the flesh finely. Bring a pan of water to the boil. Add the sweet potatoes and cook for about 8–10 minutes, until just soft.

2 Drain off the water, cover the pan and leave over a very low heat for about 5 minutes to dry out, then transfer to a bowl and set aside.

3 Mix the orange juice and crushed dried chillies in a bowl. Chop the spring onions finely and add them to the juice and chillies in the bowl.

4 When the sweet potatoes are cool, add the orange juice mixture and toss carefully until all the pieces of potato are evenly coated.

5 Cover the bowl and chill in the refrigerator for at least 1 hour, then taste and season with salt. Add lime juice for a fresher taste.

6 Serve the salsa as an accompaniment to spicy dishes. The salsa will keep for 2–3 days in a covered bowl in the refrigerator.

> **Cook's Tip**
> This fresh and tasty salsa is also very good served with a simple grilled (broiled) salmon fillet or other fish dishes, and makes a delicious accompaniment to veal escalopes (scallops) or grilled chicken breast fillets.

Mango and Chilli Salsa

This delicious salsa has a
fresh, fruity taste and is
perfect with fish or as a
contrast to rich, creamy
dishes. The bright colours
make it an attractive
addition to any table.

**Serves 4 as an
accompaniment**
2 fresh red fresno chillies
2 ripe mangoes
½ white onion
bunch of fresh coriander (cilantro)
grated rind and juice of 1 lime

1 To loosen the skin of the chillies, spear them on a long-handled metal skewer and roast them over the flame of a gas burner until the skins blister and darken. Do not allow the flesh of the chillies to burn. Alternatively, dry-fry them in a griddle pan until the skins are scorched.

2 Place the roasted chillies in a strong plastic bag and tie the top to keep the steam in. Set aside for 20 minutes.

3 Meanwhile, put one of the mangoes on a board and cut off a thick slice close to the flat side of the stone (pit). Turn the mango round and repeat on the other side. Score the flesh on each thick slice with criss-cross lines at 1cm/½in intervals, taking care not to cut through the skin. Repeat this process with the second mango.

4 Fold the mango halves inside out so that the mango flesh stands proud of the skin, in neat dice. Carefully slice these off the skin and into a bowl. Cut off the flesh adhering to each stone, dice it and add it to the bowl.

5 Remove the roasted chillies from the bag and carefully peel off the skins. Cut off the stalks, then slit the chillies and scrape out the seeds.

6 Chop the white onion and the coriander finely and add them to the diced mango. Chop the chilli flesh finely and add it to the mixture in the bowl, together with the lime rind and juice.

7 Stir well to mix, cover and chill for at least 1 hour before serving. The salsa will keep for 2–3 days in the refrigerator.

Sweet Potato Salsa Energy 154kcal/657kJ; Protein 2.3g; Carbohydrate 37.4g, of which sugars 11g; Fat 0.6g, of which saturates 0g; Cholesterol 0mg; Calcium 46mg; Fibre 4.2g; Sodium 70mg.
Mango and Chilli Salsa Energy 56kcal/239kJ; Protein 1.2g; Carbohydrate 12.9g, of which sugars 12g; Fat 0.4g, of which saturates 0.1g; Cholesterol 0mg; Calcium 40mg; Fibre 2.9g; Sodium 7mg.

Index